SHOW BIZ

FROM THE

BACK ROW

or

PLAYING WITH THE STARS

Written & Illustrated by
Bill Peterson

Ballendine Publishing

Requests for permission to make copies
of any part of the work contact:
Ballendine Publishing
4235 Glenwood Ave.
Los Angeles, CA 90065

Cataloging-in-Publication Data
Peterson, William
Show Biz from the Back Row / by Bill Peterson
284 pp.   cm.
Summary: Stories of the people with whom I've worked;
my unique viewpoint from the back row of the band or orchestra.
1. Arts, American—20th Century 2. Music—Career
3. Show Business Personalities
I. Title
NX504   2008
790.2
Library of Congress Control Number: 2008911793
ISBN: Hardcover   978-1-4363-9648-6
Softcover   978-1-4363-9647-9

Layout by Lynn Lanning
Printed in the United States of America

This book is dedicated to
my darling children Laura & Eric Peterson,
my wonderful wife Carolyn,
my friend John Williams
whose music and warmth have inspired so many,
all the musicians and stars with whom I have worked,
and my parents
who made sure I had the opportunity to succeed.

TABLE OF CONTENTS

LIST OF ILLUSTRATIONS

PRELUDE

These are the things I saw from that special vantage point I enjoyed while working with the Stars of, and participating in, this wild and sometimes wonderful Show Business.

I hope you'll pour your favorite beverage over the rocks, cue up your favorite recording by Barbra, Sammy, Dino or Frank and enjoy these reminiscences of mine...

I also hope you'll have as much fun reading about these times as I had living them.

—Bill Peterson

ACKNOWLEDGMENTS

FOR THE BOOK

First to my beautiful and patient wife Carolyn, for reading, suggesting and helping me through those days when I felt I would never get this done.

I am so grateful to my daughter Laura for all of her help and encouragement.

Also grateful thanks to my friend, novelist Bruce Wagner and to composer and lyricist Arthur Hamilton, and special thanks to John Williams, one of the greatest composers who ever graced a podium. They were kind enough to take time from their busy schedules to write some comments about my book.

I also want to thank Ms. Lynn Lanning, a friend who gives, and adds so much to this book. Her expert and caring editing, proofing and wise advice have been invaluable to me, and I am deeply grateful.

FOR MY CAREER

I'd also like to acknowledge some trumpeters that have made a difference in my career (even though they are not included elsewhere in this book):

Uan Rasey—the great 1st trumpeter who played so many of the memorable scores at MGM such as *Singin' in the Rain* and *American in Paris*, and who has taught and inspired so many of us.

Wayne Bergeron—who plays great lead, exciting jazz and has a range that seemingly knows no limits. All this and a great guy to hang with.

Gary Grant—a superb lead player who is also a marvelous recording producer and can do everything—even help a friend move!

Malcolm McNab—a trumpet virtuoso who graces so many film scores with his brilliant playing (and puckish sense of humor).

Warren Luening—who can play any style and make it look easy and sound great.

Jerry Hey—whose superb skills as player, arranger, conductor have made the difference on so many sessions.

Ollie Mitchell—who played on so many 'hits,' and after we'd run down the arrangement so many times we were nearing exhaustion, asked the leader, "You want another 'wear down' or do ya wanta make a 'Take'?"

Charlie Davis—"The Pit Bull," who is always there to encourage, tease or just pick you up when things get tough.

Chuck & Bobby Findley—who are world famous lead and jazz players and great human beings.

Tony Terran—a gifted player on anything you could want played, and who finds a "free phone" in any studio in town.

Carl Saunders—an amazing jazz & lead player, and gifted composer.

Bob DiVall—the late principal trumpeter of the LA Philharmonic and a fine teacher.

Irving Bush—Associate Principal, LA Phil., designer of trumpets and mouthpieces, teacher and great friend.

Of course there are many more, but these trumpeters stand out in my mind & heart.

FIRST CHORUS:
STEVE SPIELBERG, JOHN WILLIAMS & ME

Here it is, 1991, and I'm walking into the Music Scoring Stage at Sony Studios, which was formerly MGM. Suddenly I have one of those "What am I doing here" moments. Ever have a feeling like that?

I guess it's a flashback to when I was a kid of thirteen who wanted to play the trumpet more than anything in the world, which only seems like yesterday. Now here I am, a sixty-year-old guy in a nice gray suit and tie, going in to see my old friend John Williams and give him and Steven Spielberg, an icon in the movie business, an award. I haven't met Mr. Spielberg yet, but that's what I'm here to do.

Anyway, the moment passes, and as I open the thick sound-proof door I come back to the present reality with a jolt as I hear the orchestra finish a music cue. I've experienced lots of these moments, because I've been fortunate to have had a good career as a trumpeter and composer.

Now that I am vice president of Local 47, Professional Musicians' Union of Los Angeles, one of my chief responsibilities is to respond to the new challenges that face our recording musicians.

Films used to be scored for the most part either in Hollywood or London, but now producers are going to Canada or as far away as Belgrade and other Third World countries. What is particularly galling to American musicians is that right here in the good old USA, the Seattle Symphony decertified from the American Federation of Musicians, and now scores films by cutting Federation scale.

I have been working with the Recording Musicians Association to try to keep film-scoring work here in our town.

One idea I've come up with is to give awards to producers and directors who use our great Hollywood musicians to score their films.

The first one I think of is Steven Spielberg, the man who at that time had yet to win an Academy Award, an Oscar (it would be 1999 before he finally got this well deserved honor), but is certainly one of the most ingenious, artistic and talented filmmakers on the scene.

I contact John Williams, because he scores many of Spielberg's films as well as scores for so many other filmmakers. I arrange to give them both award plaques during a scoring session. I arrive as both Steve and John are on the podium, talking about the scene they are scoring. The orchestra contractor calls a 'Ten.'

I step forward, as John smiles and says, "Hi Bill! … Ladies and gentlemen, it's our vice president, Bill Peterson!"

I step up on the podium as the orchestra applauds.

I say, "Hi everyone! Thanks, John… all the players here know that you've recorded so many of your great scores here in Los Angeles, and we appreciate your loyalty to your fellow Los Angeles musicians. We want you to have this award on behalf of Local 47's members."

John smiles as I give him his plaque, which he shows to the orchestra.

The players applaud, and I turn to Steve Spielberg. At first I think about reciting some of my favorite films of his, but that would take too much valuable studio time.

So I say, "Mr. Spielberg, you've introduced us to unforgettable characters living through incredible adventures. Your vision has made films that really move and they've have been scored with great musicians like these folks."

Spielberg smiles almost shyly.

John Williams steps forward to say, "You know, many producers and directors would feel they were a failure if they had all this…" as he sweeps his hand across the one hundred and five musicians arrayed before us.

Steve steps up to say, "I'd feel like I've failed, if I *don't* have all of you!"

The orchestra and all of us applaud. I give him his plaque, and he clasps it close to his old leather flight jacket.

As Spielberg steps down from the podium, he very quietly says to me, "I can't tell you how much this means to me."

I am as moved as he is. It's really quite special to think that a

Bill Peterson, John Williams, Steven Spielberg

man who has accomplished so much appreciates this honor with such genuine feeling.

The ten-minute break is almost over and it's time to let John, Steve and the orchestra to get back to work.

I leave this legendary Music Scoring Stage, where almost all of MGM's great films were scored, from *Gone With the Wind* to *Singin' in the Rain* and *An American in Paris*, and everything in between.

I've played here as a trumpet player of course, but it's different being here as a Union guy. I miss the camaraderie with the other players and the sheer fun of playing music, but I feel the satisfaction of knowing that this has been a meaningful day for John, Steve and the musicians of Local 47.

♪♪♪

How I did go from being a junior high school "wanna-be" to having a career as a professional musician working in the film, television and recording studios and finally end up giving a legendary composer and director awards? Well, that's a part of *Show Biz from the Back Row…* I think you'll enjoy the stories of the people with whom I worked, and the unique viewpoint that I had from the back row of the band or orchestra.

SECOND CHORUS:
MY PERSONAL PERSPECTIVE

I have had the experience of seeing some of the biggest stars in Show Biz from a very special vantage point that you'll probably never have… from the back row of the band, orchestra, or combo that is backing them. You don't know me, and you've never heard of me, unless you find my name on some record label, but you've probably *heard* me. I'm not a famous star, but you may have *seen* me. I'm just one of those nameless, faceless musicians who play "behind" stars, either in person, or on recordings, films, and TV.

Now you need to understand that these experiences I've had first hand with the people involved are not "put-downs" or judgements. I realize that being a show biz star demands a great deal from a person, and sometimes in the heat of the moment they act the way they do, and do things that perhaps they ordinarily wouldn't. At any rate, this is my 'take' on some Show Biz Stars, past and present, as well as a short intro about where I came from and how I got to play for these folks. The first lesson that a young musician has to learn is a hard one to swallow and that is:

Music is first and foremost a business. If you're a musician, young or old, no matter how much you love to play and expect to make a living at it, you will probably be in some part of Show Biz, and it's definitely a *business*.

But it is also a tantalizing, beguiling, and dazzling *kind* of a business, not like an ordinary job, I guess. There is some kind of magic that seems to happen from the moment the lights blaze on. It can be in a Broadway theater, or when the screen lights up in a hometown movie house, or a Las Vegas show room, or the Metropolitan (or Grand Ol') Opera, or the blare of the band under the big top. And let's not forget when the curtain opens at the school auditorium stage and you see your kid stutter through his or her lines as you sit there with sweaty palms, reciting the lines before he or she does.

Then there is the rush that you get when you go to your first really big first show in a concert setting or a club, or watching a star onstage in Vegas… Yeah, there's the star!—the one you've spent your dough to see—right there in the spotlight, with a band or orchestra roaring behind them. Wow, the glamour, the excitement, and all that jazz!

So mine is a really unique view of the famous, the talented, the not-so-talented, and the One Time Wonders. It's more than the spotlight shining through the star's dress, or through Sinatra's toupee. Sometimes that spotlight shines right through the person out there, and whether you want to see it or not, you see the real person underneath all the show biz glamour and veneer… and BS.

Now this is not a "Show Biz tell-all book"—not at all. Besides, you probably know all the "who slept with whom" crap.

This is different; this is what *I* saw and experienced and felt, playing for a lot of talented people who made it to the top in the toughest, most competitive line of work, becoming and then— even more difficult—staying a star. Some of those folks probably never set foot on a stage in front of a real audience until they lost their contract at Fox or MGM, or they stopped getting film roles. In order to keep them working, their manager or agent tried to capitalize on their fame on the big or little screen by getting them booked on the stage. No one wants to be a has-been because trying to break *in* to the star echelon is *so* difficult. It's like a .150 hitter trying to connect with a 95 MPH fastball, or a quarterback throwing a touchdown pass when the clock ticks over to zero, or being a politician who has the knack of getting elected. But here are some folks who have that indefinable something that pushes them to the forefront. Maybe it's their looks, their voice, their stage door mother, or that most precious of all commodities—Talent.

Anyway this wild, fun, crazy trip of mine through thirty years of the Business of Show—Show-off, Show-down, Show-up, or whatever, needs a little back-story.

Third Chorus: My Introduction to Music Via the Big Bands

It starts in 1943, when I'm 12, and my folks take me to see a film at our neighborhood movie theater, the Studio, in San Bernardino, California. The movie is *Best Foot Forward*. Now this is a big Technicolor extravaganza that stars Lucille Ball and a bunch of young starlets like June Allyson and Van Johnson.

But the big deal for me is Harry James and his Big Band, the Music Makers. Harry has everything I think is super—he's handsome, has a great pompadour, wears a white tux coat and what really gets to me, plays a golden trumpet. The music is exciting; he plays a great swinging number, "The Two O'Clock Jump," and the dazzling "Flight of the Bumblebee." I've never seen or heard anything like him, or the big, blaring, brass section that swings so hard I can hardly stay in my seat.

We live comfortably on the forty-five dollars a week my dad earns selling meat to butcher shops for the Wilson Meat Packing Company. But now, I want a trumpet and want to play and look like Harry James—maybe I'll even get a pompadour and white jacket too.

My folks understand and respect my dream, but we can't afford to buy a new trumpet, so my dad takes on an extra job, driving a taxi cab from 10 PM to 2 AM almost every night, to earn the extra money my horn will cost. Remember this is wartime, the Japanese have attacked Pearl Harbor, and all of a sudden even this little town is at war. Army and Air Force bases spring up all around San Bernardino County. With all these servicemen around town, there is a real need for taxi drivers, so my dad signs on.

How he did it I'll never know, but every time I think how he gave up his nights of sleep to earn the money for my horn, it makes me remember just how much he and my mom supported me in following my dream. And just how much I appreciate what they did for me.

There is one problem...

All the Army and Air Force and Navy bands need musical instruments, especially brass ones, like trumpets and trombones.

Also, brass is needed first to make casings for bullets and shells and bombs, so trumpets come in a distant fourth in terms of National need. The service bands have already commandeered every trumpet, saxophone, horn, and trombone in the whole area.

But my father searches the music stores of San Bernardino and Riverside Counties for two weeks, scouting out a trumpet. He finds the last trumpet available in the whole Inland Empire.

He takes me to Talbot's Music Store in San Bernardino, where Mr. Talbot gets a dusty case down off a shelf, opens it up, and gives me a peek at a beautiful golden horn—it's not a long, dramatic looking trumpet like Harry James plays; it's an Olds cornet. It's small, and sort of stubby looking, but it is gold lacquered. I get so excited I can hardly hold it, but Mr. Talbot gently takes it and shows me how to put the mouthpiece in. I put it to my lips and pucker the way Mr. Talbot shows me; I blow and make a sound! My dad counts out one hundred and thirty five dollars plus tax for the cornet, and when we get home I proudly make this sound for my mother.

Mr. Leonard next door, who hates both music and me, comes over to see what's going on. He tells my dad that it sounds like an elephant farting. I don't care what he thinks or says—I'm hooked. Oh, along with my cornet, Mr. Talbot gives me the official *Harry James Trumpet Method*.

I immediately start lessons from Mr. Thomas, two doors down. He's a junior high band teacher who works hard all day, teaching kids all the band instruments, but he falls asleep during my evening lessons.

"Mr. Thomas, I finished the page..."

He stirs, snorts and focuses on me.

"Okay—play the next page..."

Before I finish the next page, he's out again.

I leave the dollar on the music stand and walk home.

A week later we read in the San Berdoo *Sun* that Harry James and the Music Makers are coming to town to play at the Municipal Auditorium in seven days. My mom and dad promise to take me to see my new hero, and they're as good as their word.

♪♪♪

On a Thursday night, we're first in line to buy tickets and minutes later we're inside the big old barn of an auditorium. All the seats (folding chairs) have been moved to the sides and the place fills up with dancers of all kinds: jitterbugs, teenage boys and girls ("Must be 18 or Older," the sign at the entrance says), soldiers, sailors, airmen, older men and women, and me. I get in because I'm with my folks. I've got my *Harry James Trumpet Method* in my hand. I want to show it to Mr. James and maybe get an autograph.

At 9 PM, the curtain goes up and banks of colored lights blaze onto the stage and reflect off all those beautiful instruments, as the band, with a string section and even a French Horn player, sit waiting to start. Harry James himself strides out in a tan sports coat and slacks. He picks up his golden trumpet, gives a downbeat to his band and they swing into his theme song, "Ciribiribin." I leave my folks to push through the dancers up to the stage as close as I can get. In person, I can see that Harry is a tall, slim guy, while I'm barely 5 foot 3, and from where I stand on the dance floor pressed up against the bandstand, Harry James looks to be about 10 feet tall! Now I get to see my new hero up close, and hear him play his trumpet.

After an hour, the band takes an intermission. My dad, with me in tow, talks his way backstage, and we go to a dressing room where Harry is. He's talking to a pretty blonde lady with her hair under a turban. Harry James sees my copy of his book, takes it, and signs it for me, with a smile.

When we join Mom in the ballroom, Dad says, "We saw Betty Grable!"

My mom's eyes widen and she says, "Ooh!"

But what do I care! I got my autograph! My night is complete.

We stay for all three sets, and when I get home, I can't stop looking at my book. I feel so happy.

Even now, all these years later, I close my eyes and I can still hear the clear, bright sound of James' trumpet singing out over that band.

♪♪♪

The next year brings big changes to my life. My dad starts a new career as a real estate salesman and we move from California to Canada—San Bernardino to Nanaimo, a town of 10,000, on Vancouver Island, which is the Western-most part of British Columbia, north of the state of Washington. Why this particular place? It's where both my folks are from, and where most of our relatives live. Every summer we drive up Highway One to visit all of them, and I revel in having cousins to play with, and aunts and uncles who sometimes fuss over me. Anyway, we pack up and start out for our new life in Canada.

When we get there, my folks find a two story house that is a block up a hill from the Yacht Club. It has a view of the ocean and the tip of Newcastle Island, and they decide we can afford it.

My cousin Jack hears me play my cornet. Now he's tall—6 feet 2. Jack's suave, works in a nice men's store so he's always well dressed, and also has a way with the girls. He sits me down in his folks' living room, in front of the big old Philco radio phonograph, drops the cactus needle down on a spinning 78 RPM shellac record and says,

"Now listen to this, Billy. This is important. This is Duke Ellington."

He plays me "Take the 'A' Train." I have never heard anything like this band. Where Harry James' band is smooth and tight, Duke's is wild and free. I love it.

I now have a really fine trumpet teacher, Frank Carroll, who is the town barber, but who can play all kinds of difficult cornet solos. Frank's also the conductor of the Nanaimo Silver Cornet Band, and every Monday night we rehearse all kinds of wonderful brass band music, from Sousa marches to Rossini overtures.

After my trumpet lesson, Frank's wife Gladys, smiles and says, "Come over to the piano, Billy!" Then she sits down to teach me about chords and improvising.

After a few weeks of intensive work, Frank asks me to work alongside him and Gladys with Stu Storey's band at the Pygmy ballroom on Saturday night. The Pygmy Ballroom is in the center of the downtown area of Nanaimo, and it's a popular place for the dancers to go, like my cousin Jack. He can really jitterbug, or as he calls it, "Jive." Wow, I'm so excited, I can hardly wait for Saturday night to come.

Finally, after one of the longest weeks of my life, I put on my new long pants and white shirt and my folks drive me to my first professional job! Of course I'm the youngest person in the band, but Frank and Gladys look out for me—not that much temptation is going to come my way. I'm so proud when Cousin Jack points me out to his girlfriend, while I'm up here on the bandstand. When the band swings into the Glenn Miller arrangement of "Little Brown Jug," I'm in heaven. I get to play my first "ad-lib" solo! (I'm reading the solo someone played on the record.) I stand up, and the spotlight almost blinds me, but luckily I've got it memorized.

♪♪♪

I enjoy our life in Nanaimo, but a couple of years later, 1947, I can feel some kind of tension building up. It stems from the relationship between my mother and her two older sisters, who are extremely judgmental and set in their thinking about the rest of the "family." I'm getting along great with my cousins and most of the aunts and uncles—even these two, if I don't have to be around them very much.

I kind of know that my mother and those two older sisters don't see eye to eye on a lot of things, and my folks have got this new notion that being in such close proximity is not so hot after all.

Things come to a boiling point over some insignificant issue, just like most in-family crises do, but in a small town, it's hard to ignore such problems.

Finally, my dad calls a family conference in the kitchen, and he says, "We're thinking about moving back to California, old son…"

I'm not surprised but I just say, "Oh, really?"

"Well, what do you think?"

It's scary to me that I have so much "say" in what my family does, or where we're going to live, but here it is! I'm determined now to be a professional trumpeter, even though I'm still playing my cornet. I want to come back to California, where I think I'll have a better chance to fulfill my dream. But I manage to get it out.

"I … I'd like to go back to California…"

It's decided! It takes Dad a couple of weeks to sell our home, and we pack up and move, back to San Bernardino.

My folks find a house that is pretty and comfortable and that we can afford. Everything is so different and crazy, with this big move; I miss Jack and my cousins and aunts and uncles and everything else about life in Nanaimo, on Vancouver Island, and now I have to start high school back here in San Bernardino, California.

I don't know anyone, and on the first day of classes I go to the Band Room where there's a whole sea of strangers—people kidding around with friends, others blasting away on horns and drums. But over or through all the chaos I can hear a piano playing the intro to Duke Ellington's "Take the 'A' Train." A tenor sax starts to play the melody, and I quickly snatch my cornet out and join in, at long distance, playing the trumpet fill-in licks from the recording that I know so well.

The kids stop to look and listen, and the sea of students parts so that I can see a black kid who looks up from the keyboard to see me, horn to lips. He grins at me, and so does a big, tall lanky guy playing tenor sax. He stops long enough to motion me over, and I slowly move to join the black guys.

When we finish "'A' Train," we introduce ourselves, and I find out that Billy Larkin is a wiry seventeen-year-old, with a great smile and tremendous talent. He's learned some piano technique from his mother, but he's way beyond what she can teach him. He plays blues, and swings, and he can even write arrangements. Edward Conerly is the tenor man. And Fisher Wood is the bass player. Richard Carroll is the alto sax man and he's well over six feet tall.

Every morning Mr. Harbaugh, a great band and harmony teacher, opens up the band room, and we rush in.

Billy opens up the spinet, Edward gets out his tenor sax, Fisher grabs the school's string bass and Richard gets a reed onto his alto sax. We jam the blues (I can play the blues in three keys!), then we try whatever new song one of us wants to, until the bell rings and we have to go to our next class.

FOURTH CHORUS: I BECOME A "REEBOP"

FIRST VERSE

After a few weeks of our morning jam sessions, one Monday morning, pianist Billy Larkin tells me he is starting a regular band, "The Reebops," and asks,

"Do you want to be in it?"

"Oh boy, do I!"

He says we'll rehearse this Thursday, and gives me his address.

Thursday finally arrives, and my folks drive me down to Billy's house in the "colored" section of town. They are a little hesitant about leaving me, but I insist I'll be fine. Of course they make it very clear that they'll pick me up in two hours. I can't wait to see the taillights of my folks' 1940 Oldsmobile pull away down the street and disappear into the night.

Billy comes out grinning, and says, "I'm sure glad you could make it, Pete—come on in!"

I follow him in, hug Edward and Richard, and Billy sits down at an ancient baby grand. Over it the only light is from a bare bulb which hangs from an electric wire that comes out of the ceiling. The floor is wood, just plain bare wood, not varnished and waxed like ours at home, but it's swept clean. It's a hot night so Mrs. Larkin brings us lemonade, but nothing matters as we get down to playing.

Billy smiles and says, "I wrote out 'How High the Moon'—let's try it."

We play it down, and fix a couple of things. What a great feeling, to play this tune that all the jazz groups are doing. We each get a chance to play an ad-lib chorus on these fast moving chord changes. There's nothing written out like the Glenn Miller 'stock'

15

arrangements I played with the band at the Pygmy Ballroom in Nanaimo—and what a challenge to make sense out the chords and keep on top of them as they fly by.

Then we play down another arrangement Billy has written with our band director, Mr. Harbaugh's, help. We play and play, tune after tune.

The music we make feels so right, so good that I never want it to stop. Soon the windows, which are all wide open, are filled with faces—kids, grownups, all brown skinned, smiling and nodding or clapping their hands to the music.

I have played in all kinds of places, for all kinds of people, but I have never, before or since, felt such love and acceptance as I felt that night.

The two hours go by like two minutes, it seems to me, when our cream colored 1940 Olds coupe pulls up in front. My dad comes up and into the house, shakes hands with Mrs. Larkin and my buddies, and I have to pack up my horn and reluctantly leave. I leave a part of my heart in that house, even though we are to play together so many more wonderful times.

THE REEBOPS ONSTAGE

SECOND VERSE

Our band, "Billy Larkin's Reebops," is featured in the 1948 edition of the "San Bernardino High School Talent Show" along with two guys who are funny nutty twins, The Bosley Brothers. They do an act where they pantomime to records while they make funny faces. The audience is made up of all the kids in school; they love 'em, but I'm too nervous to do anything but smile.

The mimics finish, and we walk out onstage as the curtain closes behind us. I'm nervous, but we've rehearsed our arrangements many, many times and besides, I know we're pretty good. I'm the only white kid in the band—Fisher Wood and his big string bass, Sticks the drummer, Billy at the school's grand piano (which isn't really so grand), set up behind the front line of the horns. I stand in between the two big guys, Richard Carroll with his alto sax, and Edward Conerly, with his tenor. Me? I'm five feet four now… I feel like I'm standing between two giants.

Anyway, Billy gives us his big white-toothed grin, the curtain pulls back, and Bobby Magnusson, the Class President, grabs the mike and announces,

"Now here's a great band that started right here in school! Let's hear it for Billy Larkin and the Reebops!"

The audience applauds as Billy kicks off Duke Ellington's "Take the 'A' Train." Once we start to do our thing, everything feels good, and by the end of the first chorus the kids in the audience are clapping in rhythm with us. At the end of the band chorus, which is right off Duke's recording, we swing it out, and the kids cheer and applaud.

They've never heard a swing band of kids their own age! We do the Trenier Twins' "All That Wine Is Gone," replete with us shouting and pointing into the audience, "There's a wino over here, There's a wino over there!" (We learned this tune by listening to a late night broadcast from a Riverside nightclub.) Well, the kids go nuts, laughing and clapping, especially when we point at a teacher. We're almost bewildered by the response, but I sneak a glance at Billy, who just grins and nods to keep swingin.'

It goes over great with almost everybody except for Webster

Hall, the School Principal, who stands in the wings, stage right, and looks grimmer every time we yell and point. But we don't care; we swing it out and go into the next tune.

After four tunes, we've really got the SBHS auditorium jumpin.' We look at each other, because we can't quite believe this... we never dreamed we'd get this kind of acceptance.

When we finish, we take some self-conscious bows to all the yelling, whistles, and applause. The bell rings to signal that assembly period is over, but the kids stand and yell for more. Mr. Hall marches out to the mike and tells the students that they have to go their next class, but they don't seem to be in a hurry to move out. The bell rings again and Mr. Hall gets red in the face as he bellows at them.

"GO TO CLASS!!"

Webster Hall can be heard even without a mike—finally everyone moves out and we pack up.

I go on to Accounting Class (which I am taking because my dad wants me to get some business background), but I could be going to a class on basket weaving, I feel so happy.

And I'm looking forward to sitting next to one of the prettiest of the majorettes that prance in front of us when we march at football games. I slide into my seat and look over at Gloria Masters. She looks at me, and even though I'm kind of shy and unsure of myself with most girls, I can't restrain myself. I really need for her to tell me she thought that what our band and I had done was good.

I impulsively ask her, "Did you come to the assembly...?"

She looks at me and nods. "Yes."

"Well... how did you like it?"

She touches her beautiful cheek with a slim finger and reflectively says, "You were *real* good..."

I'm glad to hear that, but I'm waiting for more. I get it. I think Gloria is going to smile at me, but she gets this look like she's tasted something bad.

She says, "...but I feel sorry for anyone that only has *niggers* for friends."

I can't believe this came out of those lovely lips. Now that mouth doesn't look pretty at all, not with that kind of stuff coming out of it. I sit still, digesting this garbage about our band and my good buddies, but it really hits me hard. I explode!

Billy Larkin's Reebops

"Well I feel really sorry for anyone that'd say anything as stupid as that, and I feel sorry for you, because you're *stupid too!*"

The rest of the period is silent… there's a wall of ice between our side-by-side desks. The bell rings and she flounces out, her nose in the air. I walk slowly into the hall, where I see Gloria talking excitedly to a big wide-shouldered dude with black wavy hair who is getting stuff out of his hall locker. I recognize him because when we're playing in the band in the stands, he's out on the field 'creaming' guys. He's Dan Goforth, our all CBL linebacker, and he's big and mean. She points at me… I instinctively start to move down the hall faster as Goforth yells at me,

"Hey, trumpet player! I wanna talk to you!"

Well, I don't 'wanna' talk to him. I take off, fast. I'm out the end of the building before he can cram his books back in. I get a glimpse of him starting after me. I'm not very big, but I've always been fast… the baseball coach wanted me to come out and play shortstop or centerfield. Now I shift into high gear, and head for … where…?

Where else? The Band Room, of course! I'm keeping ahead of the linebacker, giving him a good run for his money. But suddenly I panic, because half way across the schoolyard I hear Goforth yell,

"Hey Corny, help me catch this guy!"

'Corny,' AKA Bob Cornelius, is the quarterback on the football team, and he yells enthusiastically, "Okay!"

Now I've got two massively athletic footballers on my tail and I turn it up another notch, but I'm starting to run out of gas. My legs start to feel like they're turning to jelly. I make it to the steps that lead up to the Band Room. I hear the linebacker and the quarterback thundering up behind me, but I've had it.

Just then the Band Room doors open and attired in a fresh white dress shirt and black chinos, out strides Mr. Edward Conerly, all six feet and four inches of a black guy with big muscles. He looks at me dragging up the stairs, sees the two behemoths bearing down, and sizes the scene up immediately.

He steps down a couple of steps, and says, "Come on up, Pete, I'll take care'a this…"

The football "heroes" skid to a stop and gaze up at Ed as he slides his massive right hand slowly up to the collar of his immaculately starched shirt. I watch, frozen, on the top step. His fingers go to his collar edge, and like magic, out comes a shiny Gillette single-edge razor blade. He holds it between thumb and index finger as the bright sun glints on it.

Ed growls at them, "Now, what's your problem … *boys*…?

'Corny' and Goforth glance at Edward, his Gillette glinting in the sun, then at each other. Their macho spirit seems to melt; they turn and jog away.

Edward replaces the blade, comes back up the steps to me, puts his arm around my shoulders and says, "Let's go get us a cool drink, Pete!"

We do, and I never have any more problems with football players.

Unfortunately however it is not my last 'up close and personal' experience with racial bigotry and hatred, only my first. I've never told Edward or the other guys what Gloria really said… I figure it isn't worth hurting their feelings.

CODA

Billy Larkin joined the Army and when he was discharged he made several jazz organ albums for Pacific Jazz Records. Edward Conerly spent time on Count Basie's band, but eventually switched from sax to bass. In 1972 Eddie called me to play on Barbara MacNair's 5-day-a-week TV show. I accepted and it was wonderful to hook up again and perform with my hero, and buddy!

I'll spare you the agony of the lessons, the practice and the rehearsals in high school. I'll segue to where to my induction into music and Show Biz begins—when I play my first big-time act.

FIFTH CHORUS:
I GET TO SWING WITH THE 'KING'

It's August, 1949—I've just finished my senior year at San Bernardino High School—the Reebops are now working a steady Saturday night gig, but this weekend is different.

I've had to get another trumpet player to sub for me because my folks and I have just put our bags in the trunk of our brand new Olds Rocket 88, and are ready to go out of town.

My dad looks at me and says, "Okay, son, you're driving all the way!"

It's my birthday—I'm 18, and to celebrate I get to make my first trip to Las Vegas to hear our favorite singer, Mr. Nat 'King' Cole at the Sands Hotel.

It's a hot day, but we've got air conditioning and a great radio in this new car. I slip on my sunglasses, slide behind the wheel, key it and we leave San Bernardino behind. Everything goes great until I don't make the right turn onto the highway to Las Vegas when we hit Barstow, but that's because I'm messing with the radio to bring in KMPC—they play big band music.

My mom is Irish and excitable; her face gets almost as red as her hair as she scolds, "Bill, you're driving! You've got to pay attention!"

But my dad calms her. "Now Eileen, he's doing just fine… just turn her around, and we'll get back on the road."

Dad's one half Cree Indian, and you couldn't get him lost if you tried!

♪♪♪

When we get to Vegas, we check into the Sands. I have my own room with an ice bucket and a red velvet bedspread!

We get dressed up (I wear my new blazer), and we go in to dinner in the Copa Room.

It's all red velvet and gold fixtures, and special lights that glow up the walls. Dad says something to the guy in a tux who meets us at the door and puts something in the guy's hand. He smiles and leads us right down front! Wow! We're right in front of the stage! We order filet mignon dinners (I get served a glass of champagne), and after we finish, the lights go down, and the curtain pulls open. Now we're going to get to see Nat 'King' Cole.

But before the King comes on we have to sit through a chorus line, the Copa Girls.

My mom says to my dad, "I think they look rather common and cheap, don't you, Bill?"

My dad says, "I suppose so…"

But I can see he's watching them pretty closely. They look great to me—nothing like the girls at my school, especially in these skimpy costumes.

Then after the chorus line, I think we're going to see Nat 'King' Cole, but on comes this guy, Dave Barry, who talks about his mother-in-law and how weird his kids are, and people laugh… why don't they just put King Cole on, without all this other junk? Finally, Barry gets through, and an off-stage voice announces,

"Ladies and gentlemen, Mr. Jack Entratter and the Sands Hotel are proud to present… Mr. Nat 'King' Cole!"

The house lights dim, a spotlight blazes onto the right hand side of the stage, Antonio Morelli's band roars into Nelson Riddle's chart of "Dance, Ballerina, Dance," and Mr. Nat 'King' Cole himself strides out onto the stage. The audience claps, cheers and whistles.

I turn and grin, "This is great, Dad!"

He smiles at me, pats my shoulder, and says, "I thought you'd like it."

The King smiles his big, broad, glistening smile, and starts to sing. I listen to the brass section hit the syncopated licks, kind of like "POWS!" that punctuate Nat's smooth singing style.

He doesn't phrase like other singers like Frankie Laine, who sings right with the beat… King Cole's vocal just seems to float along somehow, sort of behind the beat, but he always comes out just right at the end of the phrase, of course. He sings one tune after another and then sits down and plays the piano on "Where or When" which swings like crazy. I love every note and every minute of it. I just pretend that that's me up there, in the orchestra, playing all those great arrangements. It sure sounds easy—almost effortless.

Mom leans over to say, "I just saw one of the trumpet players yawn. Can you imagine?"

"No I can't," I reply.

I come to a quick conclusion—maybe the trumpet parts aren't so very hard—maybe, someday... But I stop daydreaming as Nat turns and smiles,

"Thank you very much, ladies and gentlemen, will you help me thank these great musicians that travel with me, Joe Comfort on the bass, John Collins on guitar, and Lee Young on drums... and let's hear it for Antonio Morelli and his wonderful orchestra."

The orchestra stands up. Mom and Dad applaud.

Mom, who is prone to noticing every detail, says, "Look at Mr. Young's hair... I think he's wearing a toupee!"

"So what, Eileen? He's a fine drummer, isn't he?" asks my dad.

Mom says, "Well, of course. I just think it's interesting..."

I don't care what the drummer's hair looks like. I'm busy checking out the trumpet players. They are a few years older than I am, and they don't seem to be as excited as they should be, getting to play for Nat! After several more numbers the show is over.

We all cheer and clap and Nat even does a couple of encores, but as my folks and I file out of the show room with the crowd, I blurt out,

"It was great, but it didn't last long enough."

Dad knows I live for this music stuff, and he says, "You know what? You can go listen to the lounge and hear Count Basie's band—you can't go in, so just stand outside, okay? We'll be over to get you in a little while."

"Okay! Take your time!"

I'm off like a shot, going as fast as I can through all the people on their way to gamble. I can see the lights and hear the band swinging into the "One O'Clock Jump." Why would anybody want to gamble when they could hear Basie's band?

I skid to a stop and try to look cool, so I can hang out at the entry to the lounge. As I look around the velvet curtain I can see the Count smiling at the audience, and his band. I hear the whole set before Dad taps me.

"It's pretty late… time to go."

I can't argue—I've gotten to hear some great music. We go back to our rooms, but it's hard to sleep after all this.

♪♪♪

Next day we rocket home to San Berdoo, and I'm back for my first semester at San Bernardino Valley College. I practice two, maybe three hours a day, and rehearse with the other guys in the band. I just get home from a rehearsal when our phone rings and my mom picks it up.

"Yes? Yes?… Oh?… well, just a minute… he's here… just a minute…"

She hands me the receiver, and whispers, "It's a Bill Alexander… he says he's a band leader!"

I grab the phone… of course, he's the leader where my trumpet teacher Dick Dahlgren plays. Hmm! Why is he calling me?

"Hello?"

I hear this kind of loud, bored voice say, "Uh, yeah, Bill… this is Bill Alexander. I'm the band leader at the Chi Chi Club in Palm Springs. We need to add a trumpet to our regular band for a show next week. Dickie Dahlgren says you can cut it, so I thought I'd give you a call. It's for one week, and it pays $135—can you do it?"

Can I do it? Can I! I don't care if I'm going to play for a traveling flea circus… this is a real professional job! But I try to a little cool, like a pro should be…

"Well… sure… that'll be great… I mean, sure, that'll be fine… What show is it?'

Alexander drawls, "Oh, it's Nat Cole."

I feel my heart start to race, like when I get to play a solo, and I turn to my mom, who's watching with great interest, and I whisper, "Something to write on!"

She hands me paper and pencil, and I get the details. I'm so excited I can hardly stand it. I hang up, whirl around…

"Mom! I'm gonna play for Nat 'King' Cole!"

"Why, that's wonderful, honey! When?"

I tell her the details, and my mom's pretty Irish face gets almost as red as her hair.

"Your Dad and I will be there, that's for sure! Good for you!"

I call all my buddies to tell 'em the news. Edward, Rich and Billy are happy for me, and maybe a little envious.

♪♪♪

The week just drags by; I practice even more. On Wednesday my dad comes into my bedroom at 10 PM to ask,

"Don't you think you've practiced enough for one day?"

"One more page of the Clarke Technical Studies, okay?" (Even though my lips are tingling.)

"All right! Just one more. But your mother and I want to watch TV."

Finally Thursday, rehearsal day comes; Dad hands me my car keys as his suntanned face splits into a big grin.

"I had it tuned up and replaced one of your tires."

"Thanks, Dad!"

♪♪♪

Away I go, thundering down to Palm Springs in my '32 Ford, with my dark blue suit, my best white shirt which Mom has just washed and ironed, my Selmer trumpet (like Harry James plays), and my head full of dreams. I feel so happy it doesn't even matter that my car, my pride and joy, boils over twice.

The Chi Chi Nightclub is right on the main drag in Palm Springs. I park around back, grab my stuff, and go in. It looks like a movie set to me: the stage with silver and gold decorations around the sides and top and a whole lot of tables jammed around the little dance floor. In back of the tables are red banquettes, and even with the lights turned up high, it looks pretty darned glamorous to me—maybe not like the Copa at the Sands (no red velvet), but, wow… I'm playing for Nat Cole!

I climb onstage. I don't know any of the other musicians except for Dick, my trumpet teacher. Everybody's older than I am.

A big guy with wavy blonde hair comes over. He sticks out his hand and says, "Hi, I'm Bill Alexander… glad you could make it."

Finally I see my teacher and mentor, Dick Dahlgren. He smiles and looks at me closely.

"You a little… nervous?"

"Well, …yeah…!"

"Don't worry—you'll be fine."

He hands me the third trumpet book. I try to act cool—I hope my hands aren't shaking. I climb up on the riser.

Dick says, "Oh Bill, this is Cecil Read. Cecil works with Nat quite a bit, and he's gonna play first!"

We exchange hellos, shake hands. He's friendly and smiles. He's a huge guy, and old… I mean he must be fifty or so. He's taller than me, and very heavy—or, as Mom would say, rather obese… well, face it, he's so fat that his thighs roll right off the sides of the chair. He's dressed in a beautiful black mohair tux but it looks a little tight… I've heard of him; he plays in the Hollywood studios.

Then I hear him warm up, and I know why he plays studio work. He sounds wonderful. I watch as the three trombonists set up in front of us trumpets, just like we do in the Band Room.

Lee Young, Nat's drummer, comes on stage. His stingy brim hat is pushed way back on his head so I can see that his forehead goes a lot further up than it did in Vegas.

He says, "Hi fellas!"

He looks up at Cecil Read; his mouth draws down at the corners with a phony kind of concern.

He grins, "Hey Cece…! Hey! What happened to your diet, man? I hear that the tailors at Sy Devore's measure you just for the exercise, is that right?"

Cecil looks at Lee, points to his stingy brim, and says, "We're indoors, Lee—you can take your hat off—or did you forget to wear your hair?"

Lee shakes his finger at Cecil, sits down at his drums, and splatters the sticks over the snare and toms in a few licks. John Collins sits down by the piano with his guitar and Joe Comfort settles in with his bass fiddle.

Lee says, "Books should be in order—Let's get up 'Ballerina' first, guys."

When he sees everybody is ready, he turns back to his drums, and counts off. "A—one, two, three, four!"

We charge into the intro of "Dance Ballerina, Dance," and away we go! What a feeling… I'm playing the same arrangement I heard in Vegas. I'm really excited, but I concentrate on reading the notes and remember to phrase with my fellow trumpeters, and I do okay.

We run down all the charts, but of course the King doesn't come to rehearsal.

"Nat'll see you guys tonight," says Lee, as we break for dinner.

At dinner, I can hardly eat, because Cecil Read talks about playing TV and movie scoring sessions almost every day. I try to imagine what it would be like to make a living doing that instead of selling real estate like my dad.

We come back and change into our suits backstage. I rush out before the first dance set. There are Mom and Dad, beaming and smiling. I can see how excited and proud they are, and it feels good. After all, they've spent a lot of money on lessons and this beautiful new Selmer trumpet I play, just like the model Harry James plays.

"Hi Mom… Dad—I'm glad you're here."

"Car run okay?" asks Dad.

"Just great—thanks, Dad! It only boiled over twice! Look, I've got to get back for the dance music. I'll see you after the show!"

Dad raises his Cutty Sark to me, and says, "Play pretty."

I think my mother has a tear in her eye. Oh well, I'm a pro now, and I gotta go.

We play a dance set, then Bill Alexander gets up from the drums and gives the seat over to Lee Young, who smiles at us as he adjusts the cymbals and snare. Lee looks offstage to check with the King himself, having a smoke before he comes out.

He nods to Alexander, who picks up the mike, and booms, "Ladies and gentlemen, the Chi Chi Club is proud to present Mr.— Nat—'King'—Cole!"

Lee yells out the count-off for the opener … "A–One, two, three, four!" as I see Nat, his black hair shiny and marcelled, take a last drag from his cigarette, toss it down, exhale and step out beaming onto the stage in a cloud of smoke.

We thunder into the intro to Nelson Riddle's arrangement of "Dance Ballerina, Dance"—tah-dah-tah-loo-day-dah-da la da, and Nat starts to sing. I immediately lock in to his silky smooth voice;

Nat 'King' Cole with keyboard

he's just gliding along, phrasing behind the beat, and I immediately *lose* the count.

I stare at the music, there is a three bar rest, four beats to the bar, and the rests are going by—but I don't know where I am!—I don't know what bar or measure I'm in, in this first arrangement I've ever played on my first really big-time gig!

Oh my god, I'm lost… my folks are here, and Nat the King is singing, Dick's recommended me and here *I* am… I'm lost! I don't know the count! Lee Young and the rhythm section are swinging away, but Nat is so far behind the beat, he might be in another song for all I know. Then, "Pow!" One brass punctuation goes by, but it's only two trumpets, not three, that went "Pow!" I listen to Nat, but he's back-phrasing like he always does, just floating along way behind the beat.

Another "Pow!" is coming up. I've got to do something—I watch my section mates get set. I guess where the "Pow!" should be, but I'm about a half a beat late. I think I see Lee Young look up, but I'm so lost all I know for sure is that I'm in Palm Springs, making a fool of myself, and maybe even my teacher.

Finally, Cecil Read looks down at me. In a split second he sees I'm hopelessly lost, and barks out a quick cue, "Bar 22!"

I find my place and manage to join in on the next brass punctuation, another "Pow!"

I lock in and we wail through the rest of the chart. I now realize all too well, it's one thing to be part of the audience, but something else to be onstage, an actual part of the band. I'm not being paid to listen, but to play, and count!

When the tune ends, Nat greets the audience, and chats for a moment—just long enough for Cecil Read, the great studio trumpet player, to turn and look down from the empyrean heights of the first trumpet chair, at me, shriveled in my chair like a prune. Cecil fixes me with a particularly stony look.

Then he speaks in a quiet but authoritative voice. "It's best that you count, and don't listen to the act, kid!"

I feel like all the stage lights are right on me. I slide down a bit further in my chair, but Cecil reaches down, pats my knee and says, "Opening night jitters… you'll be fine."

Dick looks past the large man in the middle to grin impishly, but encouragingly. I try to smile back.

Suddenly I feel like I *am* going to be okay. We play the rest of the show, and Nat takes a moment to acknowledge the band. We all stand for a bow, but deep inside I wonder if everybody, including The King, knows how I messed up!

I concentrate on not listening to a note Nat sings! When we finish playing the bows, Dick and Cecil pat me on the back. I dash off to see my folks, who look like they've witnessed the second coming. I sit down.

Dad says, "Well, it sounded great… just like Las Vegas."

I smile as my mom pats my hand, which is still tending to tremble just a little.

"How is it, playing for him… it must be lovely to get to hear him sing, and get paid for it!" she says.

I manage to smile.

"It's just great Mom, but I'm pretty busy up there, so I don't really listen to him. You know, you *do* have to pay attention to the music!"

CODA

I never worked again with Cecil, but saw him from time to time. I worked at the Chi Chi many times, and played Nat's act many more times in Palm Springs at the Chi Chi, as well as at the Cal Neva at Lake Tahoe, but there was no thrill like the feeling of that opening night. My folks loved Nat, and saw him every chance they could. Six years later I drove my folks up to Vegas again, just after my dad had surgery, so that he got to see him one final time.

When I look back at that opening night, I remember what I thought when I saw the trumpeters playing his act at the Sands. And now I realize that nothing is as easy as it looks, except maybe losing the count, or jumping to conclusions.

SIXTH CHORUS: A NEW SET OF CHANGES

I graduate from high school, and the Reebops have to break up. Billy Larkin goes into the Army and a Special Services Unit, playing piano, organ, and singing. Edward Conerly goes with Count Basie; Richard Carroll goes into the Air Force and becomes an officer.

I get one year of junior college at San Bernardino Valley College, but the Korean "Conflict" has just broken out and a lot of my other buddies are getting drafted into the Army and being sent to Korea as infantrymen.

I want to keep playing, moving toward being a full-time professional musician. I hear of an opportunity to audition to get into the 775th Air Force Band that is in Tucson, Arizona. Now this band is supposed to be sent to March AFB in Riverside, just a few miles from San Berdoo, so a buddy and fellow trumpeter Fred Galloway and I audition and sign up. We're sworn in and we're officially enlisted Air Force men.

We're herded onto a train headed for San Antonio. We get our suitcases into the shelf and get settled when I see that we *are* in service—two uniformed Air Police men with rifles station themselves at each end of the railway car. Fred and I look at each other with sinking spirits. What have we gotten into? But all that changes when a short curly haired guy, our age, in a T-shirt come up to us. He smiles with real warmth, holds out an open box of See's Candy, sticks out his other hand and says,

"Hi…! I'm Harry Deroian from Fresno… have a candy!"

We exchange handshakes and take a chocolate. Harry tells us he loves show business, especially movies. He has been an usher in the biggest movie palace in Fresno, and he has a special favorite on the screen… Jerry Lewis!

We are treated to a one-man show of all the best comic moments in Jerry Lewis' vast repertoire of crazy, goofy, funny antics for the two days it takes our train to get to San Antonio, Texas!

♪♪♪

We arrive in Texas, and are bussed to Lackland Air Force Base to start our eight weeks of Basic Training. Fred and I are lucky to have Harry and his cousin in our outfit or "Flight." He is easily the best-liked guy in our midst, and we're lucky that our Flight Chief, Sergeant Bill Garvin, likes to hear Fred and me practice. He leaves his room to us and takes off to the Service Club.

Then after about eight weeks we vacate our nice warm barracks that we've scrubbed and mopped and made shine, and we're marched out to the parade grounds where there are brown khaki tents as far as I can see! The deal is that we're being moved into tents as we await our orders for our destinations. New recruits are marched into our old quarters.

Life in Tent City is a shocker! We manage to survive a couple of weeks in unheated tents in the freezing climes of Texas. We wake up one early morning when our ice-laden tent top collapses on our upturned sleeping faces.

Another morning I wake up to a torrential rainstorm, which threatens to bring down our tent again. My dress blue hat is floating top down in the "lake" which the dirt floor of our tent has become.

We finally get our orders, and Fred and I are sent to Davis Monthan AFB, in Tucson, Arizona.

Harry and Sergeant Garvin volunteer to go to Korea. Both our friends die in combat somewhere around Inchon.

SEVENTH CHORUS:
I MEET JOHN WILLIAMS

My buddy Fred Galloway and I arrive in Tucson and take a bus to Davis Monthan Air Force Base. An Air Police guy with white gloves and hat checks us in through the gate. Then we get dropped off at a big dingy sand colored building. We lug our duffel bags, suitcases and trumpet cases to the 775th Air Force barracks.

It's a great break for me, as we meet and get to know our other band mates… many of their parents are Hollywood Studio players.

These guys' fathers do what I dream about—playing music for a living—while *my* dad sells real estate. It seems that being around guys whose parents are working musicians is letting me look at a whole new, different way of life and making a living.

Mel Pollan, who plays great string bass, is the son of tubaist and bassist Al, who records with Marty Paich and does all kinds of studio work.

John Bambridge's dad plays string bass and tuba at Columbia Studios. John Jr. is a great clarinetist and saxophonist in our band.

John Williams' dad is a percussionist at Twentieth Century Fox Studios, and Bernie Fleischer's dad wrote and produced music for Fleischer Studio's *Gulliver's Travels*.

In later years John Bambridge worked with the Tonight Show Band on the Johnny Carson Show, and many other of my former band-mates became successful professional players.

Certainly the most famous is John Williams, who has become a most successful, respected and revered composer.

But in 1951 John goes by 'Johnny' and is also known as 'Curly.' He says it started in high school, and that nickname has carried over into the Air Force, because he has a cloud of curly red hair.

Anyway, 'John' or 'Johnny' or 'Curly' is just a marvelous pianist, and composer, and a helluva jazz trombonist as well. Best of all, a wonderful, wise and fun guy to hang out with.

John drives or hitchhikes back to Los Angeles as much as he can when he can wangle a three-day pass, or on weekends when that doesn't work, to study orchestration and composition with the excellent teacher Bobby Van Epps.

The only piano in the band barracks is smack in the middle of the day room/rehearsal room downstairs, where guys are practicing or yacking and fooling around, and John can't concentrate. Don't get the idea from this that he's unsociable or a snob, because he has a wild and wonderful sense of humor. But when you want to compose or practice seriously, you need isolation from braying trombones, squeaking clarinets and blasting trumpets. John shows the dedication and focus that he's always had, which together with his enormous talent has made him the marvelous and world-renowned composer he is today.

But he has a different schedule in those days. After band rehearsal, John takes off with a group of us who are heading for the base swimming pool. We drop John off at the Base Amphitheater, to which he has a "backstage" key. John locks himself in the Amphitheater backstage and practices every day for a couple of hours, while we cool off in the pool. I knock on the door and collect John to go to lunch.

That may not sound very special, but don't forget that this is Tucson, where it's above 100° much of the year. God knows what the temp is inside that closed up, un-air-conditioned backstage area.

I remember knocking on the door, and as he opens it, I see he's peeled off the fatigues and is clad only in his G.I. issue shorts. When I asked him what he's working on, he puts his left hand fingers on top of his right hand, both palms down, and moves the ring finger up and down without moving the other digits.

He smiles and tells me, "That!"

Just try it… It takes tremendous concentration to achieve that kind of independence.

John has a puckish sense of humor, which we all enjoy when he would 'put on' the hierarchy of the NCOs (non commissioned officers) who are in direct charge of us, and of course, outrank all of us new airmen. As an example, every morning our First Sergeant, a short but powerful man, Master Sergeant John Swek, comes through our Band barracks. You always get a warning that the good Sergeant is close at hand, because he smokes a short stubby pipe stoked with 'Three Feathers' or some such tobacco, which he laces with chopped up cloves of garlic. We always know when he's come into our bay. Now Sergeant Swek never swears or uses 'bad language,' so when he gets to your bunk, he says in his slightly inflected Polish accent,

"Alright, you daggone fiddlin' phooey, get outta that sack and get over to the mess hall and get your 'saxophone pads'!"

('Saxophone pads' is what he calls the little hotcakes that the chow line jockeys throw on your tin tray as you troop sleepy-eyed down the chow line.)

We sometimes tag along behind the good sergeant to watch the fun when Sergeant Swek comes round the corner to the alcove where Curly's bunk is situated. Swek repeats his greeting, whereby John opens a sleepy eye to focus on the little man.

John gives him a welcoming smile, props himself up on his pillow, and says in his most charming voice, "Why good morning, Sergeant! Good to see you!"

"Alright Williams. Roll outta that sack and go get your 'saxophone pads'…"

"And how is Mrs. Swek and little John…?"

The sergeant is nonplussed for a moment.

"Well, they're fine… but you gotta get up…"

"Tell me, Sergeant, what kind of a day do we have?"

Swek never quite knows how to take John, so he blusters a bit.

"Why it's a nice… daggone it, you phooey, it's time to get up!"

"But John, I'm never very hungry in the morning…"

"Well daggone it, you have to get up… we've got band rehearsal!"

"Now, what time is rehearsal…?"

"Why, the same time as every day! You know that…! Nine thirty!"

"And what time is it now, John?"

Curly, AKA John Williams

Sergeant Swek pulls out his pocket watch and says, "It's seven thirty...!"

"Let's see... I've got two hours before rehearsal... You know, John, I stayed up late last night working on a new score for the band..."

Sergeant Swek is stuck. Curly does write scores for the band. They are really interesting music that everyone enjoys playing, even Swek on his cornet. So he turns and walks away, steaming, and smoking his pipe like a chimney on fire.

Swek sends a succession of sergeants, one after another. They all like and respect our buddy, and they all fail to entice him out of bed. But at about 9 ayem, Sergeant Bill Williams, a lanky career sergeant who plays excellent jazz trombone à la Jack Teagarden, sticks his head around the corner of PFC John 'Curly' Williams' alcove and says in a low, but firm voice,

"... C—u-u-r-r-l-e-y..."

John sits up, smiles and responds, "Time to get up, huh Bill...?"

"You got it...!"

We all snicker and get on our way downstairs to the chow hall.

On Saturday nights we are assigned to play at the NCO Club, or the Service Club, which is where most of the enlisted guys go to dance and try to hit on the local lasses from Tucson.

Playing with John is such fun, really a privilege, because of his great jazz playing and harmonic sense, but also because of the humor he injects into his solos. If I play a lick which catches his fancy, or more likely brings a smile, he'll use that as a leit-motif, and structure a whole chorus on it. He doesn't do it maliciously, just as a game or exercise for his supple musical mind.

John is sent to Washington, D.C. after a year or so, while most of us stay on in Tucson.

At least I can say that I assisted John Williams, John Bambridge and the others in defending Tucson from the Korean Menace. I say that jokingly; in no way do I mean to discount the men and women who gave so much in the actual bloody fighting in Korea. We were grateful that we weren't ordered over there. We'd heard of a band that was sent to Inchon, and when the Chinese and North

Koreans stormed the base, the bandsmen were handed M-1's and told to defend the airstrip. The strip was over-run and the whole band lost their lives.

We bitch and moan about being in the Air Force, even about the fact that our band never is transferred to Riverside, California. But we are fortunate to be kept where we are, and not sent to Korea.

After we get out of the Air Force in 1952, John starts his career as a studio pianist, but is soon orchestrating for Nelson Riddle and other composers around Hollywood. John makes several great jazz albums, orchestrating, arranging and composing wonderfully. He is soon writing for TV shows and then for feature films.

I want to play in radio, television and film-scoring orchestras, like the parents of my buddies in the Air Force do. They all see that there is a good living to be made and you get to play good music with great players.

I know you don't just go to MGM or Paramount and audition for a job… you have to work your way up till someone notices you are a good player, and then, maybe…. But you have to start somewhere…

I get discharged from the Air Force and return home.

EIGHTH CHORUS: BACK HOME
TO SOME VERY SAD CHORDS

It's 1953 and it's wonderful to be home, but there's a cloud of worry and concern that descends on us very soon. My dad's having bowel trouble and pain, and my mom asks Dr. Tisinger, the best surgeon in San Bernardino to examine him.

After the exam and preliminary x-rays, Dr. Tisinger tells us, "Pete has a tumor on his colon."

Mom, who graduated from nursing school in 1928, has been working as a nurse since I started high school, and she's steadily advanced till she is now Director of Nursing at San Bernardino Community Hospital. The doctors here won't do the surgery.

Dr. Tisinger explains to her, "We have to work with you, Pete, and if anything happened... well, we want you to take Big Pete to the best man we know for this surgery."

I drive us in to Los Angeles, where we consult with Dr. William Daniel, and my dad is admitted to St. Vincent's Hospital. Dad has the operation a week or so later.

When Dr. Daniel comes out of surgery in his gown, he pulls his mask down as he comes into the waiting room.

He's very serious as he tells us, "I've taken the tumor and as much of the malignancy as I can, but I couldn't get it all."

I feel that my mom knows exactly what this means, but she has to have Dr. Daniel confirm it.

She asks, "It's metastasized?"

"Yes, it has. I'd say he has about five years."

I can see in my mother's face that this is really a death sentence that he's announced.

I feel this awful, hopeless, helpless sense of what he'll go through.

My dad smoked two, sometimes three or four packs of Camels a day for years until the surgery, but most people back then didn't understand about how deadly cigarette smoke is.

Even my mother, a registered nurse, used to smoke some herself. Of course the cigarette ads, in magazines and on the radio and even TV, trumpeted their claims that *their* cigarettes were mild, or didn't dry your throat or make you cough. and so on. I guess my folks, like millions of other people, lived in blissful ignorance of just what that stinking smoke from ciggies was doing to them.

I feel angry somehow at my dad for getting sick, even though it isn't fair, it isn't right, but there it is, and I can't deny it, even though in my heart I know it isn't his fault. Everything seemed to be going so well—too well, perhaps? But there is this aching emptiness—a feeling that there is no hope for my dad and a lot of heartache for my mother. She sees and knows from all her years of nursing what's in store for him and for her as well.

I pray and pray, and try to make bargains with this God, wherever he is, that my father believes in so much. I promise that if Dad can only be granted more life, I'll do all kinds of things, great and small. This is where I think I'll take Pre-Med, and then become a doctor myself. Perhaps with this prayer/promise in God's bank account, I can somehow bargain for Dad so he'll have more time—more of the precious life he loves so much.

Dad takes it all with his usual great spirit—he hasn't been told of Dr. Daniel's prediction, and maybe that's better.

My father has a crazy sense of humor, as demonstrated by him starting a "Beauty Contest" with all the nurses, aides and nuns as contestants. Of course when he hands out his Award certificates, handwritten in ink, everyone is a winner—Sister Matilde has the most beautiful smile, Sister Helene has the most cheery manner in the morning, Nurse Betty has the warmest way (and hands!), and so on.

Finally, after four weeks in St. Vincent's Hospital, Dad is ready to come home. All the staff loves him, and as they see him off with their best wishes, I can sense the sadness behind the smiles because they seem to know what might happen.

I cancel plans to return to school and go to work on a freight dock to help out as much as I can. I play and practice as much as possible and after a semester we three decide it's best that I go back to school. Dad's gotten some of his strength back and is back in the real estate business.

41

♪♪♪

I return first to San Bernardino Valley College to finish my Associate of Arts, then to the brand new University of California at Riverside, where I sign up to take a Pre-Med curriculum.

But my math background is sorely wanting, and when Dr. Conway Pierce, my chemistry professor, starts cross-multiplying equations on the board, all the whiz kids with slide rules around me keep right up, but me…? I'm so lost and feel such a failure that it's hard to take. I go to Dr. Pierce's office and explain.

He says, "You know, my son wanted to be a chemist, but he just didn't have it… you say you love music? Well, there's room for good musicians, as well as good doctors and good chemists, so why don't you do what you love, son!"

♪♪♪

I decide to go back to music, and see if I can become a pro. After finishing the semester at UC Riverside, and after earning four "C's" plus a "D" in chemistry, I'm accepted (just barely) to UCLA.

I find a room I can rent for $35.00 a month from a very nice couple, right across the street from UCLA and the Music Department building. With my Veteran's GI Bill money of $115.00 a month, I can make it! I really work at school, and get all "A's" and a "B." I make the Dean's Honor List.

That's when the next part of my Show Biz experiences starts.

Ninth Chorus:
"Miss Raye Regrets…"

It's June 1956, it's summer vacation from UCLA, and I've been hired to play with Matty Malneck's band at Lake Tahoe. At 7 AM a caravan of cars with guys like me, in their early 20s, takes off from Ship's Restaurant in Los Angeles (Wilshire & Westwood, close to UCLA to be exact), and drives out of town. I'm in the cavalcade driving my MG-TD, a beautiful little metallic Desert Beige British sports car that's my pride and joy.

A couple of hours later, the whole caravan starts up Highway 395, which will eventually get us toward the South Shore of the lake. It's a long trip with stops for gas and burgers and it takes 10 hours, but it's a kick. The late afternoon summer sun glitters and reflects off of Lake Tahoe so brightly that I have to squint my eyes as we drive down to the Lakeside resort. The other guys park and go in, but I drive on down to King's Beach to meet my folks who are arriving at about the same time as I.

I see my folks' Olds 98 in the motel lot. I pull in beside them as my dad and mom are lifting their luggage out of the trunk. Mom is busy organizing things, but my dad looks up, sees me, and drops the clothes bags back into the trunk, which throws Mom off.

"Bill, be careful, my best dresses are in there…"

He kind of ignores her to grin at me, "Hi there, old son!"

Then she looks up at me and exclaims, "For heaven's sake, I didn't see you!"

But now I'm getting a big hug from Dad. When he lets go, Mom moves in.

First of all she gives me the expert appraisal of not only a mother, but also a registered nurse. I know this feeling; I know she cares; she just has to check me out. Sometimes I wish she'd just give me a hug instead of the third degree. See, it is my first time away from home since I was in the Air Force. But, after all… I've been attending UCLA for two semesters, and I'm making out all right, what with my G.I. Bill and an inexpensive room across from campus.

"Have you been eating regularly? Are you getting enough sleep?'"

Oh good lord, she's starting in with me—but I just grin and say, "Yes Mom, I'm fine."

Dad squints a bit as he checks me out.

"Look at him, Eileen, he looks great!"

I get a chance to check them out, too. My dad, William also, is one half Cree Indian, and with his coal black hair and the deep tan on his high cheekboned face, he looks good considering he had surgery for colon cancer four months ago.

But the strain of Dad's illness and her job as the Director of Nurses shows in my mom's face. She's still a pretty lady, and she has started to change the color of her auburn hair to blonde. I think she looks better natural, but it's her hair, just like this is my life. I mean, I'm a sophomore at UCLA—how long is she going to check on my living habits? I help get their stuff into their motel room, but I've got to go.

I tell them, "I've got to get to rehearsal. I'll meet you at six thirty at the Cal Neva, okay?"

Dad grins, "Okay, old son," then to let me know that they're self-sufficient, he turns to her.

"Come on Eileen, let's get unpacked and we'll look over the lake and have a cocktail."

I key the MG, gun her up the hill, back to Cal Neva, and jump out with my trumpet case and mute bag and head in the entrance of the Lodge. The whole front of the building consists of huge, rustic, bark-covered logs topped by a steep slanted shingled roof, and it has a great '30s kind of vibe to it.

I go inside the Lodge. The first thing I see is a pretty young woman behind the reception counter. But the next person that gets my attention is a short guy with wavy gray hair leaning against the counter. He's maybe in his late fifties, with a flower in the button-hole of his dark blue striped suit, looking just like what I figure a "Boss" would look like. His face features a prominent nose and a mouth pulled into a kind of sardonic leer and he has a withered

Mom, Dad and me at Tahoe Sands

left arm, pretty well disguised by the special cut of his expensive suit.

I approach kind of warily with my trumpet and mute bag and ask him, "Can you tell me where the Matty Malneck orchestra is?"

He swings around and surveys me with cold steel-gray eyes, then barks, "You mus' be one'a da rat musicians!"

He jerks his good arm up and thumbs over his shoulder with, "Da meestro's in deah!"

This ain't no Harvard grad, and from what I've seen in old Warner Brothers films with Cagney and Bogie, this guy's… "da reel ting… ya know?"

I proceed on into the Cal Neva, and wend my way past banks of slot machines, along the side of the gaming area past crap and blackjack tables, turn right at the roulette wheel and find The Indian Room.

That's the Show Room where we'll be playing all the big acts. I go in and see a rectangular, high gabled ceiling room with curtains pulled back all the way along the left side. This gives me a spectacular view of the lake. Then I look at the opposite side of the room. On the right side there's a huge boulder just inside the entry, with a great big elk mounted to the top, surveying the room through glass eyes. All along the knotty-pine wall are big game animal heads mounted high over the tables packed in on the floor. This mind-boggling display of taxidermist's art is topped by a head close to the teepee: it's a huge, particularly angry looking moose gazing balefully down at me.

I look down the room to other end where there's the damndest looking teepee which has to be thirty or forty feet tall, reaching up to the gabled ceiling of the room. The stage extends from in front of the teepee. Inside it is the bandstand!

I've played in lots of strange places with unusual bandstands, like the time when I still lived in San Bernardino and worked with Tony Casas' Latin band in a joint in San Jacinto. The management of this bar had to put up chain link fence between the band and the customers because of the risk of flying beer bottles. But this is a new one. The whole scene looks like something out of an old 1930s Warner Bros. movie set.

A few of the other musicians are getting their horns out, and the drummer's already set up. I hurry as best I can around the white-linened tables, climb on the bandstand and exchange hellos with Matty and the guys. I get out the trumpet and look at the leather covered book on my stand—in the middle, "Martha Raye" is printed in gold, and in the corner is gold-stamped, "1ˢᵗ Trumpet"… that's me. I'm ready for the challenge because of my experience, but mostly because I feel confident in my ability to do the job.

Matty looks at us and says, "Okay, fellash, letch get ssstarted."

This is Matty Malneck's bilateral emission, which is a fancy name for a severe lisp. I can see he's feeling good because he's got this impish grin as he says, "Fellash, thish ish our schtar, Mish Martha Raye."

Miss Martha Raye strides out from the wings, in slacks and blouse, crosses the California/Nevada state line emblazoned in a line of glass bricks right across the middle of the stage. She gives us a big warm smile.

"Hi ya fellas!"

Some of the guys smile or mumble "hellos," but I call out, "Hi, Miss Raye."

After all, this is the first act I will be playing for here at the Cal Neva, and I want to be friendly but respectful. "Miss Raye" looks up at me with a grin and gives me a "how can you say that" kind of expression.

"It's Martha, honey, just plain Martha—save that other stuff for Sophie Tucker, okay? She's old enough that she'd enjoy having you call her Miss! By the way, I'd like you to meet my special guy, my husband, Brian McCarthy!"

A big tow headed guy with a very athletic build comes up on stage. He can't be more than a few years older than I am. Oh well, whatever. Martha grabs Matty, gives him a big old hug and squeeze. Matty looks pleased but embarrassed, as Martha tells all twelve of us in the band,

"You're working for one of the greatest guys I know!"

Matty sort of stubs his toe into the stage, but I like it. It's neat to be working for someone like Matty Malneck, whom everyone in show biz seems to love or at least respect. He's an old-time song-writer/bandleader, and a great guy to work for. Matty started out as a violinist, or as it's known, a 'sideman' for years himself. He was with Paul Whiteman's first orchestra, and later in radio show orchestras like Bing Crosby's Kraft Music Hall. Matty could see that writing songs that are used in films and on recordings brings rewards greater than being a 'sideman.' Matty started writing songs, and he wrote some great tunes, like "Goody Goody," "I'm Through with Love," "Stairway to the Stars" and "Shangri-La." Anyway, he's a nice man to work with because he knows himself what it's like to be a sideman in a band.

Now, I'm a member of Matty's band here at the Cal Neva Lodge on the South Shore of Lake Tahoe. I'm one of three, along with my buddies Tom Scott and Sanford Skinner on trumpets, and Roger White on trombone, in the show band, and this is a dream come true! I mean, to play in a band at Lake Tahoe and get paid for it? And play beach volleyball too? Wow, how good can it be?

We start the rehearsal with Martha. The band plays inside the Indian teepee on the California side of the State Line, while the Act or Star works in Nevada.

Sometimes rehearsals are a drag but this is different. Everything is great. The music's fun to play, but the wonderful part is Martha. She clowns and fools around, just to break us up. I have a hard time playing at one point when she makes crazy faces and does these wild dance steps. She even does a cartwheel. It's a good thing she has on slacks and a blouse.

We finish, and she grins, "See ya tonight, fellas!"

I can't believe it when Wingy Grober, the owner of the Cal Neva, is the short little hood in a pin stripe suit with wavy gray hair and a gimp arm that I met when I arrived. He comes out on stage.

Martha's leaving, but he grabs her by the arm, to tell us, "Hey youse rat musicians! Youse don't hafta worry about playing no third shows on da weekend, 'cause Maatha had a little trouble wit her ticker."

Martha puts her hand over her heart, does a phony swoon, then grabs up a piece of her music as if it were a contract.

She pretends to read in a very legal voice, "Miss Raye regrets that she will unable to perform more than two shows on Saturday evenings."

Then she grabs Wingy in a mock headlock, and says, "That's so's you won't work me for that third show on Friday and Saturday, just for the drunks, and then make me deal blackjack after."

48

Wingy frees himself, smooths his hair, and grins, "Yeah, yeah, awright, Martha, have it your way. Dat's what I signed."

Everybody wanders out for dinner and to get dressed for the show.

I leave them, jump into the MG, and meet the guys at Abbott's Cottages down the hill from the Cal Neva in the little town of King's Beach, which is in California. (The State Line runs right through the middle of Lake Tahoe). A couple of my buddies who've been here before have checked us into three cabins. We unpack our bags and get changed for work. Then we drive back up the hill, past the Cal Neva to the Crystal Bay Club, where we heard the food is good and not too expensive.

At 6:30, I've got my white shirt, tie and black suit on, and go out to the front entry of the Indian Room to meet Mom and Dad, who are really excited about seeing the show. Marty, the captain, takes them over to a good table.

Opening night has a really special feel about it for me. First of all, I'm playing first trumpet in the band, and that's a big responsibility, which I really enjoy.

Matty has always told me, "If the first trumpet and the drummer do their job, the rest of the band will follow."

I don't know if he says that just for my benefit, but I'm going to make sure I do my part. To start with, we have a great band. Most of us play together in Bob Florence's rehearsal band back in L.A. and nobody has an attitude. Next is the fact that my mom and dad are up here at the lake for a week to see me, and I feel proud about that. I got them a reservation near ringside. My mom waves at me as I climb up on the stand. I can see my dad smiling up at me, but it's time for me to go to work. Matty gives the downbeat, and we play his "Stairway to the Stars" fanfare and then roar into the Cal Neva chorus line number, "How Ya Gonna Keep 'em Down on the Farm, After They See Cal Neva." They shimmy and shake around the stage in what passes for dancing. Nobody falls down or hurts themselves, and on comes Martha Raye.

Martha looks great in a really low cut gown, and she proceeds to sing, dance, mug, tell stories, and clown around in a big way.

At one point Martha looks up at the baleful moose above her, and then wonders aloud to the audience, "I wonder how fast he was going when he hit the wall?"

She has the audience loving every minute of her performance. We love her too; she's the genuine article—a star that is great but doesn't take herself too seriously.

She does a tune she introduced in an old Paramount film, entitled "Mr. Paganini," which starts out rather wistfully then explodes into a wild swinging section, then after sixteen bars of so, it gets wistful again. She is rather bountifully endowed, and at one point in the middle of the really wild, swinging section she starts a high kicking dance. Right in the middle, she kicks one of her evening slippers off. She stops, snaps her top half straight down, bending her body in half like a pretzel. But as she whips down, one of her bountiful assets pops out of her gown. She quickly turns her back on the audience so she's facing the band, takes hold of the boob that popped out, gives it a little flip at us, and says,

"Don't say I never showed you guys anything!"

She deftly tucks herself back in her gown. The audience is laughing so hard they don't even know what happened. I can't believe what she just did. I'm kind of shocked, but she makes everything funny, and we all choke back the laughter as she finishes the number. After the show I meet my folks. They love it when I take them backstage, and Martha invites them into her dressing room to say hello. They leave all smiles, and I'm really grateful for her hospitality. For a lady with heart trouble who can't do a third show, she really gives it her all in two shows.

The week goes by, and it's time for Martha to close. None of us want it to end; it's been so much fun. She makes it a point to meet us personally, and I get to spend some great time with her and Matty at the bar after the shows.

Martha announces before the closing show that we're going to have a party. Now this is really something special; normally if the star really likes the band, he or she gives you a bottle of vodka, but a party?!? We play the second show, and she tells us to meet her in the Circle Bar, an intimate little lounge, which has a fantastic view

Martha Raye

of the lake. We troop in, and I see my folks having a drink. I go over to them.

"Oh hi, Mom—Dad… Gee Martha's giving a little party for the band, and…"

I don't want to hurt their feelings, but it'd be kind of embarrassing to have my folks at a band party.

Dad 'gets' it, and says, "Come on now, Eileen, let's let these folks have their party."

I look up to see Martha going around the little round bar. She announces to each cluster of people, "Excuse me, but I'm going to ask you to leave. I'm having a party for my friends in the band, and it's private. Just go out to the main lounge and tell 'em Martha sent you, and the drink is on me, okay?"

The surprised patrons get up and leave. She heads toward my folks and me. She spots us and she turns on her biggest smile, and says, "You're Billy's folks! Come on and sit down. Let me make you a drink."

My folks sit back down, and the rest of the band climb up on the barstools while Martha gets behind the bar herself.

"Don't worry, kid," she tells the astonished bartender, "I'm licensed."

She fishes in her purse, pulls out her bartenders' union card, plops it down to the bar and goes to work. She fixes my dad his Cutty and water, and makes my mom her Martini, then looks at them, then at me, and asks, "What are you having, Billy?"

She grins at my folks, "He's a big boy now, isn't he?"

It's the first time they've ever seen me take a drink, a real drink, other than a glass of wine with dinner with them. Of course here at the lake, I am a test pilot for every label of Scotch they have at the bar, but my folks don't know that.

It surprises me when Mom admits, "He certainly is, Miss Raye."

"It's Martha," she reminds my mom.

I find my voice—

"I'll have a Cutty and water, Martha."

She pours, stirs it with her finger, tests it herself, pours in more scotch, and hands it to me. She serves my folks, the whole band, Matty, Wingy and of course her Brian, who tells me after a few drinks that he's a New York cop.

My folks finish their drinks. Dad says, "We want to play the slots up the street. Have fun!"

Martha sends them on their way with, "Glad to meet you!" They leave, I relax, and the party gets into high gear.

Martha pours our drinks, test-samples them, and at the same time, tells us the funniest dirtiest jokes I've heard, and stories about everybody she's worked with, from Bob Hope and Betty Grable, to Uncle Miltie and Sinatra—everything funny.

At about three in the morning I am having a hard time focusing on the low-ball glass—or is it three glasses in front of me? I start to stagger out of the Circle Bar along with most of the other band guys. Martha however, is still going full bore—she's matched us drink for drink, and joke for joke. She looks up from mixing another highball to see me weaving my way out of the Circle Bar, and calls out in her loud foghorn,

"Where are you goin', Billy?"

"I gotta go hooome!"

I take Sanford with me. Some of the guys stay, but some of the other guys stagger back to their cars. I drive with that exaggerated slow pace that you do when you're really smashed, down the hill to King's Beach. We get to our cabins, when the phone rings.

Kathy Abbott, who runs Abbott's Cottages, comes over in her dressing gown to tell me, "It's Martha Raye. She asked for you!"

I stumble over, pick up the dangling receiver, and… it is Martha! She got our phone number from Matty.

She says, "What's the matter with you guys? There's a lot more scotch left. Come on back up!"

"Okay Martha… I'll tell the guys."

A couple of the guys can still navigate and they return to the bar. I can't pass the physical, and I pass out on the bed.

Next day, Matty tells us, "Wingy came around to the Circle Bar at 4 AM and said to Martha and whatever was left of our band, 'You're da broad dat can't do three shows? Whaddya call dis?'"

CODA

Martha hated to fly, so she and Brian drove cross-country back to New York. She took the time to send us funny postcards from several stops along the way. My folks couldn't stop talking about seeing and meeting Miss Martha Raye, and her mixing their drinks! I always felt Martha was the most generous person I'd met in Show Biz. I found it makes a big difference to your image in your folks' eyes when a show biz star recognizes you as a real person as well as an adult. I will always appreciate what she did for my image with my folks.

TENTH CHORUS: "A DAY AT THE RACES" WITH JERRY LEWIS

That famous, slightly nasal and adolescent voice calls out, "All right guys, I'm taking all of you to the races tomorrow. Meet me here at noon. We'll have a police escort. I buy lunch, but you bet your own money... Of course it's really my money, because I'm paying you! Ha ha ha!"

Jerry Lewis makes one of his trademark nutty faces—the one where he puffs himself up like a big shot. We've just finished rehearsing his act. As soon as we've hit the last notes, Jerry explodes back on stage with a burst of demonic energy and a big grin. I focus on his eyes, and he's checking out each guy in the band, getting each of our names. When he's gone through all of us, he now tells our names back to us. Okay, fine; this is one of the first times Lewis has worked without Martin. Now let's see how funny he is without Dean...

Opening night is a marathon; Jerry stays on for almost two hours, doing all the schtick you can imagine or he can come up with. For the first hour, the audience laughs and applauds, but gradually we can feel that he's simply worn them out. The comic tries to prove that he doesn't need a partner, and gradually gets into a "Grand Old Man of Show Biz" sort of presentation. Lewis sings songs straight as he sits on a stool, reminiscing. Finally he finishes and the audience applauds, but without the enthusiasm that Jerry got after the first hour. Sometimes it's hard for a performer to know when to leave 'em wanting more, especially when he has something he has to prove...

It's September 1956, I'm in my first year at UCLA, and it's Easter vacation. In L.A. I'm part of Sy Zentner's band, and here in Phoenix, it's his band, minus Sy. I hear that Sy demanded equal billing, and you just don't do that with THE STAR, Mr. Jerry Lewis, so Jerry just hires the band out from under Sy for a week. We're here for the opening of his brand new nightclub here in Phoenix. The fall semester is coming up and I have to register and pay, so this gig is a godsend. Jerry says we're going to the races? Hmm, maybe I'll get lucky on a $2 bet—that's all I can afford.

Next morning it's an unusual scene at the Casa Cockroach motel where we're all staying. I mean everybody is up and coffeed by 11:30. Everybody that is, but the jazz tenor man. I go to his door.

"Hey Dave, come on, man, it's almost time."

I pound and finally the door opens a crack, so not too much sunlight can get in. Dave Madden blinks, bleary-eyed at me. His blonde hair sticks up like straw out of a scarecrow's head.

"You go on ahead. I had a looong night."

The door eases shut. Tom Scott says, "He looks like he lost two out of three falls to that bottle of Jack Daniel's he went home with."

♪♪♪

So it is that fifteen of us pile into four cars and barrel off to meet Jerry at the club, a couple of miles away. We pull in the parking lot to see one of Phoenix's finest standing by his black & white Harley, its chrome glistening so much that it hurts my eyes. We slam to a stop and jump out.

It's a ten-minute wait before a Rolls Royce Silver Cloud purrs in.

Jerry leans out the window à la a great film director, waves a riding crop and yells at us and the cop, "Let's go, we're late!"

He pulls back inside and taps his valet Leon on the shoulder. Leon is a handsome young black man who sports a perfectly shaved head. The cop jumps aboard his bike, kick starts it, and digs out in a hail of gravel. Leon powers the Rolls away. We all dash back to the cars.

I plead, "Come on Dick, we've gotta catch up to 'em," but Dick Hurwitz's old car is cranky about starting.

Tom reminds, "We don't know where the hell we're supposed to go!"

"I know, I know—come on, damn it."

He keys the ignition again, the engine coughs and splutters and we're off—last place in a field of six. We can see the rest of our guys up ahead—way up ahead, but it should be cool; after all, we do have a police escort.

We catch up by the second intersection where we see the cop's bike, red lights blazing and siren blaring, leaning on its kick stand as he stops traffic to wave Jerry's Rolls through the intersection. He jumps back on his iron horse and races away to zoom back in front of our parade. The only problem is that as soon as he leaves the intersection, the cross traffic starts up to get through, while we're still trying to follow Jerry's parade. Dick tries to muscle through.

Tom yells, "Look out!"

We see a huge semi truck bearing down, his air horn blasting. Dick slams on the brakes, the Ford's motor dies and we have succeeded in blocking one of the main intersections of lovely Phoenix.

Driver Dick fires it up and we snake through as one guy yells, "Goddamn California driver." Another swears and shakes his fist, but we're out of there. Tom is riding shotgun. He's got his head out the window.

"They turned left at the next signal!"

We roar through three more intersection adventures, tear down a long straight speedway, to the race track turnoff. We finally make it into the parking lot, jump out of the cars, and race after Jerry and Leon, who are going through the entry.

Once inside, Jerry is at full throttle; everybody recognizes him, and he is doing himself—the knock-kneed walk, the goofy faces—he runs the comedic gamut from 'A' to 'B.' I watch and his showboating makes me feel slightly embarrassed that I'm with him. We follow Jerry to the clubhouse area. I see that even seated behind Jerry, we still have a great view of the track and the totalizator board.

We get our lunch in a box, and settle in. The red coated bugler marches out onto the grass and sounds 'First Call.'

Tom and I go to the window to make our $2.00 wager. I check the race card and pick a horse named 'Sideman.'

We hurry back to our seats to see that our pick is a long shot. We watch fascinated, as Jerry consults his racing form, and some other tip sheets, then whispers to Leon, and slips him a roll of bills. Leon turns and hurries off to a window as far from the $2 wicket as you can get. Leon gets the bet down and comes back to Jerry.

I look up at the totalizator board to see an amazing thing. The number slots are a blur—the numbers are spinning like a slot machine run amuck. I look down at Jerry. He has this goofy grin on his face.

The dizzy spin of numbers stops and the odds on one of the horses, name of McClosky, have gone from 70 to 1 to 4 to 1.

The horses enter the gate, and they're off! All the guys in the band have some of their meager cache on one nag or another, and we cheer and yell and urge our choices on. Jerry is beside himself He climbs up on his chair, his binoculars glued to his eyes; then they make the clubhouse turn.

Now he's screaming, "Come on, McClosky! Come on!"

They thunder down the stretch, and I try to see past Jerry to catch a glimpse of my meal ticket. I needn't have bothered. Sideman would have done better if he had taken the band bus. The only horse he beat was McClosky.

The rest of our day at the races went the same way. Every time Leon gets Jerry's bet down, the Tote board goes nuts and pretty soon everybody at the track is onto the fact that Jerry is controlling the Tote board and the odds. Jerry spends most of the afternoon on his chair instead of in it. I feel like crawling under the chair while he's doing 'Jerry Lewis' for the crowd. He doesn't seem to get that the crowd's not laughing now—a lot of them seem to be glaring in our general direction. Jerry eventually wins a bet, and Leon comes back with a canvas bank bag, and pockets bulging with money. The race card ends, and we wander back to the cars. I find that after all the yelling and cheering and great expectations and dashed hopes, I am exactly even… at least I've still got my $2.

Tonight is closing night, and when the curtain closes, Jerry does his 'memorization' thing: he points at each guy and tells him his

Jerry Lewis and the Odds Board

name. Then he wanders over to the wings, snaps his fingers, and Leon materializes like magic with the canvas bag. Jerry snatches it, walks back on-stage, and gives us a kind of sneering smile.

"Thanks, guys, here's your bonus."

He chucks the bag down in the middle of the stage. It lands with a thud, and Jerry walks off. Jules the band contractor gets down off the stand and picks up the bag. We all stare in the direction of the departed Jerry and then look at each other. I feel like it's another lame attempt by Jerry to be the big man.

Jules sits on the stage and counts out the money. Each of us ends up with twenty dollars—twenty dollars and a day at the races I'll never forget.

Jerry Lewis brought us a bag of money.

ELEVENTH CHORUS:
THIS JOKER IS REALLY WILD

In the fall of 1956 I'm back to UCLA to continue work on my BA, and also to play as much as I can. I'm very happy that Matty Malneck calls me to play 1st Trumpet with his band which will open at Ciro's on the Sunset Strip, where we are to back up Joe E. Lewis. He's a rough hewn nightclub comic from "The Old School." He doesn't "work dirty" as many people who are supposed to be comedians or humorists do today. I often think that the four letter words are used to cover up a lack of wit or real humor. Joe E. doesn't need that. With his red bulbous nose and eyes that have seen better days, his style is like a naughty old uncle at a family party who loves to have a few belts of bourbon and is just about to tell a slightly off-color joke.

The deep scars on his face are the result of a dispute in Chicago in the Thirties. Joe E. was a hot young comic, and a mobster/club owner, "Machine Gun" Jack McGurn, who was one of Al Capone's boys, told him he'd have to play his joint for another two weeks. Joe E. said "No!" to that kind offer, because he had a better offer at a rival mobster's club, so "Machine Gun" Jack had his hoods slash Joe's face. In fact they cut so deeply into his throat that they sliced his vocal cords. Joe was left with a rough, tough, gruff kind of voice as well as scars across his face.

Joe E.'s opening night is a Hollywood gala. Sinatra, Dean Martin, Sammy Davis and his dad & uncle, Milton Berle, Buddy Lester, and a gang of actors, singers and show folk pack the club. Joe E. starts off by raising a glass of his favorite beverage, toasting the audience as he gargles his words in that gravelly voice,

"Post time, ladies an' gennelmen… !"

(Joe E. takes a healthy drink)

Now Sinatra had just done a film based on Joe E.'s life, called *The Joker Is Wild*, and Mr. Lewis takes full advantage of that fact, as he tells his audience, "You know, Frank Sinatra made a film about my life, and I think he had more playing my life than I had living it!"

After the laughs he says, "I know that Mr. Sinatra has quite way with the ladies... and as a matter of fact, in all modesty, I myself have a way with the ladies... it's expensive, but it's a way!"

Joe E. rambles on, with the impeccable timing he's developed over all these years working the nightclubs, and he is a huge hit.

To celebrate opening night, or perhaps the fact that the sun has gone down, Joe has fortified himself with several beakers of bourbon, and after he's been on for an hour, he finishes his act and strides off.

The trombonist close to me is my buddy Bobby, and his thirst is almost as great as Mr. Lewis's, and he needs a drink *now!*

But the show isn't over yet... the chorus girls come back for *another* line number. And Joe is not finished yet either!

Encouraged by the tremendous reception from the SRO aud, he appears from the wings, stage left, clad only in his boxer shorts, adorned with red hearts as well as his patent leather shoes, socks and garters. He cuts quite a stunning figure as he sashays out to join the middle of the chorus line in their imitation of the Rockettes' famous 'high kick' ending to their number. Joe kicks manfully, left leg up, left leg down, right leg up, right leg down, left leg... When all of a sudden—Oops! A combination of bourbon, balletic short-comings and balance catches up with him, and old Joe E. goes ass-over-teakettle backwards and lands on the back of his shorts! He just sits, looking shocked that such a thing could happen to a man of his "statue." He mugs and grimaces, milking it for all the laughs he can get.

Bobby is desperate for a reviver himself, and says, "I've gotta have a taste!"

He slips out of his chair, zips to his instrument case in the wings stage right, pops it open, whips out his pint of vodka and takes a healthy slug. Matty sees him scamper back to his chair, but our leader has seen it all before with Crosby and Bix on the Paul Whiteman orchestra, and besides he's got to keep the music going for Joe E. and the dancers.

Meantime, Lewis struggles to get up, with help from the girls.

We keep playing, and Matty signals to repeat this section again. Our Star has beauties on either side, trying to pull him up by both arms. But instead of rising, he manages to pull the girls down, and the whole chorus-line with their arms interlocked still à la the Rockettes starts to fall like two lines of dominos. It's gracefully, crazily funny, and about five or six of the girls land in a heap on top him. Finally, after some more prat-falls, the dancers manage to get Joe E. back up. He then gets on the end of the line and leads them off stage singing at the top of his fractured voice!

After Joe E. Lewis closes we play some other acts (which weren't nearly as much fun as Joe E.'s) for a while, then Matty gets a job for us at Frank Sennes' Moulin Rouge. This allows me to make ends meet, along with my VA Educational benefit, and keep on with school.

Bobby Pring is a man of many talents, among them a gift of doing great celebrity voices and thinking "funny."

Many years ago he made a couple of important decisions that changed his life in wonderful ways. He stopped drinking, and kept playing as he moved to New York. He worked with Bobby Short at the Café Carlyle until Mr. Short's demise. Bobby just plays better and better each time I hear him. He plays trombone in the style of the great Jack Jenny—melodic, inventive jazz with a sly sense of humor and musicality. He now lives in Florida where he spends much happy time with his lovely lady, Anita.

Joe E. Lewis takes the chorus line down.

TWELFTH CHORUS:
SCRIMMAGE WITH A STAR

It's 1957, and here at UCLA my friends and I work hard in classes all week, just as I'm sure you've done. We also play in all kinds of musical ensembles here on campus and in L.A. But that's not enough because we're young and full of animal energy, so we get together on Saturday mornings for a friendly game of touch football. We meet at 10 AM on one of the PE fields close to Sunset Blvd., next to the running track and Drake Stadium.

It's great to just get out and throw the football around on this grass where we've drilled the UCLA Marching Band with Dr. Clarence Sawhill, the wonderful director of the Concert and Football bands with which we play. But this is "kick back" time, just relaxed fun and games.

So it is that one Saturday we're pretending to be footballers, laughing, teasing each other and throwing lazy passes before we divide up and scrimmage. But a group of New Arrivals, six guys, roughly our age or a little older, come onto the field and the youngest, a handsome kid with a nice smile and great hair, asks if we'd like to play a pickup game of touch football. We look at each other and say, "Sure." Now I look closer at the other guys—a couple of them are big and athletic looking. Okay, we'll see how good *we* are.

They kick off to us, and I get the ball. I've always been blessed with good foot speed so I take off toward our opponents' goal. But I'm kind of shocked when I get about ten yards, only to be touched by a pair of rock hard big hands that strip the ball out of my grip. One of the big guys grabs it and laterals it off to the good-looking kid, who races down the field to score a TD. He comes past us and grins, without even a hair out of place.

All right… so it's only one score. We're down but not out of it.

They kick off to us; Tom receives the ball and takes off. We try to run interference, but our opponents go through us like we weren't even there. Tom doesn't get too far when the other guys 'touch' him hard. He fumbles, but falls on the ball. We huddle and decide to do one of our special running plays, where Tom takes the ball from center then flips it out to me about five yards to his side, but they are on me almost at the same time as I get the ball. I fall on it. The bigger athletic guy and the rest of his team immediately smother me. Oof! I hang on to the ball for dear life, and hope to god I don't have anything broken. So much for our trick play.

On the next play, another ball slapped out of one of our guy's hands. This time it's Don, a tall, lean trombonist from Bishop, California, who happens to be one half Indian. He comes back to our huddle, shakes his head and asks, to no one in particular, "Where's Sanford?"

Sanford is a trumpet player who is not particularly gifted athletically, but he's big, strong and although he presents no threat as a runner, he has one redeeming talent: he can throw a perfect, tight spiral that can go like a bullet for thirty or forty yards.

No one knows his whereabouts, so we play on... and it becomes a travesty of a game. Every time we have the ball, the other guys make one of us fumble. They pick up the ball, get it to the kid, Mr. Good Looking, who doesn't seem to have even worked up a sweat, but he's scoring all the points. As for our team, we all look like we've faced the L.A. Rams or the Chicago Bears and gotten trampled. We're sweating like mad, our tongues hanging out, and these guys are cruising, especially Mr. Good Looking... his hair isn't even mussed. By about a half hour into the game, the New Arrivals have run the score to something like 72 to 0.

Now I wish we were out here on this field in our band uniforms, just doing football game day formations; playing our horns and marching around... that's something we all know how to do; anything but trying to play football—this is sheer humiliation. But nobody wants to give up or give in! Suddenly, after yet another touchdown by these guys, we see a ray of hope. It's Sanford, driving up in his Volkswagen 'bug' convertible. San's car is unmistakable—it caught fire a while back and he's never had it painted, so it resembles a Wehrmacht staff car that's camouflaged with streaks of grey, black and brown. We affectionately know Sanford as 'Bear'—

a big teddy bear. He lumbers over to us, followed by his yappy little dachshund, Gretchen, who I named "Gretch the Wretch" because she snatched a small steak off my plate one day at San's and ate it. Sanford has a distinctive way of talking, not quite 'country,' but almost—sort of reflective.

He apologizes with, "Wull, golly fellas... I'm... (He rubs his chin)... sorry I'm late, but wull... I guess I just... over-slept and..."

I cut him off with, "San, we need you to do one thing!"

"Wull... what's that?"

"We want you to wind up and throw a long pass right down the middle of the field!"

"Wull... don't I get to... warmup? ... ya know, throw the ball around a little?"

"NO! That'd give away what we're gonna do!"

"Oh—oh... so this'll be sort of a kind of a—surprise, like... right?"

"You've got it! We're losing and you're our only chance to score at least once on these guys!"

"Wull... okay... ! Just... like... throw the ball right down the middle of the field... Who am I throwin' it to?"

"ME!" I tell him. "I'll get out there and Tom and Don'll trail me. All ya gotta do is throw it long. They won't be looking for that!"

"Wull... okay!"

"Bear, just say 'One–two–three–Hike!'"

Bear nods, and we line up as Gretch moves closer to her master.

"ONE–TWO–THREE–HIKE!"

Bear gets the ball, and steps back as he cocks his arm. I sprint as fast as the wind down the field, but there's no one chasing me, and there is no ball coming downfield to me. I turn to see what's happening; it's like a slo-mo comedy. Gretch has waddled right behind her master just Sanford the Bear steps back. He trips over Gretch the Wretch, and falls backwards just as he throws the ball with all his might.

The ball goes about thirty yards into the air, but only about five yards past the line of scrimmage. I race back to try to catch the ball. I get under the ball, ready to gather it in, when suddenly a huge paw looms right over my head—the ball floats right into the big

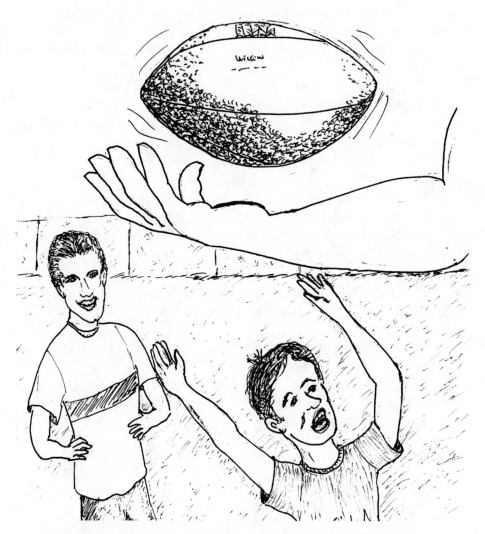

The ball floats right into the big athletic guy's huge hand. He grabs it out of the air, then hands it off to Mr. Good Looking…

athletic guy's huge hand. He grabs it out of the air, then hands it off to Mr. Good Looking, who streaks untouched into our end zone.

I look at Bear lying on his back in the grass. Gretch is licking his face. I figure we've taken enough of a licking ourselves.

I tell Mr. Good Looking and his cronies, "We've had enough… we're gonna go for a beer. Wanta come?"

The kid grins, shakes my hand. All the guys exchange hand-shakes.

"No thanks, we're gonna see if we can get another game."

Tom comes over and stares hard at the kid then asks, "Isn't that guy" (he points at the biggest of the athletic guys) "…isn't he Paul Cameron?"

Mr. Good Looking grins, and nods.

"Yeah he is…"

"And aren't you…?

"Yeah, I'm Rick Nelson… thanks for the game, guys!"

We learn later that Paul Cameron, the All-American footballer who played for Coach Red Sanders' team, is now Rick's bodyguard, and the other guys are all ex footballers too.

We retreat to a nearby tavern. Over a cold one or two we start to laugh at ourselves, at the game, and even at the Bear's attempt to throw a bomb.

As I remind our banged up team, "Let's see what Ricky or Cameron can do with a trumpet, huh?"

It's a rationalization, I know, but it's one way for the UCLA Band's Brass Section to move on after our game with Ricky Nelson and the Star's All Star Varsity.

THIRTEENTH CHORUS:
MARLOWE, MICKEY, VIKKI & ME

Matty's gigs at Ciro's and the Moulin Rouge have finished, and I go home on Sundays to see my folks. My dad is not doing so well... just as the surgeon told us. I take him and Mom in to Los Angeles to see Dr. Daniel again. He does a proctological examination and x-rays. He tells us the cancer has metastasized more. I take them home to San Bernardino, where Mom can look after him when she gets through her daily routine as Supervising Nurse of the Surgical Wing at San Bernardino Community Hospital. I'm worried, but there's nothing I can do for him. I'm here in Los Angeles, and I drive home and see him and Mom as often as I can.

That makes it hard to do what I have to do—to balance school and musical work, and get out to see my folks. But I know I've got to concentrate on what I need to do... Right now, it's time to practice—warm up my trumpet chops. I've played this routine my teacher, John Clyman (first trumpeter at 20th Century Fox Studio Orchestra), gave me months ago, so long that I know it by memory. So I plop this mystery novel onto my music stand, while I go through the lo-o-o-o-o-ng tones, and all the rest of the routine. If my teacher could see me reading a book while I'm playing his routine, he'd kill me, because I'm supposed to just concentrate on my sound, but he can't, so I read as I practice.

It was a warm day, almost the end of March, and I stood outside the barbershop, looking at the jutting neon sign of a second floor dime a dance joint. A man was looking up at the sign too. He was big man but not more than six feet five inches tall and not wider than a beer truck, a forgotten cigar smoked behind his enormous fingers.

Street people gave him darting side-glances. He was worth

looking at. He wore a shaggy Borsalino hat, a rough gray sports coat with white golf balls for buttons, a brown shirt, a yellow tie, pleated gray flannel slacks and alligator shoes with white explosions on the toes. There were a couple of colored feathers tucked into the band of his hat, but he didn't need them. Even here on Central Avenue, he looked about as inconspicuous as a tarantula on a slice of angel food.

I nod my head in awe at the way Raymond Chandler describes his character and scene so well in *Farewell My Lovely*. This is a new kind of detective novel for me; I've read Sherlock Holmes, but those stories are all set in London and it's hard to relate to hansom cabs and Victorian England. This book by Chandler has a hero who is different. He's Philip Marlowe, a private eye who lives right here in L.A; he's smart, tough, brave, and cynical because he's seen it all. Above all, he's honest—he still does the right thing, no matter if he gets slugged or shot at for doing it. To relax he works out famous chess games late at night. How cool can you be? Marlowe meets really exciting people like this big guy, Moose Malloy, and he solves murders and mucks around in the seamy underside of my hometown.

I wish somehow I could have these kinds of adventures, and be a part of this wild, thrilling part of life that might be going on right now, but, let's face it: I'll only ever read about it. I guess deep down I'd like to be tough and cool like Marlowe, instead of just a trumpet player—okay, so I'm dreaming. I look at my watch, and I know that it's time to get back to my own real world—of long tones and scales and arpeggios. I have to go to rehearsal in an hour.

It's Spring of 1957; I'm a sophomore at UCLA in music, and at night I play trumpet at Gene Norman's nightclub on the Sunset strip, The Crescendo. Gene Norman runs GNP Records, a jazz label; he has a disc jockey show on KMPC in the afternoon and most nights he's at the club. I'm grateful I'm earning a living in the music biz, instead of working in a store or something to get through school.

Today we're going to rehearse Vikki Carr, and it should be fun. The regular band of trumpet, sax, bass, drums and leader Bob

Armstrong on piano will be augmented; for this gig we'll have three trumpets, a couple of trombones and four saxes. It'll be good musically, and the other players are excellent. Every week or so, I see some celebs, but maybe I'm like Philip Marlowe in one way. I guess I'm kind of jaded by Hollywood's glamour crowd; it's pretty boring after a while watching famous folks get bombed. It is not like what Philip Marlowe gets involved with. Maybe I was just born too late for all the good stuff.

Here at UCLA not much happens that's really thrilling like what I read about. It starts to rain as I cross Thayer St. to my rented garage, put my trumpet case and my new book into my trusty '52 MG-TD, and struggle to get its balky canvas rain top up and the side curtains in place.

I go up Gailey Ave. and turn east on Sunset Blvd. My little sports car whizzes along through the curves and puddles as I head for the Sunset Strip. I pull up into the vacant area under the big billboard right across from the Crescendo. I grab my trumpet case out of the MG, and dash across Sunset through the rain and afternoon traffic, into the club.

The waiters are setting up the tables. I can smell the fresh linen and the air is still cool and clean and everything is shiny. I can see the bar man setting up and I like the neat rows of bottles on the bar back and the glasses gleaming, all set up for the night's festivities. I move to the back of the club and climb up on the bandstand.

"Hi Bill!"

"Hi Jay," I reply to our lead alto man, Jay Cooper, who is also just getting started as an attorney. I clamber over a chair to the trumpet section, as I kid one of the trombonists, a big burly guy who has a shoulder bag.

"Hey Big John, I love your purse!"

Tom Scott, another trumpeter, good looking with dark wavy hair, is already there. He's always reading. He's already deeply engrossed in a *History of the Civil War*.

"Hey Tom, have you read any Raymond Chandler?" I ask enthusiastically.

Tom looks up as if I'd asked him if he read Dick Tracy.

"Oh… yeah… that detective…"

"Marlowe! Philip Marlowe! I just got into it, and…"

But there's no more time for literary discussion. Andy Thomas, Vikki's conductor (a little guy with a quick smile, and an excellent pianist/conductor) passes me the trumpet books. I take the first book, pass the rest along, and we start to run down the music. Everything goes smoothly, just like it should. After all, the parts are straight and this is a good band. Miss Carr is diminutive, beautiful, and redheaded and has a sweetly plaintive voice full of emotion. She smiles at the band—a pretty lady with an emotional, vibrant style, a good singer and a nice person. We smile back and exchange hellos. We finish rehearsal and break for dinner. Tom and I go across Sunset to a coffee shop and eat.

Tom asks, "Did you read in the paper about that guy Johnny Ranelli, the gangster that got shot at some supper club last night in the Valley?"

"Yeah, they say it was a gang type of rubout! "

"Maybe Mickey Cohen did it," I answer.

Tom says, "Could be… the guy that got hit was supposed to be one of the mob."

We finish and hurry back across Sunset as the rain showering down makes halos round the lights that illuminate the billboards all along the Strip.

We get inside, get a couple of bar towels from the barkeeper and dry off for the dance set. After a half hour of subdued show tunes and muted swing, it's show time.

Leader Bob Armstrong tells us, "Take five, guys."

We get down from the stand, and just have time for a drink when he calls us back. There seems to be a little more urgency tonight than just an ordinary opening night, but then this is show biz, so go figure. We get back on, and I realize I didn't make a pit stop, and we're going to be stuck on the stand for at least an hour or an hour and a half.

I stage whisper to Armstrong, "Bob, I've gotta go, before the show starts!"

He, of course, comes back with the stock line to such a plea, which is, "What's the matter with you? You knew about this gig two weeks ago!"

Everybody laughs, and he nods, "Go ahead, but hurry up."

As I get off, I notice two guys with wide brimmed hats and

dark suits just coming through the front entry, into the club. They blow past Sandra, the good-looking blonde in a gold lamé outfit, who runs the hatcheck. These two keep their hats on, but they get the big time treatment from Mario, the trim, gray haired maitre d.' He ushers them toward ringside, but the bigger of the two peels off and beats me to the men's room at the side of the joint. In fact he must be in more of a hurry than I am, because he shoulders his way past me coming out as I start in through the shuttered doors. I go on in; maybe he just wants to wait because all three urinals are in use. I duck into a stall and get ready to unzip, when I see a leather bag on the back of the toilet.

I kind of mumble to myself, "Hmm, it kinda looks like Big John's..."

I pick it up, unzip it instead my pants and glance inside. Whoa! Inside is a great big blue-steel pistol—a Colt .45, I think. I zip it up and set it back gingerly. I can hear Armstrong chiming his signal on the piano that it's time to go, which means I don't get to go. I'm more concerned and really scared by what I've found; I mean Philip Marlowe does this every day, but trumpet players don't find guns just lying around. Maybe this is one of those things someone sees, but is not supposed to see. It happened in *Farewell My Lovely*, and the guy ended up dead, shot through the head.

On the way back to the stand, I grab Mario, the maitre d' who is seating a couple of customers, and whisper in his ear, "Mario, I just saw a .45 automatic in the men's room. It's in the middle stall."

Mario gives me a quick look, and says quietly, "Okay, kid."

He doesn't miss a beat. He seats his party, then turns and heads for the men's room.

I get on the stand, but I could have taken care of business, because they are holding up the show. Vikki is nervously peeking out from behind the partition which shields performers and the kitchen from the audience.

I ask Armstrong, "What's going on?"

He shrugs, "I guess some big shot is late."

Finally I can see some little flurry in front by the door.

"Jeez, I wish they'd hurry up!" I tell Tom.

A party has just come in, and Mario brings them down front, then turns and gives the high sign to owner Gene Norman who is standing at the back of the club, a small spot glowing down off his

...a great big blue-steel pistol...

wavy gray hair. Now I see another guy with a wide brimmed hat being led to the ringside table. He is covered front and back by the other two wide brim guys. They wait till Mr. Big parks it, then they look around the room, and sit too.

Gene Norman turns to the house mike, and in his most mellifluous radio tones, says, "Ladies and gentlemen, the world famous Crescendo is proud to present the Liberty Records recording star, Miss Vikki Carr!"

Andy gives the downbeat and as we swing into her opener.

Tom whispers during a four bar rest, "Hey! That's Mickey Cohen, the gangster!"

I sneak a peek.

"You're right, Tom!"

I notice that the guy that pushed past me from the men's room looks up at me. He leans over to tell Mickey Cohen something. What could it be? Is it something to do with that damn gun? I don't need any more pressure than what I've got bladder-wise, right now!

Vikki's act goes perfectly. After she kills the audience with her new hit, "It Must Be Him," Tom leans over to say, "Vikki and Johnny Ray are the only singers that can sing and cry at the same time."

I don't care about that; I've got two things on my mind. One is, I've gotta go bad, and the other is, what about that automatic in the men's room? Did I leave fingerprints on the case? Could that be the gun that a mobster like the three sitting right in front of me used to murder Johnny Ranelli?

♪♪♪

We finish the act, she does an encore and I am dying; I need to go more than the audience needs another song. She finally quits, and before the last note of the bows echoes out, I am off and running for the men's room. As I move, I see Cohen's party get up too. Oh lord, now what? But I can't linger; I've got to go. I dash in past Jose, the little Mexican guy who is the attendant, and thank God, all the urinals are vacant. I make it, and unzip just as the big wide brim guy comes through the door.

He glances at me, checks the rest of the room, then gestures with his thumb to Jose, and barks, "You! Outside!"

Jose manages a nervous smile, and scrams out the door. After Jose has exited, Mr. Widebrim nods to someone at the door. In comes Mickey Cohen! I've seen his picture in the paper, but he is bigger and stockier that I thought. He's got a real five o'clock shadow, which is kind of covered up with powder. He's still got the hat on, and to my complete terror he sidles up into the urinal compartment next to me. Now there are only three people in here. Mickey Cohen, his big bodyguard Mr. Widebrim, and me. I can see the headlines in tomorrow's *Times*—

HOLLYWOOD MUSICIAN MURDERED IN NIGHTCLUB RESTROOM. GANGLAND SLAYING SUSPECTED!

And even worse is that fact that I can't even pee! I'm too scared to let go! Mickey has no problem. He finishes, and then he reaches inside his coat, not fast, just real relaxed. Oh God, I did find something I shouldn't have, and now I'm going get my head blown off. I grit my teeth and glance frantically around. What would Philip Marlowe do? He probably wouldn't be here in the first place and if he were, he wouldn't be in the vulnerable position I'm in! I turn back to watch with a feeling of horrified fascination, as Mickey Cohen's hand comes out of his coat in a kind of slow motion. Now I know how Philip Marlowe feels, when the heavy has the drop on him. But instead of a blue-steel automatic, he is holding a little can of Johnson's Baby Powder! With his other hand, he pulls his pants out and sprinkles the powder into his pants, and a cloud sprays up. I can smell the scent. Then he proceeds to give the can to Mr. Widebrim, who shakes some more into Mickey's hands. Mickey then pats his face to cover his stubble. He turns, washes his hands like a surgeon, takes a towel from Widebrim, and dries his hands. He throws the towel down, glances at me, and says,

"Now you can say you took a leak with Mickey Cohen… Take it easy kid."

He turns and follows Widebrim out.

I'm shaking like a leaf in a high wind, but finally—finally, I can let go! I have never experienced relief like this, and I'll bet Marlowe never has either! I hear the familiar chiming signal from

Mickey Cohen

Bob Armstrong's piano but right now I don't care if I never get back on that damned bandstand. All that matters is that I survived this insane night of Marlowe, Vikki, Mickey and me!

CODETTA

Jay Cooper has become one of the most respected attorneys in the music biz field. Tom went on to do records, TV and film scoring, and is still playing. Big John now carries his shoulder bag to gigs in Texas. I was inspired to read all seven of Chandler's novels and even wrote a script myself, called *Knifepoint*, about a tough, jaded, but dedicated detective... and, oh, me? I have had a great career just being a trumpet player.

FOURTEENTH CHORUS:
THE CODA FOR MY DAD

I stay in school, and keep working at the Crescendo on a show to show basis, but one night a few months later, my mother calls my landlords and Mrs. Collier brings me to the phone.

Mom says, "I think you'd better come home. Your father isn't doing very well…"

I call a sub for my gig, and roar home as fast as I can. Dad is heavily sedated, but he sees me, tries to smile, and says,

"Hi old son…"

Then he lapses into his drugged state—God, it's so hard to see him like this… the guy that played ball with me, and bought me a cornet and a boat, so I could have what I needed and wanted. The dad that explored the islands just offshore of Nanaimo, and taught me how to fish, and walk like an Indian through the forest so as not to frighten away the animals in the wild.

He's so thin, his once tanned face now pale and gray. I can see he's in pain in spite of all the morphine, and looks so sick. I start to cry… for him, for Mom and for me too.

Eventually I fall asleep, but my mother, bless her heart, somehow stays awake beside him. At five AM, she gently wakes me, without saying a word, and I go back into their bedroom. Dad's breathing is labored, rattling and it's a long time between breaths. I hold his hand, and watch and wait, and pray. Finally, he takes a last breath, and Mom and I both sit looking at the man that was husband and father, then we just break down.

I don't know how my mother has done it… to work all day, to be in charge of all the nursing care for three floors and a surgical wing—a whole hospital full of sick people—then come home to nurse him all afternoon and at night too. To watch him die, slowly day by day, inch by inch—this husband, this partner, this man whom she loved so much and so deeply... that must have been the most difficult thing to do in her life.

A few days later we have the funeral, and I stay while family friends and my Aunt May come and stay with us. After a week I have to go back to school and playing the trumpet.

But a big part of my life has changed... that man that I always loved and looked up to, is gone. All I have now are photos of him in our boat, smiling as we fish, or explore, and the memories of everything he did to make my life fuller, better and more wonderful. I will always be grateful that William Rowland Peterson was my dad.

FIFTEENTH CHORUS: NAT 'KING' COLE, COBINA & TIPPY & SHOW BIZ GLAMOUR

"Thank you for asking me to come."

"Gee, you're welcome, Mom. I'm just glad you came."

I look at my mother and know that I did the right thing. She looks tired and older than her fifty years. This is the first summer since my dad died last fall that they won't be going on a trip together. She looks so sad and lost most of the time, and she's alone except when she's at work or I can get home on weekends. So I invite her to take a week off from her job as Director of Nursing at San Bernardino Community to come to Lake Tahoe where I am playing in Matty Malneck's Cal Neva show band.

It's 1958, I'm in my junior year at UCLA, and I'm lucky enough to have the perfect summer job for somebody like me that eats, sleeps and dreams of being a pro trumpet player and someday, a studio musician. I mean, here I get to play first trumpet for lots of big acts, like Sinatra, Tony Bennett, and Sammy Davis Jr. I am really happy to be doing this; it makes me feel like I'm really making progress professionally. I'm proud that I can pay for the cabin for my mother, and take her to see the shows we're playing. Of course she has a rather innocent outsider's view of all of show biz. For instance, she tells me,

"I just love Cary Grant and Irene Dunne in those movies like *The Awful Truth* or *My Favorite Wife*... They get into such funny situations and say such clever things."

I feel a little twinge of sadness that she can be gullible about the way things work, and yet so good at what she does, which is making sure her patients get the best nursing care at the hospital.

It's about 7:30 in the evening, we're backstage, and my mom is meeting some of the guys in the band. She's smiling but a little lost, and I sure hope she'll have some fun tonight, because the headliner is Nat 'King' Cole, who was always my folks' favorite. If I can, I'll get Nat to say hello. He's a superb singer and musician, and a regular guy (he loves baseball)—the band really loves to play his act. But the rest of the guys and I also get a kick out of the opening act.

Mom asks, "Tippy and Cobina? Now are they the two telephone operators that are so cute on the Jack Benny program?"

"No, not exactly. They are two chimpanzees."

She can't believe it.

"Why would Nat 'King' Cole have monkeys on the stage with him?"

I'm supposed to know everything.

"Mom, Nat doesn't work with them... oh, you'll see."

I knock on Nat's door; he graciously comes to the door in his tux.

Nat the "King" is very regal but kind, as he shakes Mom's hand and says, "Very glad to meet you, Mrs. Peterson."

I thank him. She has a dazed smile that will last the rest of night.

As she walks away, she manages to say, "If only your father could have been here."

"I know, Mom."

I guide her from backstage toward her seat close to ringside. Just then Roger White, one of our three trombonists for this show, rushes in; he's running late. Roger has a blonde crew cut, and all the girls around the club think he is good looking. He gives Mom his great smile.

"Hi, Mrs. Peterson, I'm very glad to meet you."

Mom smiles too. "It's very nice to meet you!"

Roger hurries by to get his trombone out. I can see Mom's impressed with the whole backstage thing.

She's about to float back to her chair, when she turns to me and says, "I just don't understand why Nat, or you, for that matter, has to play with monkeys!

I have that sinking feeling—she'll never get it, or understand show biz.

"I've got to go to work, Mom. Here, Jerry'll take you to your table."

My buddy, wavy haired and sleek in his captain's tux, takes my

Mom meets Nat 'King' Cole.

mom's hand like he was conducting the Queen to her throne.

I turn back, get the horn out, get the lips vibrating a little, and climb on the bandstand. Matty smiles, gives us the downbeat, and we're off.

We power our way through the line number. The ten Cal Neva lovelies prance and smile their way around the stage as we roar through "The South Rampart Street Parade." They dance off to meet those male members of the gaming audience who can afford their company.

Then Matty gives the downbeat for Tony Antonucci and his two chimps, the unpredictable Tippy and Cobina. They are seated in special tall chairs on wheels. His pretty wife, Maria, assists. She wheels out Cobina and he does the same with Tippy. They sit and make faces at the audience while he brings out a little capuchin monkey with a hat, named Mick, who is seated at a small electric organ attached to a high chair. Mick and his instrument are on wheels too, with a power cord to provide power to the organ. I get a kick out of the chimps and the little guy, Mick, but there are ego problems even in the world of monkeys. Tony told me that the chimps have gotten so they love the applause they get, but that they resent Mick's star turn, and would kill him if they had the chance.

I'm shocked; I say, "But Tony, they're so funny!"

Tony tells me, "Listen, don't kid yourself. They're really strong— either of those chimps could break your arm if they wanted to."

Wow, I have a new view inside show biz, and a new respect for the animal kingdom.

Anyway, Mick plays "People Will Say We're In Love" on his little electric organ and we try to accompany him, note for note. Now this monkey does not have the greatest sense of rhythm, so as he looks around at Tony or the chimps, or the band, and the audience, he plunks out the tune, in a kind of random way—but you can tell what he's been programmed to play. No matter how long the pause between notes he gets them in the right order. "Toot –too—toot—toot-toot, toot…" Matty just tries to conduct so as to catch each note and it's usually a source of amusement when we try to stay with this Van Cliburn of monkeydom.

Maria leaves Cobina and goes off stage for some more props. Tony is working with Tippy, who is getting laughs while Mick is picking out Rogers and Hammerstein. Cobina has been left alone. She looks around, and then with a really toothy chimp grin reaches down and grabs the thick power cord which attaches to Mick's chair and organ. Cobina starts to reel Mick in like a fish on a line. Mick the monkey feels he and his whole setup moving backward. His rhythm gets even more erratic.

"Toot-toot—toot, toot... eek... awk..."

He hits two or three clinkers in a row. Cobina pulls him closer, closer... We're really struggling to stay anywhere close musically. Tony looks up to see Mick almost within Cobina's powerful grasp. He secures Tippy, and rushes over to rescue Mick. He pops Cobina upside the head really fast, and wheels Mick out of harm's way. Maria comes back with the props and the chimps do their thing, balancing, grimacing, tossing, and catching, and the audience loves it. After all, it is monkey business.

Finally, Tony and Maria bring the chimps back upstage, so Mick can do some comedy bits with Tony.

We are playing more monkey music, a kind of a fast circus piece. Cobina is on her chromium-padded stool, right beside Roger, the trombonist, who is on the outside. I steal a glance over, and see Cobina is watching Roger pump his trombone slide in and out, in and out. I haven't got time for anything more than a glance. This gallop we're playing is fast!

But apparently Roger's good looks are not lost on any part of the animal kingdom, because next time the other three trumpets and I have a breather and the five saxes are blasting away, soli, I see Cobina give Roger a big chimp grin. She bats her eyes and in a flash, leaps off her chair and into the astonished Roger's lap, just as he moves the slide out fast to the farthest point on the slide, seventh position. Cobina whips out her long arm, grabs the slide and flings it off the pipe and sends it zinging past the band, right onto the ringside table right down front. The gold slide slithers down the white tablecloth. It sends drinks crashing over, as the patrons jump back.

Tony dashes over, grabs Cobina by her long chrome chain, and jerks her, but Cobina does not want to leave her beloved. She wraps her arms around Roger's neck. She looks like anyone being torn away from the one she loves. Tony frees Roger from her amorous embrace, and a waiter hands Roger back the slide to his trombone.

Cobina starts to reel Mick in like a fish on a line.

He fits it back on, and as Matty yells, "Bows!" Roger finds that the slide still slides. I look out to find Mom in the audience. She's laughing so hard tears are rolling down her face.

The dust settles, the animal act disappears, and after a respectable pause, Matty announces (I omit the lisps),
"The Cal Neva Lodge is proud to present Mr. Nat 'King' Cole!"
We swing into the opener. Mr. Cole comes out, and proves once again what a unique artist he is. The audience loves him, which is just how I feel about him—a great singer, pianist and a truly gentle man.
We finish the show, and Jerry brings my mother backstage.
My mother brushes past me to Roger, and says breathlessly, "Those monkeys are so funny. I see why Nat would want them on his show. How do you do that, Roger? Did you have to practice a lot to be able to do that?"
Roger looks at me, and I have the same feeling, which is, "Don't try to explain." Roger just gives her a wry smile.
"No, Mrs. Peterson, it just happens naturally."

CODA

My mother relaxed and seemed to start to take a renewed interest in life and going on. She found she could enjoy things, a little bit at a time.
Cobina had to be phased out of the act, because she became more and more unmanageable and mean; perhaps it was a case of unrequited love. Anyway, next time I played the act, Tony had a new chimp, named Tippy. Tippy seemed content, but Mick the monkey was never quite the same—his sense of rhythm was permanently disabled, because he kept looking over his shoulder. Wouldn't you?

SIXTEENTH CHORUS:
THE BACK ROW BOYS GET REVENGE

"God, look at that snow, Sanford!" I tell my buddy and fellow trumpeter, a big burly guy, Sanford Skinner.

San nods and rubs his chin, "Well yeah, we're gonna have a white Christmas."

It's Christmas week, 1958, and I've been able to work at clubs along the Sunset Strip pretty steadily throughout the school year. Now it's school break time, and I've gotten called for work by bandleader Will Osborne... we're going to work Tony Martin's act for ten days at Harrah's Club on the South Shore of Lake Tahoe. I've gotten Sanford on the gig. He's a big lovable guy who has put in so many hours in the practice rooms when he was a student at UCLA that I'd tease him to get a cot and just live in there. He'll be playing first trumpet, I'll play second and another player will come in and play second so that I can come home and start school after the first week. That way I won't miss any classes, but I'll make some extra bread. I've also met a girl that sings with a great group in Harrah's lounge, across the street from where I'll be playing. Patti is pretty, and as the leader of her group introduces her every night, "Here's Pretty, Perky Patti Richards!"

As Sanford and I look out the coffee shop window the bright sunshine glistens on the pure whiteness that covers everything—it even drapes the huge neon marquee outside that announces that Harrah's presents Tony Martin. Tony is a big star on the night club circuit, but I'd rather hear Sinatra.

"Wull, uh, when do you go back?" San asks.

I remind him,

"I've got to be back at UCLA in a few days."

It's Christmas break from school, and this is a chance to have the fun of playing with Will's band. The size of the band changes with the demands of each act; this show the band will be two trumpets, a trombone, four saxes and, added for Tony's act, four violins.

It's a nice break from being a junior at UCLA, where I've been cracking the books and enjoying the school routine. I'm a little worried about missing days of classes; UCLA is not like high school, but Tahoe in winter is fantastic and I need the money to keep going to school. This way I get back to the books, and Sanford will be established playing first trumpet. I've been doing a bit of a selling job to my leader, Will Osborne, on Sanford's behalf, because he hired me to play first and doesn't know Sanford. I assure Will that Sanford will be able to do the job very well.

After all, San could use the gig, and he's been on lots of road bands, and when he gets the 'book' down, he does fine.

I check my watch.

"It's time to get in to rehearsal."

"Wull yeah… I don't wanna be late," San says as he lumbers along with me into the South Shore Room.

The place looks pretty bleak in the afternoon; tables stripped of their linen and silver finery. Two of the saxophonists look up as we climb on the bandstand.

"Hey, Sanford, how ya been?" asks Bob Crandall, the lead alto man.

"Bob! Good to see you!" Sanford grins.

Don Davison offers San a can of beer. Sanford grins and takes it, but I grab it, and stick it out of sight under the stand as Will Osborne comes in.

"Hey!" Sanford protests.

"Gee, San, you don't drink in front of the leader—especially on the first rehearsal," I scold.

"Uh, oh, yeah, you're probably right."

Will greets us, "Hi fellas!"

"Hi Will's" are returned.

We all love Will. He was the leader of a band during the golden days of the big bands, and did films and their radio show with Abbott & Costello, and did other radio shows too. But most important, he's a fine musician who is a really good guy, one who cares about the musicians who work with him.

Al Sendry, Tony Martin's conductor, comes with Tony's music

in a box. Al is slim and intense; he's got a towel around his neck. He's a good musician, and as usual he is almost vibrating with energy. "T.," as Al calls Tony, has a beautiful voice and his fans love him, but he is very difficult to work with—nothing is ever good enough for Mr. Martin, and he never lets anybody think it might be. I mean, it's great to be a perfectionist, as Sinatra is, but T. has such a smarmy kind of attitude, as if he was looking down at you as a mere musician. This from a guy whose real name is Al Morris, who played pretty sad clarinet in some San Francisco hotel's ricky-tick "Mickey Mouse" band before he was "Discovered" as a singer and went on to MGM to do musicals.

I feel that working with Tony Martin makes Al a little edgy. He spots me, grins, hands me the first trumpet book, the second to Sanford.

"Glad you're here, Bill!"

I worked the act just last summer at the Cal Neva Lodge and it went well. I appreciate the compliment, but I remember what a pain 'T.' was—an incredible ego and a kind of condescending manner with the band and the audience.

I swap books with Sanford when Al moves on; now he's got the lead trumpet book and I have the second book, but I don't have a chance to tell Al what's going on, because now Tony Martin makes his entrance. He is the "Star," and he looks the part. He's got a great tan, and his clothes!… Well, I wish I had his slacks, sports jacket and loafers and he had a wart on the end of his nose….

We get up the opener arrangement, and Al warns us, "This first tune segues fast to an eight bar mambo bit."

I remember you have to shove in a cup mute right after you finish the opener—this is so T. can do a little Latino dance step with his hand to his navel, down front. I guess it's supposed to be sexy; it's T.'s kind of BS show biz style, but the ladies, young and old seem to love it. Maybe I'm feel a little jealous, sitting here kind of anonymous in the back row.

Anyway, I remind Sanford, "This segue thing comes up real fast—why don't you put your cup mute on the music stand so you can get it fast?"

San rubs his chin as if this was something to ponder.

"Yeah—uh—wull… okay!"

Al Sendry counts off the uptempo opener chart. The band

swings into it, Tony croons his way through, and we end up on the last chord. We don't rehearse the segue like it'll be in the show. So the rehearsal plods along, like rehearsals do, and T. does his usual bit. His mike level is too soft, not enough highs or lows or whatever; then he starts on the band! The drums are too heavy, the band is not watching the dynamics, and brass section is way too loud! I know what he wants. T. wants us as soft as a mosquito peeing on a Kleenex.

He says, "Fellas, my music has to be played with refinement. This is not a jazz band, you know..."

This is T.'s "I'm an artist" act, so I tell the brass section to play softer and aim the bells of their horns into their music stands so it'll be softer.

Sanford does okay, as we go along, he plays the parts, but Al Sendry looks at me questioningly... he knows I'm not playing lead. We finish and San and I hurry off to get dinner and change into our black suits. We stop at the bar for a little Jack Daniel's antifreeze, and then we're ready.

♪♪♪

It's a special opening night, because it's the first time the club has tried to stay open in the winter, so all Harrah's brass is at ringside—Candy Hall, the entertainment director; Bill Ring, the Veep; and Bill Harrah, the owner himself. I think it's kind of amusing that they should be sitting four feet from a leak in the ceiling which goes "drip-drip-drip" right on the stage. Harrah is unhappy.

I hear Harrah's voice rumble up from ringside.

"What the hell is this?"

Bill Ring, the VP, tells the Boss, "There's some leaks in the roof, and the heat from the show room is melting the snow, and it's coming through..."

Harrah growls, "Well, damn it, fix it!"

"Bill, I've had a crew working on it!"

But even a millionaire can't stop Nature taking a leak—the roof leaks merrily away.

Will Osborne announces Tony pain-in-the-ass. We charge through the opener, Sanford hits the high note on the end. So far so good, I think. Al cuts us off, but I guess Sanford is relishing the fact that he nailed the high note because he isn't ready for the segue.

Al cuts us off, leaps up from the piano bench, jams his hand into the air, yells, "Hit!" as he gives a downbeat.

San is so surprised, he says, "Oops!" and drops his cup mute.

The mute hits the floor with a clunk. Now Sanford is faced with a big choice. I can almost hear what he's thinking,

"Should I play the part open, without the mute, or should I go ahead and get the mute and put it in, and then play it?—Hmm!"

The wheels in San's head are turning, but by the time he gets his horn to his lips it's too late; the boat has sailed and the segue vamp has begun. I lean over to play Sanford's lead part, but because I've been watching him drop the mute, I'm late getting to it, so the band plays five or six bars without the first trumpet part. I figure, "Big deal, the show will go on."

But instead, T. stops in mid sexy dance step, and suddenly I sense disaster. I guess Mr. Martin feels his music has been violated; somehow his Show Biz moment spoiled. Who the hell knows what lurks in the hearts and minds of stars? (If they have them!) Anyway, T. turns toward the band; he looks really pissed. He marches back, and the show has ground to a stop.

Al Sendry pleads, sotto voce, "T…! No!"

But this doesn't stop Mr. Martin. He pushes between Bob, the alto player, and Don, the tenor man, right up to Sanford in the back row. I always figured we were safe way back here in the back row, but nobody is safe from a 'Star's' wrath. I can see that San's sweating like he's run a 10 K.

Tony puts the microphone to his lips, looks at Sanford like a cobra about to strike, and hisses, "It goes like this! Ta-ta-ta, ta-ta-tah-dah! *Got it?*"

He glares at Sanford for what feels to me like about an hour. Finally he turns and stalks back to the front of the stage. Al plays a vamp as Tony slips back into his suave act, and chats with his audience.

That's fine for T., he's shown everybody what a big deal he is, but I have to deal with Sanford. He looks shell-shocked.

I turn to San, who looks stunned and sort of out of it… he just says, "I fucked up!"

Tony Martin at the mike; saxophonist in shock.

I look at him.

"Hey, you can't let this bastard get to you."

But I can see Sanford is dazed—he is deep into it.

"I fucked up…"

He's just sitting there with his horn in his lap, repeating, "I fucked up…"

This is now apparently his mantra. It's fine, but we've got a show to finish playing.

"Come on San, you've got to play the show. You've got to play lead."

What I'm really thinking is, "You've got to play first because I've got to get back to school!"

Just then, Al Sendry yells back to me, "Bill, *you* play lead."

Oh God, I can't believe this is happening… the best-laid plans, etc… Al kicks off the next tune as T. runs through his 'charming' show biz drivel. I reach over, flip the next chart up in Sanford's book, and play the lead part. After about eight bars, Sanford comes back from his slough of despond, and starts playing the second part, which I already had up in my book.

We get through the show, but it's awkward because Sanford never gives me the book, and I haven't got the heart to take it, so Sanford turns his music, and I play it. I turn my part over, and San plays it. Finally, I take the lead trumpet book back on a break, and slip San the second book. We get through the show, and play T. off. We go back to the band room, and start to talk over the scene, when our leader, Will, appears, and motions me out. I go into the hall, and Will says,

"Tony would like to see you. "

I walk down to the door with a star on it. I knock, and Al Sendry opens it. I see Tony in an incredible silk dressing gown that probably cost more than I would make in a month.

"You wanted to see me?"

T. smiles at me, as he arises from a couch, and motions me to enter.

"Bill—" (good grief, he knows my name, but his voice is like

96

Sanford wilts as T. points.

a snake oil salesman) "—I really must have you play first trumpet for me!"

Hmm, what's he got in mind? Does he want me to travel with him?

He smiles and goes on, "At least till the end of the week when we close."

"But I've got to get back to UCLA!"

"I understand that you feel you need to, but this is my act—my engagement!—and I'll make it worth your while."

"Gee, the other guy will do just fine, Tony…" (Now that we are on a first name basis, I feel pretty confident). "Just give him a chance."

He really turns on the charm and persuasion.

"Out of the question, Bill, I must have *you!*"

Now I realize how he must have captivated countless leading ladies such as Alice Faye, Betty Grable and Cyd Charisse.

Luckily I keep my head, and say, "I'll have to think about it."

I leave the presence of the great one, and wander off into the night, back to the bar for a drink with the guys, to ponder the wonders of show biz.

♪♪♪

Later I am back in my little motel room, feeling no pain, but boy, do I feel guilty. I mean, here I got Sanford to come to Tahoe at his own expense, for a job that blows up in his face. I'm working on my guilt, when suddenly there's a knock on the door. I open it, and there's my bandleader, Will Osborne. He looks very concerned.

"May I come in, Bill?"

"Sure."

He's got a paper sack in his hand. He hands it to me; I unwrap the fifth of Jack Daniel's.

"Thanks! Would you…?"

"I could use one."

Will collapses his lean frame into a chair. I get two glasses and pour.

"Tony has made a big deal about what happened tonight with Bill Harrah… The result is, either you stay or he'll get Leighton

Noble's band to replace us."

"But, Will, for god's sake! Sanford just screwed up a little. It wasn't the whole band!"

Will waves a tired hand at nothing.

"The bastard has the power. I'm afraid it's all up to you."

I look at this guy who is like a father to all of us. There's no contest.

"Of course I'll stay, Will."

"I'll see that you get an extra week's pay, okay?"

"You don't have to pay me that, Will!"

"Tony Martin's paying for it."

"In that case, how about two weeks… Hey, wait a minute, how about Sanford?"

"He's going to play the week out on second trumpet, and he's going to get paid for two weeks, all right?"

"All right!"

It's a week's pay Sanford wouldn't have gotten since we will close in a week anyway. The week goes by, there is peace in the South Shore Showroom, and the roof springs leaks on a nightly basis.

♪♪♪

It's finally closing night, and tomorrow morning I will drive back to Los Angeles and school. But first, tonight I have a plan to wreak revenge on our beloved star, and I know exactly what to do and when to do it… When Tony sings "Fascination," only the strings play—the brass section is tacit, so we switch off our stand lights every night at this point. I know what I must do.

Sanford and Rog the trombonist watch me, fascinated, as I take the mouthpiece out of my horn and pull the tuning slide out of the leader pipe. Now I have a foot-long tube, slick as a rifle barrel. Then I tear a strip off the bottom of Tony Martin's precious music and stick it in my mouth. I chew it up till it's just right. I wad it up into a nice, tight, wet little pellet. I turn my horn around backward so the bell is over my shoulder. I pop the wad into the end of the pipe closest to the bell, and take careful aim at the back of the star's neck. As T. reaches for the big high note, the high point of the song...

"It was Fascination, I know..."

I take a big breath, then put all my power and energy and hatred into the blast. My pellet rockets out, straight on target.

"Splat!"

I score a bulls-eye right in the nape of Mr. Martin's neck. He claps his hand back there in an involuntary move, as he cuts the note off, with a kind of strangled release. Just the guys beside me, Sanford and Rog, the trombonist on the other side know what I did! Now I'm little scared. Will he figure it out? Will he march back to the trumpet section? But what I hoped for happens. He looks up at the leaky ceiling, glares at Al Sendry as if it was his fault, and finishes the tune. It's a small victory for the boys in the back row, but we enjoy the Moment.

CODA

I return to school, and work like crazy to make up the work I've missed by staying the extra week and a half at the lake with Mr. Martin. Another trumpeter takes my place, and soon Will is offered and accepts the position of Entertainment Director at Harvey's Wagon Wheel Casino next door.

Sanford? Well, he comes back to Los Angeles, but soon gets a gig with Tex Benecke and the Glenn Miller Band and Show featuring the Modernaires.

He finally marries a Swedish girl, and moves to Sweden where he plays in a radio orchestra until he retires.

What ever happened to Tony Martin? Not enough to suit me. I can understand that his Act is most important to him, and he wants it played perfectly, but not to give Sanford another chance, and to threaten to get a *whole band* fired, is way above and beyond the way things should go. That's how I feel!

SEVENTEENTH CHORUS:
FUN WITH LONESOME GEORGE

I turn our car onto the road up to Lake Tahoe. I look over at my brand new wife, Patti. She is beautiful, blonde and right now her pretty green eyes are sparkling. She looks and smiles at me.

"We're sure lucky this all worked out."

I look over and give her hand a squeeze.

"We sure are."

It is the summer of 1959, and I have just graduated from UCLA on June 15th. Two days ago Patti Richards and I got married. I met Patti last summer at Lake Tahoe, where she was singing with a group and I was playing in a band. Now we're newlyweds, driving up Highway 395. It's a gorgeous summer day.

A few days earlier, we're having lunch in Westwood, planning wedding things, when Patti asks, "What are you going to do for a job this summer?"

Up till now, I've been so busy finishing up school and preparing to get married, I haven't really thought about the new obligations that a married man has; now I have to get a job.

"I'm going to call Matty—maybe he's got something."

I make the call right then—there's no time like the present for a man with responsibilities. I call Matty Malneck, the bandleader I worked for last summer at the Cal Neva Lodge. I tell him Patti and I just got married.

He says, "Bill, congratulations… I heard her last summer. She sings great, and she's very attractive. You know, I'm working the lake again this summer. Would you like to play first trumpet?"

"Sure I would."

"Maybe you can help me get a band together."

"Of course."

Matty is a great guy to work for—a quiet legend in the music biz, a small, unassuming man that all the stars know because of his songs. He is the composer of "Stairway to the Stars," "I'm Through With Love," "Shangri-La," "Goody, Goody," and a whole host of other songs. So life could not be better. I have a Bachelor's degree, a new bride, and a job. Patti, who is a wonderful singer, is going to work at Harrah's on the South Shore all summer, while I'll be at the Cal Neva, a legendary gambling casino on the North Shore. Our future is assured, at least for the summer of '59.

We crest the hill, and catch our first sight of the lake.

"Oh, it's so beautiful," she says.

"You're right. Tahoe's got to be one of the prettiest places in the world."

Patti suggests, "Why don't I drop you off at the Cal Neva for your rehearsal, and I'll look for a place for us?"

"That's a good idea—you've been up here more summers than I have—you know the lake a lot better than I do."

I ease our '52 Olds down the long drive to the Cal Neva Lodge, with its great old rustic look of bark covered split logs. Patti pulls away and I go in. I see Wingy Grober, the owner of the Cal Neva that I met last summer. I move on, trumpet case and mute bag in hand, and meet Matty and the other early arrivals in the Show Room. The rest of the band comes in, and we set up to rehearse the act music for our first show, George Gobel.

Johnny Mann, George's music director, says, "Hi, fellas."

He tucks his long legs under the piano, and we start the rehearsal. George pops in, says 'hello' to us with a shy grin, and drifts out, looking casual but dap in a turtleneck and expensive looking slacks, probably from Sy Devore—I wish I could afford some—maybe at the end of the summer when we have made our pile.

Tonight is opening night, and we play the opening act, a singer named Marion-something-or-other, who goes through the usual repertoire of pop tunes with all the affectations but none of the soul of a Sarah or an Ella.

But when we swing into George Gobel's quirky theme song, from his sleeper hit of a TV show, the audience perks up. I find his puckish style completely irresistible—he has only to say "Good evening, friends," and I laugh. He tells a couple of stories, and I am on the floor—he gets me right in the funny bone. After all the comedians I've worked—the "Jackies" and "Joeys" and "Bobbys,"

George is fresh and clean and original, and he's funny—who can explain "funny"? Anyway I do laugh a lot, and George notices me, up on the trumpet riser in the back.

He says to me, on mike, "Don't hurt yourself there, Spanky."

I grin at him, and he goes on with his act, which is a master-piece of understated whimsy, self-deprecating, like when he was a fighter pilot in the South Pacific. He tells of being in a line of other Curtiss Wright P-40s, waiting to take off. Unfortunately he was daydreaming for a moment, which is a dangerous thing to do in a 4,000 lb. fighter plane with a 1,500 horsepower engine and a ten foot prop spinning, which is poised to roar down the runway. George lets up on the brake, and his plane taxis forward, right into the tail section of the plane in front of him.

There's an inquest. A granite jawed captain demands of little George how he could have done this.

George explains, "I don't know, your honor. I was sittin' there, minding my own business, when all of a sudden the guy in the plane in front of me backed right into me." (Remember that WWII airplanes could NOT back up—they could only go forward, which is the point of the joke!)

Lonesome George talks about mean old Alice, his wife, and later in the act, George announces,

"I'm going to play my guitar and sing a song for you. Now I could just have my guitar sitting out here, but this here is a big time act, so I have someone who brings my guitar out to me... I figure, it's my act and I can do whatever I want. Charly, will you bring my guitar out, please?"

On cue, out comes one of the most luscious looking show-girls I have ever seen, in spangled tights, carrying a guitar. She hands George the guitar, gives him a kiss on his forehead, turns and exits—that's all. George looks at the crowd with a self-satisfied smile; they laugh, and he launches into his song in a high, clear, wistful tenor.

"All is well, for it is spring, flowers bloom and bluebirds sing..."

At this point, one of the reed players tweedles a high trill on his flute. George stops his song, turns slowly to look at the musical intruder, and then starts again—again, another trill. George moseys back to the 'triller' and deadpans, "If you play that instrument to

Charly brings Lonesome George his guitar.

kill time, you have a wonderful weapon."

After the second show, which makes me laugh even more, George stops me backstage, and asks, "Spanky, you sure are having a good time... are you getting paid for this?"

I grin and allow as how I am.

George says, "How about you and me go have a drink... you do drink?"

I assure him I do, and after I give Patti a call to tell her what's happening, we go out the front entry of the Cal Neva, right past Wingy Grober. He is so surprised that he almost drops his cigar. After all, "one a da rat musicians" is hanging out with the star of his club.

We wend our way up the street to the Crystal Bay Club, where the maitre d' seats us, and fusses over George. George asks what I'd like.

"I'd like a Cutty Sark."

George's eyes twinkle, and he points to the white tablecloth.

"Just line up eight chocolate covered Cutty Sarks, right here for me and my friend Spanky."

The guy is puzzled, but hurries away and returns with eight straight shots on a tray. I am not used to hanging out with celebrities, so I'm a little flustered, and don't know exactly what to say.

I tell George, "I just got married."

George listens at my story, then says, "I'll always remember my first girl friend, Wilma. I used to take her out on my bike. Old Wilma, she'd sit up there, in the wire basket. I'd pedal and she'd ride... old Wilma waffle bottom, I used to call her."

George keeps telling stories, and I laugh so much I have tears in my eyes. George polishes off most of the Cutty Sarks, but I do my best to keep up.

Suddenly, the maitre d' appears at George's side and whispers something in his ear. George pulls out a couple of bills, hands them to the guy, and says, "Spanky, I gotta go."

He gets up and I follow him out. Right at the curb in front of the club is a big blue Caddy convertible with the top up. As Lonesome George and I arrive, the Caddy's door opens, swings wide and a pair of shapely arms reach out and "Charly," the guitar-bringer-outer pulls little George inside—George may not be lonesome tonight. The Caddy pulls silently away, leaving me to contemplate the full meaning of being a star and having your own act.

Patti picks me up, and she looks beautiful. She's still got her gown and special makeup. I give her a hug and a long kiss—after all we are newlyweds.

I ask, "How was your night?"

Patti is just bursting to tell.

"You'll never guess! Sammy Davis Jr. came in for our late show. Everybody was excited even though we tried to act like it happens all the time."

I'm impressed, but when I tell her about my adventure, she says, "I can't believe it—that's great! What did you talk about? What happened?"

Patti wants all the details and tells me about our apartment. We have lots to talk about as we drive home, with the moon reflecting the entire length of the lake, spangling the surface with silver moonbeams.

Two nights later, George's world changes. "Mean old" Alice, his wife arrives, together with her and George's spiritual advisor, Father Patrick Flynn, of Our Lady of Perpetual Guilt church in Encino. George is still funny as ever, but I think he's a little more wistful when Charly brings him his guitar and gives him her ceremonial peck on the forehead.

EIGHTEENTH CHORUS: THE WILDEST! — LOUIE PRIMA & KEELY SMITH

It's the summer of '59, and Wingy Grober has booked the hottest lounge act in the world into the Indian Room at the Cal Neva Lodge.

Now this is a novel thing, because there are unwritten rules that there're two different kinds of acts. There are the groups that work in the Lounges in Vegas, Reno and Tahoe, and then there are the "Main Room" acts that work the big rooms in these venues. So it's really unheard of that a Lounge group is booked into a Main Show room even up here at Lake Tahoe.

Of course Louie Prima and Keely Smith have broken all records in Las Vegas with their band, Sam Butera and the Witnesses. Louie's a trumpeter/bandleader from the Swing Era. He saw that when the Big Bands were dying, he had to come up with something new and fresh. His answer was to incorporate a little band style from the '40s… a style that originated with leader and composer Louie Jordan and his Tympany Five, which both black and white audiences loved and which led to a string of hits.

Prima's band plays some of Jordan's great, funny songs, original tunes like "Caledonia" and "There Ain't Nobody Here But Us Chickens," all played at a wild boogie-shuffle tempo.

Louie Prima incorporated this crazy, fun music style into his band, The Witnesses. Sam Butera's the leader, a good tenor player who is from New Orleans, as is the whole band. Louie and the guys have blended all the funny routines that evolve in a Lounge as those with talent for comedy come up with great funny bits to fill the four hours or so that they have to entertain the people. "Little Red," the trombonist, blows the hell out of his trombone while swinging upside down on a trapeze above the band. The whole thing is like a manic three-ring circus with touches of all the great comic tradition of the Brothers Marx, Laurel & Hardy and all the rest. Add to this Louie's frenetic jumping-around-never-still-a-

Keely Smith, Louie Prima and the band

moment movement and mugging and you have a great swinging band and a wild leader.

What elevates this act is that there has to be some conflict, some fly-in-the-ointment, like Stan Laurel's inevitable screw-ups, or Harpo's constant shenanigans. Miss Keely Smith is the reason that the whole thing really works. She is a complete contrast. Louie features Keely, who stands calm and still, never changing expression, except for an occasional look of annoyance at Louie's mugging. Louie calls her "The Indian" and with her classic features, coal-black hair done in a distinctive style and slim trim figure, she looks the part. Boy can she sing! She has a clear but emotionally swinging style that is mesmerizing.

So, because they are a self-contained act, our band, the Matty Malneck Orchestra only has to play for the "Cal Neva Lovelies," the chorus line that clumps and kicks its way through the opening dance number to start the show. Tom Scott and I play two-man beach volleyball during the day, or splash into the lake (which feels ice-cold), and have as much fun as 'twenty something' year olds can possibly have.

As a result of too many hours in the blazing sun, too much practicing during the day and probably not enough sleep, I go to practice after beach ball, and my lower lip *splits*! The crack is deep and long, and really sore, and this not what you want to have happen as a trumpet player. I can't get my lips to vibrate—in fact, I can't even make much of a sound. All that comes out is a sound like a wounded water buffalo. I do have to play the Chorus line number, so I race to the drugstore and buy a bottle of Campho-Phenique® and apply it to my lip. It stings like crazy, but I still can't make a sound on the horn. What am I going to do? My trumpet player colleagues can't offer any advice, but I get a wild idea. Louie Prima has been a trumpeter longer than I've been alive and has lots of experience with trumpeters in his various big bands... so I jump in the MG and drive up to the Cal Neva to see if I can find him.

I check in with Matty, who tells me he thinks Louie is down by the pool. I work my way through the Casino and down to the pool. The pool is along the side of the Lodge, and has a very distinctive feature: the line of demarcation—the State Line—runs right through the middle of the pool, marked by a line made of tile. But right now, I'm not interested in geographical markers. I want to see

Mr. Prima, and hope to god that he has something to help me.

Sure enough, I see Louie with his bathing cap covering his very bald pate. He hanging on the side of pool, kibitzing with some of the Cal Neva bosses. I wait for a break in the jokes and patter, and then I come over to Prima. I re-introduce myself and tell him my problem. Louie is very responsive.

He says, "Lemme get out of the pool…"

Louie climbs out and I show him my 'wound.'

He nods, and tells me, in his husky Italian-New Orleans patois, "Yeah, I had one'a dese myself back in '48! You did da right thin' puttin' that stuff on it…"

"But even though I don't have to play your show, I still have to get through the Chorus Line number, Louie!"

He pats me on the shoulder and nods with real understanding.

"I understand—now here's what you do… Take your horn an' play down into da pedal tone range. You play soft, you rest a LOT, and mos' important, you *puff* your cheeks out…"

I'm like every brass player who ever took a lesson—"DO NOT EVER PUFF YOUR CHEEKS OUT!"

Louie can read my mind; he smiles and says, "Yeah, *I know*, Bill … Ya *never* do that… but the people that told you that, didn't see the split you got in your lip. You just do like old Pops tells ya! I'll take a look at it before the show."

"All right Louie, I'll do it! And thank you very much!"

I turn and streak home, grab my horn and drive out along the lakeside road, and pull off onto a dirt road that leads into the forest. I park, pull out the horn, and remind myself to take it easy. (The so-called "Pedal Tones" that Louie advised are the notes that you can play which are below the normal lowest note on the trumpet. These notes vibrate your lips like mad, and make the circulation really flood the lips.)

I do an easy hour or so, resting a lot, then go back to the cabin, pour more liniment on the split and take a nap.

Before I leave the cabin for work I do the "Puff the cheeks, play low pedal tones, play soft and rest a lot" routine. I can get a sound, and it feels better. I really feel encouraged.

I get to work and check in with Louie. He gets me under a bright light in his dressing room and checks out the split.

Then he asks, "How's it feel? Can you get a sound?"

I'm excited as I tell him, "Yes! This really works, man!"

He grins and slaps me on the back.

"Why sure it does... You don't think Louie gonna tell you wrong, do ya? Us trumpet players gotta stick together!"

"Well, thanks so much, Louie!"

We shake hands, and I climb on the bandstand with a little more confidence. I back off and play a little softer and easier than usual. We do the "Stairway to the Stars" fanfare and the Chorus Line number, "South Rampart Street Parade," and all the notes come out fine!

We get off the stand as Louie, Keely and Sam and the Witnesses come on-stage. Louie glances over at me, and I nod. He gives me a "Thumbs up."

And I stay on to watch one of the most entertaining shows any time, anywhere!

Sam and the Witnesses open the show with an uptempo flag-waver, "When the Saints Go Marching In"... And then Louie enters the fray with "Just a Gigolo" with all the mugging and funny stuff... he says some lines in Italian and Sam the tenor man mimics him. Keely leads the vocal responses, but looks at Louie like he's crazy. She then does "I Got It Bad and That Ain't Good"—Louie echoes her line with, "I got it good and that ain't bad!"

Between tunes, which you could never characterize as a "lull," Jimmy the drummer has slipped on a gorilla head mask, and as the spotlight finds him, he starts "discovering" the drums. The "Ape man" hits a top cymbal with his paw, and reacts to the sound—then he lifts the cymbal to look underneath to see what caused it... then he picks up a bundle of drum sticks, and tosses them at the snare and tom toms. He reacts to the noise; then finally, he start playing a jungle drum beat very much like Gene Krupa's famous solo on Benny Goodman's "Sing, Sing, Sing" (which Louie Prima co-wrote), and the band gets into it. Jimmy tears off the mask eventually; then they swing it out...

If you haven't seen or heard this group, do yourself a favor—buy a CD or a film, and at least experience the fun, nuttiness and out and out swing that Louie, Keely, Sam and the Witnesses generate. (It'll put a smile on your face... it did for me back then and still does! I'll always be grateful to Louie for helping me when I really needed it!

NINETEENTH CHORUS: MEETING MR. SINATRA

I'm back with Matty Malneck at the Cal Neva Lodge at Lake Tahoe—it's 1960, and it's a beautiful summer, but we're especially excited because Frank Sinatra is playing here this season. He's coming off a whirlwind tour to benefit the UNICEF Children's Fund, accompanied by a quintet of great studio musicians from Hollywood. I'm looking forward to playing the great arrangements of Billy May, Nelson Riddle and Neal Hefti.

Most acts will rehearse their music in the afternoon, but not Frank. Matty tells us that Sinatra likes to rehearse late at night, or later, early in the morning. Well, he's the Man, and we'll do whatever he wants, so we come into the old Indian Room, with the band inside the giant teepee, for a 2:30 AM rehearsal.

Bill Miller, Sinatra's pianist and conductor, passes out the books containing those great arrangements. We start in with the guys who toured around the world with Frank, but without the Man himself. It's not unusual for the star not to come to rehearsal when he or she has a guy like Bill Miller to handle things. So we play down the charts and it's a blast. Then, about 3:30, the back door of the Show Room opens and in strides Sinatra, with a drink in his hand.

As he moves through the tables, he calls out, "Hiya, fellas!"

He gets on stage and motions Miller to kick off the next arrangement. We play it down as Frank just listens.

Then he tells someone off-stage, in the wings, "Okay, bring it on!"

Eddie, a guy in his forties, with a creased face and wavy, greased hair, is the maitre d'. He obediently rolls out the portable bar onto the stage, as Franks tells us, "Eddie's the bartender—anything you want, he'll pour it!"

I can see from the expression on this nose-over from New Jersey's face that he hates having to be there and he really hates having to pour drinks for the band. But he's here because of Frank and he knows there's a lot of money to be made from the high rollers that will want to see Sinatra. There's a pause, I can feel that Sinatra has made us an offer, and it behooves us to take advantage.

It's up to me, so I call out, "I'd like a Jack Daniel's, rocks!"

Frank grins at me, and says, "Okay! What do the rest'a you mugs want?"

The ice is broken and the guys in the band start calling out their drink orders, as Eddie pours and burns.

We rehearse a lot more, and I have a really satisfying time of it, which I'll get into in the later chorus, "The Sinatra I Knew." But this "Chorus" has to do with my taking the job a little too lightly, and taking my abilities too much for granted.

♪♪♪

We are into the fourth day of Sinatra's engagement, and he likes the band, loves Matty and everything is going well. However I have a big argument with Patti one evening before it's time to leave the South Shore of Lake Tahoe and drive around to the North Shore to go to work. I have a drink of Scotch from the jug of Cutty Sark that Lennie Hayton gave me on Lena's closing night. I get unreasonable, jealous and become a real jerk; I throw reason and caution to the winds—I'll show her just how mad I am and how much I hurt. I drink the neck out of the fifth of Cutty Sark and refuse to eat the steak she's cooked for us. My trombone playing buddy, Big John Wanner, who's going to drive us to work comes by, sees what condition my condition is in, and asks Patti what happened. She explains, but I'm still declaiming my great pain and righteous anger.

He says, "We've gotta go… got any coffee?"

Patti helps get me into John's MG-A, then rushes back to get ready for her gig with Jack Ross and the Dick Lane Sextet at Harrah's, just a couple of miles from our apartment on the South Shore. I manage to spill most of the coffee as they stuff me into the little sports car, and off we go, with John making all manner of barbs, to which I am too plastered to remember or respond.

Now the road around the lake is curvy and John is driving fast, because my scene has gotten us off to a late start. I look out the side

Sinatra opens the bar.

of the racing MG, but everything is a blur… I start to feel awful, I'm queasy, dizzy and the Scotch is sloshing around my empty stomach. Suddenly I know I've got let go. I mumble something to John, who reaches over and holds my head out of the car and over the road. I barf big time and will not dwell on all the loathsome reactions. We get to the Cal Neva, and John carries his trombone case and my trumpet case into the side entrance to backstage. He searches for coffee and I work my way along the backstage, and realize that I am now at work, where I am the first trumpet player and the contractor of the band, and I am drunk! All this, and an important realization now comes flashing along the booze numbed synapses of my besotted brain: I have to play for Frank Sinatra, the King of Show Biz, the Chairman of the Board, in about thirty minutes. I'm having trouble focussing, and standing up, but now the "Flight or Fight" response starts to kick in!

As I gulp the cuppa John's brought and the adrenaline starts to flow, I make my way up on the bandstand. I open the 1st Trumpet book and look at Matty's "Stairway to the Stars" fanfare and mini overture; the notes are pretty blurry but I know the piece from memory so it'll be okay. Next come The Cal Neva Lovelies, but they're dancing to the same music as last week. I can play that by ear, for heaven's sake. Then Buddy Lester, the scar faced comic, comes next. He opens for Sinatra and he runs out on stage singing "Fine & Dandy" in his barroom baritone, while the band just sits there. No problem—oh, I have to play the old bugle call, "First Call" after he tries to play it on his horn, but messes it up.

Oh boy, it's Show Time and now the full realization of what I've done hits me… I'm the guy in the band with the most responsibility, and here I am "Shit-faced"! God, what an idiotic thing to do… but Matty picks his baton and looks up and gives the downbeat. Thank god I can play the horn okay—not great, but passable. Matty finishes his opener, and then kicks off the line number. I just play it by ear, or memory, or whatever it takes and get through it pretty well—it's not difficult thank god. But I can feel that as I blow and take deeeeep breaths that the booze ain't goin' away… I'm still stoned!

On rushes Buddy Lester, singing his own opener. As usual, he runs around the stage frantically, singing and occasionally looking back at the band and yelling, "More trumpets!"

It's all part of the gag. Meanwhile I've got the driest mouth this side of the Mojave Desert, and as Buddy gets into his act, he grabs his beat-up old trumpet up off its stand, and goes into the audience, doing schtick with the customers. He stops, sets up the bit, then launches into his awful version of "First Call." He looks into the bell of the horn as if it was its fault, and not him. Now, I'm on. I stagger up out of my chair and all of a sudden I'm so dizzy and light-headed I feel like I'm gonna pass out. Lester stands there waiting for me to show him up, and so I put my horn to my lips and try to play the call. Oh my god!—I crack three of the first four notes and I sound almost as bad as Buddy. I weave back into the chair, and Buddy finishes his act.

We play him off, and as he rushes past the bandstand he looks up at me with an angry scowl and shouts at me, "I wanna see youse later, pally!"

Next, I open up Sinatra's book. Now I have to read the music! Bill Miller comes out of the wings and smiles at us, then kicks off the opener. I know how it goes, and I get through the first eight bars, as Sinatra comes onstage... so far so good! Then there are eight bars of rest, where the trumpets don't play. But for the life of me, I can't count the rests—"One, two, three, four; two, two, three, four; four, two, three, four"! I lean over to Al Biales, a good player I go to school with at UCLA and tell him.

I say, "Al, you gotta play the act... I can't count!"

He looks at me with real fear in his eyes, as he says, "You've got to! I can't play some'a the high notes... Look, I'll count 'n tell you when to come in!"

So that's what we do! I can play the parts and Al leans over on the rests and cues me like,

"One, two, three, four; two, two, three, four; three, two–PLAY!"

It works and I stagger through the act... I'm able to make the "Luck Be a Lady" altissimo part. Sinatra doesn't seem to notice, and after he finishes and we play him off, I stagger off the bandstand. I'm soaked in sweat, my mouth feels like a desert caravan had walked through in their bare feet, and I'm sick.

Of course my chauffeur/trombone buddy invites me to the bar for some more Scotch. Of course I eschew his kind offer and make my way up the hill to the Crystal Bay Club where I am able to hold down some eggs, toast and coffee.

After a walk in the cool air, I'm able to navigate and go back to the Cal Neva. I find Buddy Lester in the lounge and apologize to him… "Sorry, man, I was sick!"

Most important, I play the second show without screwing anything up. All the way back to South Shore, John has a great time commenting, but I don't care. Thank god he got us there, and Al helped me through the most embarrassing and stupid night of my professional life.

TWENTIETH CHORUS:
THE GREAT SAMMY DAVIS

Sammy Davis, Jr., is coming to the Cal Neva. But he's coming with an awful burden; he's working for the first time since he was in a terrible car accident on the way from Las Vegas to Los Angeles.

He's brought to San Bernardino Community Hospital (where my mom is Director of Nurses), in the middle of the night.

After emergency surgery in the early morning hours, in which the doctors have to take the smashed eye, which is hanging out of its socket, my mom goes in at 5 AM to see to Sammy's care. He's in recovery, and still unconscious from the anaesthetic.

When he wakens, he's told what has been done. He has lost an eye. Davis is in pain and shock, and sure that his life as an entertainer is over. My mom comforts him as best she can in her quiet, loving way, but Sammy doesn't have time for much quiet time. A parade of friends from Hollywood, Beverly Hills and Palm Springs starts that just doesn't stop. Frank Sinatra is one of the first to come see Sammy.

He tells his buddy, "Sam, we're gonna be working together just as soon as you're able!"

My mom has the unenviable job of making sure that Sammy gets the R&R time that he needs, but Sinatra understands and helps in his own way, making sure that not everybody gets in to tire Sammy out.

I hear from Mom that once Sammy is allowed to get up, he visits all the other patients on his wing of the hospital, saying hello, cheering them up and kidding around as much as he can.

Both as the Director of Nursing and as a plain human being, she is absolutely amazed at this little guy's spirit and caring for other people. Sammy is finally released and goes home to his home in Los Angeles, where he is eventually fitted with an artificial eye. He also dons some very hip glasses, and true to his word, Frank puts Sammy to work.

I get to experience the thrill of watching and working with one of the most talented generous performers for whom I have ever been privileged to play. It's the summer of 1959, and Sammy is booked into the Cal Neva Lodge for ten days. I've had the misfortune to have a car accident on Highway 395, around Bridgeport. I smashed up my Triumph TR3 sports car coming up to the lake at 3 Ayem, without pausing to sleep. Patti comes to get me after several hours. As a result, I haven't had any sleep for two nights, and come to rehearsal tired, but relaxed.

I've never played for Sammy, and I get to the Cal Neva, sit down and open the 1st Trumpet book. I find some rather challenging charts, but I'm so relaxed I just take a big breath and sit up straight, just like my teachers have always told me to do! George Rhodes, Sam's pianist, conductor and music director kicks off the opener, and our band roars through the arrangement without a hitch… I hit the high notes on the end, and both Sam and George smile at me. I return it… I really feel good, being part of this show.

Sam has his own drummer and guitarist who travel with him, and it's a pleasure to play with them… they swing!

This is Sam's opening night, and everything goes beautifully; the packed Show Room loves Sammy Davis (no longer the "Jr." tacked onto his name), and his incomparable dancing, singing, mugging, impressions… he even plays the trumpet and drums.

The SRO audience won't let him leave, and Sam honors their cheers and applause as he does encore after encore. He finally thanks them once again and begs off.

Backstage, Sammy is radiantly happy! This is his first gig since the accident. The next night I see him backstage and do something really thoughtless… I mention to him that my mother was Director of Nursing at the hospital he was taken to after his accident. It is a terrible mistake. It's something he's put behind him, and my

Sammy Davis

mention of that awful time must have brought the whole horrible accident back to him. He backs off and I shrink back, feeling like such a fool—such an insensitive fool. I apologize, and just stand there. After what seems such a long time, he reaches out, pats my arm and finally says softly,

"It's alright, man… it was a bad time—but your mom was cool."

I bite my lip, nod my head, and say, "Thanks Sam. She thinks you are the best, and so do I."

But troubles seem to dog Sammy. Lake Tahoe's forests catch fire, and the power lines to the North Shore are fried. Across the lake we can see Harrah's dozen or so searchlights blazing up into the smoke choked summer night sky, powered by an auxiliary unit that's huge. I hear it's big enough to power every casino, club and gas station as well as all the surrounding homes… (That's right, those electric pumps that bring the gas out of the underground tanks, through the pumps and into your tank? …They're out of commission too, courtesy of the great fire).

On our side? Nada—nothing. Oh, the Cal Neva Lodge *has* an auxiliary power source too; it's an old World War II Army generator, run by a balky old gas engine, all of the rig still painted camouflage colors. It provides just enough power for the lights in the casino, and one spotlight for the show room.

The usually crystal blue of the lake is a dirty smoggy gray tinged with red. The fire is so widespread, blazing through the dry firs and pines, that even the sun is obscured. From time to time there's this red ball that shimmers up there behind the clouds of smoke. People hold handkerchiefs to their faces as they walk between clubs during the day.

There is one Union Oil station that can pump up gas by hand or something. The owner charges the then unheard of price of $2.00 a gallon for the precious stuff, and people who have to leave are paying it. It does everybody's heart good to learn that an exec of Union Oil went in, asked for gas, got his 5 gallons and tried to use his credit card to pay for it. When the station operator would only accept cash, the exec introduced himself, and had the owner booted out within a few days.

Sammy has gone through too much to be deterred by the fire. He goes on the first night of the fire, jokes, sings, dances, does everything in his arsenal to make folks forget what's happening outside, and by god they come! Our "handicapped" club is hurting business across the lake, and the former co-leader of Patti's group, Dick Lane, is Entertainment Director at Harrah's.

He can't understand what's happening; after all Harrah's has Lawrence Welk! So Dick gets in touch with me through Patti because the Harrah's bosses don't understand that one little black guy with a broken nose and one eye is outdrawing Mr. Welk and the thirty or so people he's putting on stage every night.

Dick needs to know how many people we get over here, across the lake at Cal Neva. I take great delight in giving him a call each evening to tell him that the show room is jammed! Not that I care that Wingy Grober and Sanford Waterman are cleaning up, but that the Swingin' Sammy Davis is outdrawing Mr. Welk and his cornball band… Talent will out; and it will outdraw the watered down pap that Welk is serving up.

We suffer through the forest fire for a week, then suddenly one night the rain comes—a deluge that knocks the fire down. The power guys can get in and restore all the poles and lines.

In a couple of days much of the electrical service is restored, and we finish Sammy's gig with a great party on closing night.

TWENTY-FIRST CHORUS:
"DIRECT FROM THE BAR—DEAN MARTIN!"

Sammy Davis closed last night, and we're in the wigwam band-stand at the Cal Neva Lodge for an afternoon rehearsal with Dean Martin. We're playing the 'line' number for the Cal Neva Lovelies, a little ditty entitled, "How Ya Gonna Keep 'Em Down on the Farm After They See the Lake?" The dancers (so-called) are singing the lyrics to this epic as they try to keep time and dance. This is not the Radio City Music Hall Rockettes, it's obvious, and they sure ain't the Ray Conniff Singers either. They clump around through the choreography that Gina, the Line Captain, who *is* a good dancer, has drilled and rehearsed with them. But you can't teach graceful movement to a dancer with two left feet. As far as singing goes, it's hilarious! Every once in a while they land close to the same note together, but most of the time, it's like the worst junior high or middle school chorus you ever heard.

However, the girls are good looking for the most part, and they do have good legs. I strike up a conversation with one girl because I'm curious about their view of their role here at Cal Neva. The reason is that at the beginning of each season at the Lodge, Matty tells me to instruct the band in the "Facts of Life" when it comes to the showgirls and "dancers." I'll paraphrase Matty's instructions…

"Look fellas, the girls are here for the entertainment of the bosses and the high rollers. Leave the girls alone, and don't get involved!"

Later he proceeds to tell me the inside story.

It seems that a few years ago, a bandleader from San Francisco had this gig before Matty. This guy got into a relationship with the Line Captain at that time. The trouble was that she was the "girl friend" of a guy named "Bones" Remmer, who was serving time in the Carson City slammer for income tax evasion. "Bones" sent word to the bandleader to lay off his girl, but the bandleader

124

figured that he and his lady friend were safe because "Bones" was behind bars. WRONG!

Even after two warnings, the bandleader still treated them with complete "ignortion." One night soon after the warning the "lover boy leader" walked into his cottage after work and a date with his girlfriend. Two guys stepped out of the dark and grabbed him and held him one on each arm, while a third guy stepped in with leather gloves on and punched the guy so hard that he cracked a couple of the leader's ribs.

They walked silently out into the night, leaving the guy lying on the floor. When the leader was able to get up, he called his girl friend, told her to be careful, and that he was going to take care of the situation by driving to San Francisco immediately to see his buddy, the District Attorney in the City. He'd come back to the lake and they would be free to run off together. She agreed, and he left for Baghdad by the Bay.

The next morning, he met with the D.A., who told him the facts of life! The D.A. told the leader that he had no jurisdiction at Lake Tahoe—"It's another county—it's another *state*, for godsake. Just stay away from Bones's girl, keep your nose clean and stay away from those Good Guys."

But our hero ignored the DA's advice. He roared back up to the lake, saw the girl and they made plans. After the second show that night, they planned to run off, but strange as it may seem, after she went to his cottage, the bandleader went missing.

Matty was summoned to lead the band in place of Lover Boy. Later that summer, two guys were out in a boat fishing for lunker trout in the lake. They were really excited when they hooked into one… they struggled to reel in their brass fishing lines, but when they brought up their catch, it turned out to be the former band leader with his feet in cement. Any questions?

After hearing this real-life melodrama, I have a hard time getting my mind back to the business at hand, which is rehearsing an act.

The guys come back from a 'Ten,' and Ken Lane, Dean's conductor/pianist is passing out the books, so I take the first trumpet book and settle back to the routine. We're about to start when Dean Martin himself arrives, suntanned but looking a little the worse for wear. He grins at us, then says 'hi' to the Cal Neva Lovelies, who are hanging around close to the stage.

Dean looks at Ken, who assures him, "He's on his way…"

We don't wait long to find out who "he" is… it's the local doctor from King's Beach. He strides onto the stage, pulls out his stethoscope and gives a quick listen to our star's ticker, then tells him to go into the dressing room.

Dino just grins, shakes his head 'No,' and says, "Naw, let's get it over with…"

Apparently Dean yanks his slacks down and the girls titter as they see his shorts. The Doc takes a syringe and a long needle out of his bag, pulls the shorts up and swabs Mr. Martin's buttock, then jabs the needle in.

Dean can't resist, and does a series of expressions of surprise and pain that would make Barrymore proud. Ken nods his head—he has seen it all before, as Dean hoists his slacks back up and the dancers giggle.

Dean announces to the assemblage, "Just a little shot'a bourbon…!"

But the medico won't let that pass.

He announces, "It's vitamin B-12…!"

The Doc leaves as Dean wanders off to receive a drink from someone, and we get down to the business of playing the charts, without the attendance of Mr. Martin!

TWENTY-SECOND CHORUS: "LADIES AND GENTLEMEN—MISS LENA HORNE!"

If you're old enough to have seen Lena in person, you treasure the memory. If you're not of an age, perhaps you've seen her in the PBS Special which celebrated her 80th birthday. Even if you get the film *Cabin in the Sky*, and just watch and listen to her sing "Stormy Weather" you'll get a feeling for and about her. Of all the stars I've worked with, Lena Horne is one of about three people I've played for that I'd buy a ticket to watch and listen to... she's that good!

It's 1960, and Lena is going to open at the Cal Neva, in the brand new Celebrity Room which Frank Sinatra has had built and which he opened. For the past ten days we've been playing for "The Rat Pack"—Frank and friends: Dean, Sammy, Joey Bishop and Peter Lawford. They all end up on stage, after opening night. Of course it is manic fun, no holds barred, no prisoners taken, no one, especially Sammy, left unscathed. It's been orchestrated chaos, reminiscent of the Brothers Marx, and the jam-packed showroom crowd loves every joke, bit and song, two shows a night... but today's another day, and this afternoon rehearsal is for Lena's opening night.

I'm in the top row on the highest riser with the other two trumpeters. Just in front are the three trombones and down on stage are the five saxophonists. Matty brings Lennie Hayton, Lena's husband, out on stage to the conductor's stand, and says in his funny lispy kind of voice (he has a problem with esses),

"Fellaish, meet Lena'ish musical director, Mr. Lennie Hayton!"

Lennie smiles his warmly wicked smile and says, "Hello fellas! We caught Frank last night... the band sounded good!"

We reply with grins and a couple of "Hi's" and "Thanks."

Lennie opens his leather bound Conductor's folder, and tells us, "The book's in order so let's start with the opener."

Lennie counts off the uptempo chart, Lena's drummer and bassist kick right in, and we roar through the arrangement... It's so well written, it's a breeze. I nail the high note on the end with authority and Lennie looks up at us with a nod and a smile. I can feel he's more than satisfied—maybe even a little impressed. But I catch myself before I get too puffed up because Lennie was the Music Director at MGM Studios, where he worked with many of the best players in Hollywood. He and Lena met while they were working on *Cabin in the Sky*, and later married. After that he left the studios to become his wife's musical director—he does all the arrangements. I look at him and notice that there is something about him that reminds me of a satyr. I mean Lennie is a handsome, rakish looking guy with a perfectly trimmed Van Dyke beard, and he looks cool in his "Bev. Hills" casual attire, but he has these wicked, slanting eyes that seem to see through you.

Lennie looks up at us, smiles that smile that seems to say, "I know all about it," then turns to the wings, smiles again, and introduces us to...

"Fellas, Miss Lena Horne!"

Out onto the stage walks Lena—the most beautiful and stunning woman I have ever seen. She smiles a smile at us that all of us almost luxuriate in, and purrs in that exquisite voice,

"Hello, guys... glad to see ya all."

She's wearing high heels, black slacks that fit better than any glove you ever saw, a white silk blouse with her hair in a white turban. Miss Horne simply radiates a kind of unforced, lovely, sensuous class, unlike some Hollywood stars that either don't have the style and grace, or the incredibly gorgeous face or figure that Lena has been blessed with. She has a tall Collins glass filled with a white liquid in her hand and she takes a sip.

Emboldened by Lennie's knowing warmth and Lena's open, "natural woman" attitude, I smile and call down, "Is that milk you're having, Lena?"

She chuckles, shakes her head but asks, "Would you fellas like to have a glass of 'milk' like Lena's got, too?"

Since I started this, I grin back and nod, "We'd love to, Lena!"

She signals a waiter, and in a few minutes, when we take a break in the rehearsal, we enjoy a rum & Kahlua punch, courtesy of the lovely Lena and the gracious Lennie. Lena drifts off after being with us for a few moments, as Matty and Lennie reminisce about the music biz.

Lena and her glass of 'milk.'

We take a break from the rehearsal and some of us wander into the Casino. There we see a guy in dungarees, a blue boat rope for a belt, a striped T-shirt and a Captain's cap, playing all the hands on a high roller Blackjack table. The guy seems to be having a very good time, aided by a steady series of cocktails the pit waitresses keep plying him with. He has stacks of chips, silver dollars and greenbacks all over the table. There's a crowd beginning to gather to watch the action, and I figure he'll never be lonely with all that dough. I ask my buddy the pit boss who this is, and he tells me it's Gar Wood, whose company manufactures heavy road building and earth moving equipment as well as the famous Gar Wood speed-boats. Time to go back and finish our rehearsal, but it's been fun watching a really "High" roller in action.

Opening night is exciting, and the whole band is "up" for the challenge of playing Lennie's charts with the fiery accuracy that they require. It's probably how a baseball team feels when it gets ready to play the New York Yankees… if you can't get up for this, you can't get up for anything!

The opener roars by, Lena riding the rhythm effortlessly, but with that special vital intensity she generates.

Then we're into the second tune. One thing I become aware of as we back her torchy, sexy rendition of "The Man I Love" and of course "Stormy Weather"—Lena never plays on her beauty or sensuality to get to the men in the audience. Instead, she plays to the women, doing a song by Julie Stein, I think, which has a little zinger for some man whose big talk is not being backed up by his action in the boudoir, in which she goads him with a throaty kind of snarl, "Hey Dad! Get up off your launching pad!" The audience absolutely loves her, especially the women… somehow she becomes like their champion and their ideal at the same time.

This is in direct contrast to poor Diana Dors, a blonde sexpot Brit who made a few films and did some shots on the Sullivan and Tonight Shows. But what a contrast when she worked this room. First of all, her gowns were of a very revealing décolletage and she played directly to the men. When she leaned over to the guys at ringside, her boobs were almost in their faces! The women with them simply hated her, and the response was anemic.

But Horne? When she insinuates her way through "When I Take

Lena Horne

131

You Out in the Surrey with the Fringe on Top," halfway through her act, she paints such a picture… of a ride every woman would love to take with that special man, and you can feel from the crowd that *everyone* is on this ride, right *with* Lena. I have never experienced, before or since, a performer who has such complete control over an audience as Lena can exert on a crowd. Everyone, all of us, musicians, listeners, busboys and waiters, even the jaded pit bosses gladly went right along with this paragon of musical and physical perfection for an hour which always seemed much too short.

After the show a few of us go out to see a lounge group playing behind the bar. It's a beautiful girl singer who at the time was married to Dick Haymes, the singer. But the big attraction is Gar Wood, at the bar. He has his winnings piled up in front of him, and he is really swinging now… he looks down the bar, first one way, then another and loudly invites everyone,

"Hey there, have a drink with me—on me!"

Of course the customers are anxious to respond and the bartenders get very busy. As Mr. Wood turns and calls out with a stoned good humor, I see that one of the girls who hang out around the Casino is sitting cozily pressed close to Mr. Good Time. Every time he turns and waves his arm to offer more drinks, she nimbly snatches some more of his chips, which disappear almost before you can see it, into some pockets of places in her dress which most women don't have.

Suddenly Wingy Grober appears at our side. He watches for a moment, then he steps forward fast like a prizefighter seeing an opening. He grabs the back of her bar stool with his gimp claw of a hand, spins her around in a dizzying circle, and as she comes face to face with him, her belts her with a right cross that lifts her off the stool and lands her on the floor. Just as quickly two guys in blue shirts, bandoleers and boots, appear and grab the fallen female, one under each arm, and take her through a door at the end of the bar that I didn't even know existed.

Wingy turns and mutters disgustedly, "Broads!"

Two days later we see the chip snatcher at the bar. She has bruises, scrapes and a shiner, and sits very quietly sipping a cocktail.

Wingy clips the 'B' girl who was stealing chips.

One night, I'm backstage just before the show and I hear a shriek! It's like a short scream, and it's coming from Lena's dressing room. I thought I saw Lennie with Matty out front, so I run to the door and pound on it, and yell,

"Lena! Are you okay?"

The shrieking stops, the door opens, and Lena peeks out at me. Now, for a split second I'm embarrassed—maybe Lennie wasn't out front! Maybe they were... Oops!

But Lena just smiles and with that laid-back, almost touch of the South in her voice, she says, "Ah'm fine, honey."

"Well I thought I heard you sort of scream, and I..."

Lena reaches through and pats my arm as she reassures me with, "Oh thanks... that's nice of you to worry, but that's just me warmin' up..."

I guess I look a little unsure or confused, so she explains, "A couple'a screams is the quickest way I know to warm up... besides, you know that ain't Grand Opera we're doin' out there, honey."

She smiles, shuts the door gently and as I wander off to the bandstand, I realize that Lena is a woman of many vast and mysterious wiles and charms, and Lennie is a very lucky man. They may not be doin' Grand Opera out there, but they are one hell of a Class Act!

TWENTY-THIRD CHORUS: KEELY COMES ON

Keely Smith is a marvelous singer; her records have been played steadily from the period she was featured with Louis Prima, Sam Butera and the Witnesses, till this very day. Keely can be heard on every "Good Music" radio channel as well as on cable TV's channel of "Singers & Standards."

I first saw and heard Keely when she *was* with Louis, as his partner and his wife. They worked back in the lounges of Las Vegas and were a smash hit, and so Wingy Grober has booked them into the main room of the Cal Neva, The Indian Room, as the featured Act. They don't disappoint expectations… The Indian Room is packed every show and the audiences love the act. Louie is a bundle of energy, constantly in motion with wisecracks and dancing around like a wild man. Sam Butera and the Witnesses provide a rambunctious but musically solid background for Louie and Keely, and Sam steps into the spotlight for burning hot tenor solos.

Then there's Keely… she stands as still as a statue, seldom changing expressions and completely ignoring her stage-mates' antics. The wilder Louie and the guys get, the more deadpan Keely plays it.

Louie calls her "The Indian," and she plays her part to perfection. When it's her turn to sing, she unleashes that beautiful voice that features an unusual little Creole, or Southern, turn of word and phrase.

She sings Duke Ellington's beautiful ballad with end-of-phrase comments by Louie. When Keely sings, "I Got it Bad and That Ain't Good," Louie jumps on-mike between phrases and bursts out with, "I Got It Good and It Ain't Bad!" Keely and Louie sing the great Mercer-Arlen tune "That Old Black Magic" in their unforgettable uptempo version. In a temporary lull between their hit songs,

Jimmy Vincent, the drummer, who used to date Keely (when she was Dorothy Keeley before Louie met her and renamed her "Keely Smith"), sneaks into a gorilla mask and the spotlight finds him tapping the cymbals and the drums like a curious ape. Every guy in the band has a role to play and they are marvelously funny. Keely keeps her onstage persona intact even when everybody else is convulsed with laughter.

Keely and Louie's marriage ends and Keely goes out on her own. Frank Sinatra has always liked her singing and signs her to his own record company, Reprise Records. Her first album, "Little Girl Blue," arranged and conducted by Nelson Riddle, is a hit, and in July of 1963, Sinatra also books her into the new Show Room, The Celebrity Room.

This act is a joy to play—the Nelson Riddle and Billy May arrangements of the great tunes are *so* good, and Keely is one terrific singer.

I notice Keely checking the trumpet section at the rehearsal and she mentions during one of the breaks that she thinks I look like the Los Angeles Dodger's pitcher, Don Drysdale, who is affectionately nicknamed "Big D." I can't see the resemblance and I'm a few inches shorter than Drysdale but Keely won't be dissuaded... so when she introduces and thanks the band every night at the two shows, she says (I will try to present a phonetic interpretation of her accent),

"Ah wanna thank the Matty Malneck aahkestra, an' 'Big D' up theah playin' lead trumpet."

It's a little embarrassing as the other guys in the band smile or snigger at the special mention I get from our star, but there is no way to ignore her rather meaningful come-on look which she bestows on me twice nightly.

I've invited my mother up to stay for a week or so, and she comes up and joins my wife Patti at the first show of Keely Smith's at the end of the first week. Keely chooses this particular show to look at me for a poignant moment after she thanks the Matty Malneck orchestra. She announces over the microphone, to me and to whole crowd, including my wife and mother, in a very sexy tone,

Keely Smith

"Big D, you're wastin' a whooole week here, baby!"

I want to slink down behind my music stand, but I can feel my face getting red, and there's no place to go.

After the show, I meet Patti and Mom in the Casino...

Patti looks at me questioningly, but my mother questions me out loud.

"What was that all about—what she said on stage...?"

What do you say when you've been 'hit on' by a show biz star? I finally shrug my shoulders, shake my head and just say,

"I really don't know... I guess it's a case of 'unrequited lust'!"

That seems to satisfy her, but Patti waits for more.

I turn to her directly and remind her, "You know where *I've* been all week, honey!"

The rest of the gig goes by without any further event, but Keely keeps on with her introduction of the band and... me! "Big D..."

TWENTY-FOURTH CHORUS:
SINATRA & THE RAT PACK

It's 1960, and I've got the band all set before I leave for Lake Tahoe. I've hired two other trumpeters, two trombones, four saxophonists, and a pianist, bassist and drummer.

But when I call to tell Matty the band's set, he says, "Frank's opening the new room. Hire a bass trombonist and a baritone sax man… Oh, and we'll need eight violins, two violas and two celli also…"

I get some good advice and contact Sid Sharp, a fine violinist and contractor, who gets the strings for me. I get the extra sax and trombone guys, and we all arrive at the lake for an afternoon rehearsal in the Indian Room. We get set up, not in the huge teepee like the old showroom, but in a beautiful state-of-the-art Show Room as fancy as any in Vegas. Now we've got a bandstand like Vegas rooms feature.

Matty motions me over to tell me, "Lisschen Bill, Fffrank doesshn't want anyone in the wings or backssstage during the show! Tell the fellassh, will you?"

I say sure and face the orchestra to relay Matty's message. The musicians all listen and nod assent. Freddie, our lead alto saxophonist is busy doing schtick so I make *sure* he gets the word. But Freddie likes to smoke a lot of grass and sometimes he's hard to reach.

I have asked him in the past how he plays so well 'stoned' and he gives me a glassy smile and tells me, "I practice stoned!"

It's time to work—I climb up to the back row, take my spot in the middle of the trumpets with the three trombonists in next level down. It's the catbird's seat as far as I'm concerned, because the lead trumpet sets the tone, the pitch and time for the rest of the band.

As Matty always says, "If the first trumpet and the drummer

play together, the rest of the band will follow."

Bill Miller is Frank's long-time pianist and conductor. He's a tall thin guy with graying hair and the palest complexion you've ever seen, so pale in fact that Sinatra sarcastically calls him "Sunshine Charlie."

Bill passes out the book of music, one for each player, as Irv Cottler, who always travels with Frank, finishes setting up his drums, tries a couple of "Pings" on the top cymbal, a crunch on the snare and a few snaps of the hi-hat, and we're ready for action.

Bill says, "I don't know what order the old man'll wanna go in, but get up 'River Stay Way from My Door.' I'll have the order for the show later."

He kicks it off, "A–One, Two, Three…"

Irv plays a drum fill, "Ta-da-ta-la-dat!" as Miller finishes the count off, and we're into it. I don't know what to compare this feeling to, for folks who have never had the thrill of experiencing it, but when a great drummer propels a good big band in a well-written arrangement, it's exhilarating and thrilling as this is. I can feel the beat, hear the guys and me, swingin.' Even without the Voice to sing the song, playing the arrangement is a real kick.

We rehearse some more of Frank's tunes and take a 'Ten.'

When we go back in to continue rehearsing, I'm surprised to see not Bill Miller, but Ken Lane, Dean Martin's pianist/conductor is now at the piano.

I've played Dino's act before and Ken says hi to me as he hands out Martin's music. Ken is a fine accompanist and a good guy but he has the worst rug I have ever seen. The "hair" is almost white, and looks like a helmet on his head… the rug doesn't quite fit and sticks out at the back of his head. Oh well, that's show biz…

We run through Dino's arrangements, and as he finishes the last tune, I see George Rhodes, Sammy Davis' conductor breeze in.

So this is going to be what Frank & friends did at the Sands in Vegas. The Big Three—Sam, Dino & Frank—book-ended by Peter Lawford and Joey Bishop are doing to do this thing they called "The Summit" down in Vegas.

We finish rehearsing all three guys' arrangements in three hours (with a couple of ten minute breaks), and it's a bit of a blow,

Dino, Sammy and Frank

a little test of us brass players' "chops." ("Chops" is a musician's shorthand for the embouchure or lip formation that one forms to make a sound on a horn). One, or rather two (!) of the reasons that the rehearsals go so quickly is that neither Frank nor Dean show up for the rehearsal.

Sammy comes on stage with all his usual energy; he's friendly and funny as always, but he is also very serious when it comes to the music. But he's such a consummate pro, and our band is good, so we play everything down one time and then we're through till the dance set and the Cal Neva Lovelies' chorus line number before the first show at 8 PM.

When I come back from dinner at 7:30, I see the parking lot of the lodge is jammed. I have to side-step my way through the casino and slip into the Show Room past all the well dressed folks who are trying to attract the maitre d's attention in order to slip him a twenty for a table. That's the usual deal, but tonight, it's fifties and hundreds that find their way into Eddie's moist mitts.

Then a "Captain" escorts the suckers (these guys are collecting a tip into the hand each has turned palm up behind their backs, if the party wants a 'better' table).

I go in, and the backstage area is crowded with Frank's people. Matty has given me a rundown on who's who and what's what.

"Jilly" Rizzo, Sinatra's buddy, restaurateur and sometime body-guard, is directing traffic by bullying, yelling and if necessary, shoving people, as Frank comes in through the back door.

Songwriter Sammy Cahn, his balding head gleaming and his wise eyes wary behind the hip glasses, is right behind the Chairman of the Board.

Skinny Amato and Hank Sanicola are two guys who seem never too far from Frank. Skinny Amato owns the 570 club in Atlantic City, and has always been a big supporter of the singer. Hank Sanicola is a "manager" and front man for whatever Frank needs.

He directs the Captains where to seat the party, depending on how much "juice" they have, or how big the tip is… The whole place is a mob scene… people jostling to get inside, and those inside pushing or being pushed to get to their table. I hold my trumpet case up, and slip past folks and onto the stage.

The rest of the band is there, as are the string players. They are mostly in their forties and fifties, and they are discussing the crowd backstage, as well as the several hundred who are flowing in. I get in front of the orchestra and announce what Matty asked me to.

Al, the trumpet player on my right, a big, heavyset guy who is going to UCLA with me, comments that he had a hard time finding a place to park.

As I get my horn out, I see something in the wings that I hadn't seen since we first rehearsed Frank's act in the early hours of the morning, last season. It's a portable rolling bar, replete with low-ball glasses, an ice bucket, fifths of Jack Daniel's, Smirnoff and Scotch, a water pitcher, a seltzer siphon and assorted other bar standards. Now I see Sammy Cahn adorning the rolling booze cart with cue cards with jokes written in felt tip pen.

I turn to Al and say, "It's gonna be a wet night tonight!"

We are ready to go at the 8 PM show time, but the crowd is still squeezing their way in. Matty tells me he's seen crowds like this when he worked with Al Jolson back in the early Thirties, and he looks unimpressed as he leans wearily against the grand piano, his baton held in limp fingers.

The small tables are jammed close together, and we watch what looks like two reindeer with antlers sticking up in the air, but it's really just busboys weaving through. Each guy is carrying two chairs in one hand and a table in the other.

Right behind them Eddie is yelling, "Hurry up you schmucks! C'mon, let's go! Goddam it, MOVE!"

Now I'm positive that these Hispanics don't understand the word "Schmuck," but they sure as hell get Eddie's message in any language. They push past waiters trying to take orders, bumping tables and spilling already served drinks, past complaining customers as they lurch toward the stage.

The busboys land the tables and jam chairs under them and retreat, following Oberleutnant Eddie, who marches back to his profitable post at the door.

Matty watches and turns to us and says, laconically, "These guys have no respect for the Proscenium Arch!"

Eddie surveys the room from the maitre d's post at the back of the room. I can see that there is no conceivable way to jam one more tiny table into the joint. Eddie looks up to Matty, and gives him the hi-sign—thumb and index closed to a circle. Matty sighs and turns to us. He raises his hand, and by god, the maestro has a baton in hand, instead of the pencil, which he usually uses to conduct! This is a sign that this is the big time, or respect, or… whatever—I never ask him, and he doesn't explain.

He gives a downbeat and we launch into the "Stairway to the Stars" fanfare.

After the ending chord, he cuts us off, grabs the mike and says in his inimitable "bi-lateral emission" style, "Ladiesss and Gentlemen, the Cal Neva isssh proud to pressshent—(drum roll)—the Cal Neva Loveliessssh!"

Matty downbeats us, and we swing into "Everything's Coming Up Roses."

Most of the Cal Neva Lovelies would not qualify for the New York City Ballet or Sadler's Wells, or even the Rockettes, but most of them are good looking if you don't get too close. Without exception, they all have big boobs and long legs, and what else would anyone want from a chorine, especially here high in the Sierras.

Anyway, the ladies manage to get through their number without bumping into each other. They troop off to a smattering of applause; we all know that all these people didn't jam in here to see a program of balletic perfection. All of us are here because the hottest thing in Show Biz is Sinatra and his Friends, Dean and Sammy!

There's a drum roll as Matty grabs the mike and announces, "And here he is, Ladiesss 'n Gentlemen… The Ssshtar of our Ssshow, direct from the bar… Dean Martin!"

Ken Lane downbeats the uptempo version of "Oh Marie," while Dean ambles out, a low-ball glass in one hand, and a cigarette in the other.

The band fades and Ken leads Dean into "Drink to Me Only That's All I 'Akx'—Ask, and I Will Drink to You!" (His intentional fumbled phrases are funny and a part of the act, of course). He looks at the audience, which is laughing and applauding as Ken counts off the opener.

We play a repetitive vamp as Dino looks around—his whole attitude is, "Where the hell am I?" and finally asks his conductor, "How long I been on?"

The folks respond and he launches into a whole set of "Special

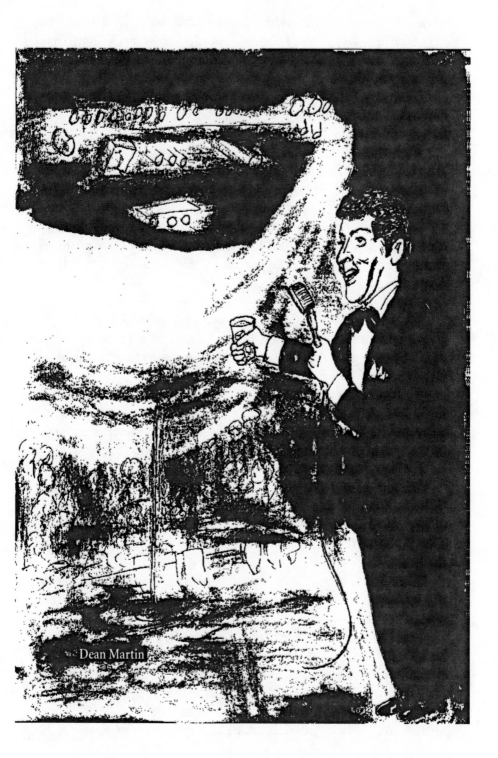

Dean Martin

Material" lyrics set to "When You're Smiling," but changed to "When You're Drinkin'!" Then we modulate to "The Gentleman Is a Tramp." More "inside" jokes about his agent, the Biz, booze and the swingin' life.

Dino says, "Here's a song that my very good friend Tony Bennett asked me not to sing, and that's why he's not my very good friend—he's one'a dem Eye-Talians—the worst kind…"

With that he launches into a straight version of "I Left My Heart…" (If I gotta finish the title for ya, ya got no business readin' this book)… then he jumps into a swingin' "Gonna Sit Right Down and Write Myself a Letter."

I sneak a peek to the wings, stage right, and see Frank lighting up a cigarette and taking his low-ball glass of Jack Daniel's from Skinny Amato. I can feel the intensity radiating from the man. Then Mr. Martin launches into "Volare" and closes with "On an Evening in Roma."

We wail out the ending as he saunters off and I happen to glance over to the wings, stage left and see Gloria, Freddie the sax man's blonde good looking wife, scoot in, wearing a black dress. Her eyes are locked onto Frank.

He comes onstage to an uptempo vamp, a finger popper, and the crowd roars at him. He's like a firecracker… the energy is intense and he hasn't sung a note—yet! He grins at the uproar, turns to Matty and does a perfect Matty-esque impression…

He lisps, "Sssshwing, Matty… !"

We jump from the vamp to the chorus of Matty's own tune, "Goody, Goody!" and Frank shows just why he *is* the Chairman of the Board… he swings! He goes right into "Chicago, Chicago, That Toddlin' Town." No special material—Sinatra just pours out the lyrics.

Then Frank intros "When Your Lover Has Gone" and reminds the audience, "A lotta guys have cried in their beer over this one…"

Frank's voice has some huskiness and a crack or two in it, but he tells the story of the song direct, to the point and with that special understanding he has for the lyric.

The crowd settles in and listens quietly—appreciatively, then they applaud warmly, and that invisible bond Frank can form with an audience is established. Sure, he chases broads, drinks, messes around with some hoods like Sam Giancana, but when he sings a ballad, particularly a torch song, everybody knows that this is the real thing... both audience and performer recognize it as Sinatra thanks the audience.

Frank tries a little humor but he doesn't have the easy genuine funny approach Dino has... so he tells about an upcoming release of his album with Count Basie, and gives 'em a taste with a swingin', roarin' arrangement by Neal Hefti of "Please Be Kind!"

We finish the tune, and Sinatra saunters over to Matty and teases him, "Ladies and Gentlemen, thisssh issh our Maesssshtro, Matty Malneck... he's the only guy that gives a shower when he introduces you."

Matty blushes as the crowd snickers, and Frank goes on with, "Sshay what wasssh the name'a that song you wrote during the War?"

"You mean, 'Ssshlewfoot?'"

Frank presses him, "No, no, the other one!"

Matty almost stubs his toe on the stage in embarrassment, but comes out with it—"You mean, Ssshigted Sshub, Sshank Sshame"?

Frank cackles at Matty's embarrassment and the audience joins in, but we in the orchestra don't like to see our leader, Matty, made fun of. After all, he's a good guy—but Matty just grins—after all, Sinatra recorded "Goody, Goody" and Matty's royalty checks have increased very nicely, I'm sure, because of it.

Matty launches us into a rockin', swingin' chart by Nelson Riddle of "You're Nobody Till Somebody Loves You!" Frank rides on Irv Cottler's driving drum beat, swings it out, and exits on bow music, which also brings on Sammy Davis Jr.

Sam glances back where Frank just exited, and says, "I know that guy from somewhere"... then he intros himself, saying, "Good evening, ladies and gentlemen, I'm Johnny Mathis!"

He does a beautiful "What Kind of Fool Am I" with real vocal passion, and like everything he does, he pours his heart and soul in it.

Then he swings "You're Out of This World," and kids with someone who takes his picture, à la Jerry Lewis.

As our band wails the instrumental section, Sam does a great eight bars of dancing. Coming back to the vocal, he quips, "I'd like to see Sidney Poitier do that!"

He finishes his tune, and starts a medley, but Frank and Dino are back!

It's got to be difficult for this diminutive black man who has chosen the Jewish faith and who has faced all the slings and arrows of racial prejudice, to be accepted by the Show Biz hierarchy. It's not a matter of talent—Sam has as much or more than almost anyone, but he's had to prove himself more than most do.

Because of that, Sam laughs at Frank and Dino's taunts and teases long and louder than anyone, and puts up with their really demeaning lines, like Frank's, "Go sit in the back of bus!" but Sam has a come-back—"Jewish people sit in the back of the bus!" Frank, not to be topped says, "No, Jewish people *own* the bus!"

Sammy has his large tinted glasses on so his artificial eye is not noticeable. You have to hand it to him; he's gone against all the racial and social barriers in town. Here he is, a Jewish black man who married the blondest actress in Hollywood, Mai Britt.

Sammy flies across stage with all the balletic bounce that Barishnikov could muster; Dino weaves his way out, and grabs Frank's mike away from him, looks at the audience, which is already howling and applauding, and drawls,

"What are alla you doin' in my dressing room ...?"

At this point, Sammy deftly sets down his drink on a piano and skips over to Dino, and jumps up into Martin's arms! Dean catches and cradles him as he turns to Frank and the audience and says,

"I wanna thank the NAACP for this award..."

Frank cracks up, grabs another mike and starts doing impressions, pushing, driving, as he is trying to do Cary Grant's Cockney dialect first with, "Ju-dy, Ju-dy..."

But it's a little stiff, and Dino pushes Sinatra away and picks it up, but instead of trying so hard, he just throws it away, but with just the right inflection.

"Ju-dy, Ju-dy, Ju-dy..."

Dino gets a laugh, has a sip, as Sammy starts in.

Just then Frank glances stage left and sees Gloria standing there, smiling, and enjoying the act. He grabs up a low-ball glass, shoves some ice into it, then turns like a baseball pitcher picking a runner off first, winds up and fires the glass at her! Gloria, now looking like Little Orphan Annie, stares at the missile headed at her face and passes out. As she slumps to the floor, the glass smashes into

Frank throws a glass...

the cement wall behind her, and ice and water rain down on her. Two of Frank's guys grab her and whisk her away.

But of course the show goes on! Sammy is the master of this metier, and he starts into one of his bag of impressions, when Frank interrupts him and puts him on the lowest of the three stools that are out onstage. Sammy bounces off and starts singing "The Birth of the Blues"—but no one ever gets a chance to finish a song.

There are a lot of insults aimed at Sammy, like when Dino asides to Davis,

"You're lucky to be out here with us, you putz!"

I wonder if somehow these two guys, great entertainers in their own right, are perhaps a little jealous of Sammy's talent at dancing, singing, doing impressions and generally capturing an audience.

The madness, mayhem and madcap mirth goes on and on... Each of them starts the first couple of lines of classic pop tunes— with a twist.

Dino sings, "Love Walked In, and scared the S-s-s-shadows away..."

Sammy counters with, "Did You Ever See a Jew Jitsu... Well I do!" and dances furiously.

Frank waits for the pandemonium to quiet down a bit, then starts his classic saloon song, seriously, "It's a Quarter to Three, and there's no one in the place except you and me..."

Sammy and Dino take over, right on pitch and on the beat with, "So Stick 'Em, Joe...!"

After a bit, Joey Bishop and Peter Lawford wander on-stage, and the audience greets the newcomers with yells and cheers. Joey does some one-liners and Sammy goads Lawford into tap-dancing with him.

They end up singing "Luck Be a Lady Tonight" and exit. Of course they do a couple of encores. They finish up with their arms linked and doing a high kicking routine as they stagger off to absolute bedlam from the audience.

♪♪♪

After a few nights of this, I notice that Joey Bishop's deadpan one liners get a few laughs, and Lawford has a few funny lines

The Rat Pack: Dean Martin, Peter Lawford, Sammy Davis, Frank Sinatra, and Joey Bishop

which someone, maybe Sammy Cahn, has written for him. Sammy Davis works hard at everything—he sings when he gets a chance, dances like mad and gets laughs with his put-ons and impressions. But Dino gets the laughs—effortlessly and easily. Frank works hard and just doesn't get the same results on the "laugh-meter" (if there were such things onstage, but we can hear the difference in the back row).

One night before they start, I overhear Frank and Dino talking offstage. Frank seems a little put off by the response he's gotten from the crowds, and he tells Dino,

"Hey Dage," (the affectionate contraction Frank and Dino called each—short for "Dago"!) "let me do the jokes you've been doing!"

Dino shrugs and says, "Okay…!"

When they start the act, and Frank does Dino's lines, Sinatra still doesn't get the laughs he covets.

After the show, I overhear him ask Martin, "I don't understand, Dage… I'm doin' your stuff, but I'm not getting' the laughs…! What the hell is it?"

Dino has a drag from his ever-present cigarette, a sip of his drink, then looks Sinatra in the eyes, and tells him,

"… 'Cause you ain't funny, Frank…!"

If anybody else in the world had said that to Frank Sinatra, the 'Chairman of the Board' would probably have belted him in the mouth, but Sinatra just took it. He stared at his buddy, then shook his head and shrugged. Mr Sinatra knows that he is the premier singer of American Popular Music, bar none! I guess he was satisfied with that… comedy isn't something you learn—it's a talent, just like Frank's … Dino has a way with timing a line, and Frank has a way with singing a song so you feel it right down to your gut.

CODETTA

This summer a couple of us save our dough so we can eat in the Cal Neva's great steak house. It's usually full of high rollers, but I know the maitre d' and even the head chef, a burly red headed Russian guy who likes me.

We have just opened with the McGuire Sisters, and we see a rather stocky guy with horn rimmed specs who seems inseparable from Sinatra. My buddy the pit boss tells me that this newcomer is Sam Giancana, one of the major bosses of the Mafia.

The first night after payday we head for the steak house and one of those great New York cuts. We get to the entry and we can see Sinatra and his girlfriend Juliet Prowse at a big table with Sam Giancana and his girl friend Dorothy McGuire. These couples are book-ended by Jilly Rizzo, Frank's buddy and bodyguard, and Skinny Amato, who owns the 500 Club back East where Sinatra started his comeback. Frank also had his buddies, Dino and Sammy D., come in and work the 500 Club, either with him or solo, at what I hear is a lot less than they can command in Vegas.

Anyway, we are set to go into the steak house when I notice two large guys in blue shirts, black 'trooper' style pants and boots on either side of the entry. I start forward followed by my buddies but one of the big guys steps forward, holds up his hand and says, "Not tonight, fellas!"

We shrug and retreat to more friendly dining environs.

CODA

Since "The Rat Pack" or "The Summit" as Sinatra likes to call this clambake, opened, Marilyn Monroe has been coming up to hang out. She is working in Reno with Clark Gable and Montgomery Clift on the film *The Misfits*, which has been written by Marilyn's husband, Arthur Miller. I don't know what her relationship with Miller is, but she sits next to Sinatra or one of the Kennedy brothers after they "sneak" her into the showroom.

The band and Matty are ready to start the show, but we sit and wait. Then after an interval, the curtains at the showroom entrance part, and we can clearly see the tousled blonde hair of Monroe. She pulls a scarf over her hair, and she's led down near ringside, where she sits next to Sinatra and across the table from one or the other of the Kennedy clan. Now the show can start!

Frank Sinatra, owner of the Cal-Neva Lodge in 1959, with Marilyn Monroe. Former owner Wingy Grober is standing in the middle.

TWENTY-FIFTH CHORUS: "COME UP AND SEE ME SOMETIME"

It is August, 1961; I'm two years out of UCLA, a full-time musician, and I've been trekking back to Lake Tahoe every summer. Patti is on the Vegas-Reno-Tahoe circuit with Jack Ross and the Dick Lane Sextet.

I'm working at the Crescendo nightclub on the Sunset Strip. Right now I'm practicing every trumpet player's staple exercise book, the *Herbert L. Clarke Technical Studies*, number one, metronome marking 108—ta, da, da, da, dee, dee, dee dee, da da, eight times in a row—I know this thing by heart. While I practice, I watch Channel Eleven's Afternoon Movie show, hosted by Ben Hunter, a vaguely charming guy with a bad rug. But today it doesn't matter because he's unspooling *My Little Chickadee* starring my personal favorite comedic actor and life hero, W.C. Fields. He's one actor who wrote much of his own stuff, and who once summed up a difficult life problem in a film like this:

"There comes a time in every man's life, my dear Oswald, when one has to grab the bull by the tail and face the situation square in the face."

I watch as the great man blusters and bumbles along on the screen, but I realize he's having a harder time stealing scenes than he usually does because of his sexy, sarcastic, worldly, and very funny co-star, Mae West. At one point she bumps into one of her many admirers in the film—it's full body contact, from bosom to knee bone. She pulls back, coolly surveys the embarrassed suitor, and drawls,

"Do you have a pencil in your pants, or are you just glad to see me?"

I finish the exercise, check the clock; it's time to drive to the Crescendo for the afternoon rehearsal. I put my trumpet back into the case, close the front door of my little house in the wrong end of

Encino, jump in my Rambler station wagon and wend my way up Laurel Canyon to the Sunset Strip. I park in the vacant strip across from the Crescendo and walk through the club, past waiters setting the silver on the fresh white tablecloths for dinner tonight.

I jump up on the stand, exchange hellos with Bill Douglas the drummer, Andy the bass player and Jay the alto man. Bob Armstrong, the pianist/leader looks over the top of his glasses at us. Everybody gets quiet, because this means an official "leader" type of announcement. Last night there was a rumor that Gene Norman, the club owner, might close the joint for a few days. Maybe we're on notice; this new kid Wayne Newton hasn't been drawing flies. But instead, Bob, who has two expressions, the "you're fired" one, or a smile like a horse when it pulls its lips back to glom onto a carrot, unveils all his teeth as he smiles at us.

"Fellas, we have an extra gig—a rehearsal—a *paid* rehearsal with Frank Werth down in Santa Monica tomorrow afternoon. Any of you can't make it?"

"Who we playing for?"

"It's a surprise... wait'll tomorrow."

Of course I can make it—nobody's ringing my phone off the hook with record dates. I do know that Frank Werth is a very well schooled composer of very serious music who wrote the scores for one of my favorite radio shows about a tough private eye, *Richard Diamond*, starring Dick Powell, and which featured his brother George on trumpet. George would come in cold, on the air, on a high C sharp, then he'd roar through this cadenza into the theme, also a very exposed and difficult trumpet solo. The music was very contrapuntal, very technical sounding. If he writes that hard for his brother, what'll I have to play?—But that's the fun of this business, I remind myself—you know, whatever they write I'm supposed to be able to play.

Bob gives us directions to the gig tomorrow, and then we start to run over Joanie Sommers' music. I start to wonder who we're rehearsing tomorrow, but there's no time now. We open up the books, and run down Joanie's tunes. She sings great, the charts are good, and the afternoon whizzes by.

Next day, I motor along Wilshire, to Ocean Ave., and down the California Incline, a steep turnoff to the Pacific Coast Highway. I love the blue sky day and clean ocean breeze, but I snap out my reverie to glance at the address on the paper, and all of sudden, I see I'm there. It's a two story white place, with lots of glass brick and rounded corners. I pull in to see the other guys parking in the big driveway that stretches toward the beach and a four-car garage. I park and get out. The drummer and bass player carry their equipment to the door where Bob, the leader is waiting for us.

He smiles as I ask, "What a pad! Whose place is this?"

He rings the doorbell and grins toothily.

"Mae West!"

I'm about to say something, when the door opens kind of majestically. The door opener is a small man, in his sixties or seventies, with a deep tan. His white hair is very neatly cut and combed, but what's easy to see is that he is in fantastic shape no matter what his age is, with a weight lifter's arms and chest bulging through his T-shirt. He looks us over a little disapprovingly—he can see we're just a bunch of out of shape, pale faced, dissolute musicians—but he nods and says,

"Welcome…! Miss West is expecting you. My name is Guy. Come in, gentlemen—right this way. Mr. Werth is already here."

He leads us inside. The place looks like a movie set for an ocean liner. The furniture is blonde, streamlined, on polished wood floors, and there are lots of chrome and windows shaped like portholes. Guy leads us through the entry and into a long room where two monkeys with leather collars are leashed to a long chrome rail which runs between two wooden supports in the middle of the room. There are all kinds of fruit in dishes laid out on the floor, which is covered with newspapers. The monkeys are running up and down, fighting with each other, chattering at us, then they leap up to swing on the bar. When nature calls, they just relieve themselves at will on the newspapers or the floor or wherever they happen to be. The place smells of overripe fruit and monkey shit. Mercifully, Guy leads us past this mess, down a hall into a large room, sort of a den or playroom, with a fireplace and white leather couches and a white baby grand arranged around a large bare floored rehearsal area. The room is dominated by a metal spiral staircase, which curves up to the second floor.

"Sit down, gentlemen. Would you like a refreshment?"

The drummer asks for a scotch and water. Guy looks at him

like he'd ordered a strychnine on the rocks.

He says stiffly, "Miss West allows no alcohol to be served. A Coca Cola or water, perhaps?"

We order up Cokes and he glides away for the refreshments. I turn to see Frank Werth standing by the fireplace mantel. He's a gray-haired gent with glasses, in rep tie, sweater and blazer. He is very professorial looking—someone I'd have seen in the UCLA Music Library. Right now he looks like he'd be more comfortable giving a lecture on the color of Mozart's eyes, or what Beethoven liked for breakfast, than passing out music to a bunch of night club musician types. He tells us rather apologetically that he has written a Las Vegas show for Miss West and that we're here to run it down for her while he shows her the songs and material. Guy comes back with a tray of drinks. He passes them out, then, very gravely, announces,

"Miss West will be with you shortly. Excuse me."

I take a look at the music. I see there's no *Richard Diamond* type cadenzas for the trumpet, thank god, it's all straightforward show type stuff, and we turn to our drinks, and talk about the house and the monkeys and whatever. A half-hour goes by, and I can see Frank Werth is getting antsy. He checks his watch, and Guy comes back to check that we haven't tried to spike the drinks or molest the monkeys.

Frank asks, "How much longer? I've got to get back to town."

Guy stiffens, pulls himself to full height, and announces, "Miss West is a very busy star. She will be with you as soon as is possible."

Now I don't know how busy Mae West is—I haven't seen her for years, except for this morning. But I have no place to go, so I sit back and watch.

After another fifteen minutes, Guy glides back in and announces, "Miss West will be appearing in a few moments."

He oozes out, and we wait another five. We hear a door close up above on the next floor, and we turn back to the spiral staircase to see a pair of pale pink slippers, then the bottom of a nightgown, also pink, appear on the top stair. Miss West is coming down to see us, at last.

Her steps are slow, and I can see that the whole bottom of the nightie is water spotted. Now I can see her. The skin of her face

Mae West makes an entrance.

is stretched so tight, I'm afraid it'll crack. Her eyes are like slits, with exaggerated long black eyelashes that curve up toward her corn-yellow blonde hair. I suddenly feel kind of sad—sorry to see her like this. But she seems glad to see all of us. She eases down the stairs, makes the curve of the stairs with a kind of voluptuous wiggle. Guy has reappeared magically. She smiles at him, then us. The skin doesn't crack. Her voice is low and slow, with that same insinuating sexiness as in the movie.

"Hiya fellas. What have you got for me?"

We get ready to play. Bill settles behind his drums, Bob at the piano. Frank goes to Mae with the score in his hand. She waves off the score pages, but extends her hand—Frank is the perfect gentleman—what can he do?—he kisses her hand. He starts to point at the notes on his score, but she waves it aside, and undulates over to a big chair and sits down, like a sexy queen. Her voice still oozes with sexual innuendo.

"Let's hear it, boys."

Frank gives a downbeat, and we roar into his score. We play the music, but I start to get a sinking feeling as Frank talks the song while we play. The music and lyrics are as stiff as Frank looks. We finish the song, and Mae looks at Frank Werth as if he was trying to sell her a Bible. Bob, our leader, looks like he wishes he was under the piano bench instead of on it. He starts to give a downbeat to the next tune, but Frank stops him. He turns to Mae.

"Now Miss West, this next song is a love ballad which you sing to the leading man."

Frank stops his pitch when Mae holds up her hand.

"I don't sing no love songs to nobody. They sing 'em to me, honey."

Frank mumbles, "Of course, Miss West, I meant…"

"Go ahead, honey, don't let me slow ya down."

Frank kicks off the next tune. Thank god, it's an up tempo show biz two beat thing, oom-pop, oom-pop, oom-pop. It's the only thing we've played that even vaguely sounds like Show Biz, or even fun. As we finish, Frank jumps in immediately, selling hard.

"Now, you see this next tune has a double fugue with a contrapuntal duet between you and the men's chorus behind you, and then we go into a stretto in augmentation, and a codetta with…"

Mae waves her hand to stop him, and gets to her feet. She sashays slowly over to Frank, who is mopping his forehead with his handkerchief, leans her head to the side, and nods at the score in Frank's hand, as she asks,

"Where are the jokes, honey? I don't need no stretchos—all I need are the jokes."

Frank doesn't know what to say to that, so he turns back to us. We charge into the last tune, and I want it to be over even more than Bob, Frank or Mae West. We finally clank to the ending, hit the last chord, and start to pack up. Frank starts to talk about the score, but Mae turns to us; her eyes glint through their slits, and she drawls out the side of her mouth,

"Thanks, boys. Come back and see me some time."

CODA

Frank Werth kept writing more wonderful serious contrapuntal music for orchestras. We never did come back to Mae's house, but one night, about a year or so later, I saw her in a ridiculous film called *Myra Breckinridge*. Everything was bad, except for Mae—she just played herself, and did her own material too, like when she gave advice to the ingenue. Mae told her, "A good man is nice to find—but a hard man is even better."

TWENTY-SIXTH CHORUS:
SID CAESAR AND 'LITTLE ME'

It is 9 o'clock in the morning in July of 1964, and I am sitting in the pit of the Los Angeles Philharmonic Auditorium, getting my trumpet out of the case, along with thirty other musicians. I feel really happy to be here as I dig the mutes out of the mute bag, because this is a good job and a nice step up from playing the night club circuit here in L.A. and I'm also going to work with Irving Bush, a wonderful player and friend. We are getting ready to rehearse a new show, called *Little Me*.

I turn and grin at Irv, "This should be good, huh Irv?"

Irv smiles, "I hear the show is pretty funny."

As the rest of the orchestra exchange "Good mornings," we hear a commotion at the narrow little door which is the entry to the orchestra pit. This is on the side of the pit where the string section is, to the left of the conductor's podium. In the middle of the pit are the woodwinds, who are kind of under the stage, with their backs to it, while the brass section, with the trumpets up front, are on the right side, with the percussion behind us. We have a pretty good view of anything that happens down stage.

Irv and I turn back just as a music stand crashes over. We see a heavy-set guy cutting a swath through the string section. It is our fellow trumpeter Pinky Savitt, who plays second at Warner Brothers' studio. He is making his entrance with his customary aplomb, lurching and bumping into people with all the finesse of a freight train arriving in the pit.

The string section players hug their valuable instruments protectively.

Bernie Kundell, the concertmaster complains, "Hey Pinky, watch it, will you?"

Pinky has more the build and face of a guy you'd buy pastrami from in a kosher meat market than a trumpet player. Pinky turns to look at Bernie.

"Oh–uh—sorry."

But Pinky's trumpet case swings out like an unguided missile, and hits librarian Harry Stitman. Now Pinky would have scored a direct hit on Harry's ample stomach, but instead Pinky hits the twenty or so leather bound orchestra folders Harry is passing out that contain the show music. The folders go flying, and Harry explodes in his warmest New Yorkese,

"Hey! Watch it, will ya, ya putz!"

The exertion of bending over to retrieve the books makes Harry's chubby face and bald head look like a really red tomato growing out of a starched white shirt. Harry is the percussionist who has been brought from New York to L.A., and has been assigned the extra goody job of librarian, or book passer-outer… (it pays extra). As if there weren't at least a dozen or more percussionists right here in L.A. that couldn't play the tymps and xylophones and stuff that a show requires. But this morning Irv and I talked to Lou Adrian, the skinny fiddle player who is the contractor of the Civic Light Opera orchestra.

Lou tells us in his best confidential secret style, "Ya see the reason they brought Harry Stitman all the way from New York is that he has a special part in the show for which he has rehearsed with Sid Caesar himself… besides, Harry is Charlie Sanford the conductor's brother-in-law."

This of course just goes to prove that there is no nepotism in the music business. Anyway, when Pinky sees whom he's whacked with his case, his whole attitude changes.

"Oh Jeez, Harry, I'm sorry—I didn't know it was you!"

Harry straightens up with, "Ya mean ya wouldn't a hit me if ya knew?"

Pinky throws up his meaty paws, one of which still holds the deadly trumpet case. Pinky is able to knock a clarinet player's music off the stand and onto the floor as he protests,

"Ah, no, no, Harry… I didn't mean that way. I heard Charlie might be comin' ta L.A. ta do a TV show and I wanted ta meet ya both…"

Harry fends Pinky off with, "Ya sure got a great way'a meetin' people!"

Irv and I watch as Pinky lumbers through the next endangered section, the French horns and trombones.

Irv asides to me, "Ah yes, the Marx Brothers in *A Day in the Orchestra Pit*... watch your trumpet—here he comes!"

Pinky finally arrives breathless after cutting this swath of destruction through the orchestra and plops down on the other side of Irv.

I call over to him, "Mornin' Pinky! How ya doin'?"

Pinky mumbles back, "Oh hi, Peterson..."

He turns to Irv and says, "Say Irv, did Lou tell you that you was playing first?"

Irv smiles, and nods, "Yes, Pinky, Lou asked me to play first."

"Oh," says Pinky with a disappointed look on his face. (Playing first pays more and it's a coveted position.) "I thought maybe he'd want me to..."

Pinky gets his horn out, drops three or four mutes which roll under other peoples' chairs. We are helping retrieve the mutes when a man of fifty or so mounts the podium. He's dressed in casual clothes but expensive, and he arranges a towel around his neck. He picks up the baton, holds it in his right hand with the point pressed into his left. He gives us his best 'New York charming' smile of condensation, as if he's come to the West Coast to deal with a bunch of musicians who couldn't possibly be as good as the guys in the Apple are.

Anyway he starts with, "Good morning, everyone! I'm Charles Sanford—I did *Your Show of Shows* with Sid, and it's a pleasure to be here... now, we've got a lot to do, so as soon as you have your book, let's get started! ..."

He sees that Harry is still not ready to go, so he demands, "Harry? How much longer?"

Harry mumbles, "If that klutz hadn't made me drop da music..."

Maestro Sanford gives Harry an imperious wave of his baton, "Just hurry up, Harry..."

I love watching "important" people modulate from one persona to another.

The music gets passed out, and we run down the overture, and the rest of the show. The music is very good—why not? Charles Strouse of *Bye Bye Birdie* fame wrote it and it was orchestrated by the great Ralph Burns, who wrote much of Woody Herman's best stuff. Everything about the show musically is wonderful—except for Charlie Sanford. He not only looks and acts so up tight you'd think we were doing brain surgery or live TV, but he conducts with all the grace and style of a man afflicted with both St. Vitus's Dance and arthritis at the same time. To call this guy stiff would be a compliment. Anyway, we are pros and we can adapt to almost any conductor, even this guy.

After the morning's rehearsal, Lou yells out, "Lunch! Everybody back at one thirty!"

Irv gives me a subtle wink, then turns to Pinky, "Ah Pinky, would you like to get a sandwich?"

Pinky ignores the invitation—his head swivels around to find Harry, anxiously. Harry is behind the brass, encircled by his tymps and xylophone, but I see there's an interesting addition to the regular paraphernalia. There's a two foot square hunk of black slate, mounted on a tilted drum stand with a microphone just above it in front of Harry's high drummer's stool. Sitting on the slate are a pair of shoes with metal taps on them, à la Fred Astaire.

Pinky calls back, "Hey Harry, how 'bout I buy ya lunch—I owe ya one, okay?"

Harry looks up from some personal reverie, sees a free lunch staring him in the face, and shrugs, "Okay… it's your town—you know something close?"

Pinky smiles, "Trust me."

Irv turns and nods at me, "I think Pinky is going to be Harry's personal L.A. tour guide. Shall we?"

In the afternoon, Sid Caesar and the rest of cast come to rehearse with us. Sid seems a little nervous, and even on a break, when I venture, "Hi, Sid!" he sort of backpedals and looks like I might put the bite on him for a five spot.

Then he gives me a quick smile, and stutters, "Uh, uh, …hi!"

Sid moves away into his dressing room with the star on the door. But that star on the door is justified when we get to see him in action.

♪♪♪

Little Me is a show about the intimate memoirs of Belle Poitrine (formerly Belle Schlumfert), an aging silent film star who has used every person and every casting couch in town to advance her career, and finally become the darling of two continents. Belle meets each of seven characters Sid plays. Sid becomes all these guys, who are her lovers. He is brilliant as he changes into the "too good to be true" snobbish Noble Eggleston, who sings to Belle, "I love you, even though I'm filthy rich and dirt poor." Next he becomes the crusty old millionaire, Cyrus Breakwind, and from Oberleutnant Heinrich Von Steuben-Strudel to Jean Val Jean, the singing, dancing French star of stage and screen. This bit in the show is Harry Stitman's opportunity to shine—to show L.A. why he has been winged in from Gotham for this show. Sid, as Jean Val Jean, is about to be poisoned by his ever-loving Belle. She has fallen in love with the new movie Tarzan, Letch Feely, and would like Jean out of the way. But Jean doesn't drink from the poisoned wineglass right away. Belle watches breathlessly as he brings the glass to his lips, then suddenly toasts everyone. Of course Sid expands the bit each night with more hilarious bursts of double talk Gallic toasts and gags. He prepares to drink again, then impulsively cries out,

"But first—We dance!"

At this cue Sid starts to tap dance furiously on stage. He looks like a great star dancer who suddenly becomes a sort of berserk one man chorus line. Meanwhile, in the pit, the great Harry Stitman grabs up the pair of tap shoes by the soles. He uses the taps on the heels to beat out about three minutes of tap dance effects on the big black piece of slate in front of him. Of course it's a chance for Sid to stretch this out, and he is at his hilarious best. We can all enjoy it in the pit, because all that happens is Sid on stage and Harry in the pit, pounding away. It is funny, so maybe Harry is worth all the extra expense. Anyway, at the end of the dance Sid downs the whole glass in one gulp, and does the funniest bit of writhing while he dies I've ever seen. He ends up in extreme downstage position—collapsing so that his head hangs over the stage apron, into the orchestra pit. As he gives his last gasp, Belle flutters around the stage, pretending tragic loss, while Sid opens one eye and winks at us. Just another Caesar touch to this, the best show I've ever played.

No wonder that this all so good; the whole wonderfully funny and hip show is based a book by Patrick Dennis who wrote *Auntie Mame*, with the stage book by Neil Simon. Need I say more? Suffice to say, once Sid is in one of these characters, he is fantastic, not nervous or self-conscious.

On opening night it is all we can to do concentrate on playing, because he breaks us up time after time with his genius for comedy. I am having one helluva great time playing in a good orchestra, getting very well paid and seeing and hearing some of the funniest stuff I've heard. A far cry from backing some so-called comedian named Jackie or Bobby or Buddy who tells mother-in law jokes.

It's a funny thing though… when we in the orchestra enjoy the show or laugh it seems to upset the Maestro. Charlie Sanford will lean down to us with a warning finger to his lips—to "shoosh" us not to disturb the wonderful madness on stage. Oh well, such are conductors. Anyway, while Irv and I are enjoying this terrific show, Pinky is making great strides in becoming Harry's best friend in L.A. The fact that there's a rumor floating around the pit that Charlie Sanford will come west for a new show with Sid has nothing to do with Pinky's cultivating his new friendship, I'm sure.

On the first Saturday, we have our first two-show day, which means we play a matinee till four thirty, then relax and go out for dinner. Pinky decides that it'll be safe to let Harry have dinner with some of the rest of us. Harry is probably anxious to meet some other players too, so we go to an Italian restaurant and five or six of us gather round at the bar, and yack it up while we have a drink before we sit down to dinner. I watch little Harry bend his elbow faster than when he pounds out the tap dance fireworks in the pit for Sid.

Irv and I watch bemused, and I remark, "I wonder if Pinky is covering the bar bill Harry is running up?"

Anyway, we meander over to a table, and eat. Harry washes down the pasta with a few glasses of vino, and we all stagger back to the theater. Irv and I walk around a bit to stretch and clear away the fumes, but Pinky and Harry go down to the orchestra room. It's curtain time, we are all in our 'respectable' positions, and Maestro Sanford gives us one of his phony smiles, followed by the stiffest downbeat in the music biz. By now, we've got it cold, and we plunge into the overture, at about eight PM, feeling no pain. The show rolls along, the audience enjoys it and loves Sid, and all is well.

However, at one point where there is a break in the music while dialogue is happening on stage, just before Sid's Jean Val Jean dance bit, I feel a trombone slide tap me on the backside. I turn and Roy Main grins and gestures behind him. I look and then nudge Irv too.

We have just enough time to see Harry Stitman, slumped on his drummer's "high chair." Harry's eyes are closed; all three of his chins are resting on his tux shirt. The scotch, all the pasta and the red wine have done their work. Harry is deep in the arms of Morpheus—all alone by his xylophone. The tap shoes lie forgotten on the slate, as Harry belches lightly and then settles down to snooze and snore just audibly, as Sid builds into his famous Jean Val Jean tap dance number. Sid stops his sip, cries out, "But first we dance!" and starts to tap dance like a demonic Fred Astaire. Charlie Sanford, the conductor, turns to give one of his patented stiff wrist downbeats to the percussionist of our august musical group. Does he see a wide-awake, alert, dependable, highly paid professional percussionist who has been flown to L.A. to do tap dancing in the pit? No! Instead he sees his little short fat brother-in-law who is as comfortably fast asleep as if he was conked out on the sofa at home, ignoring his wife!

Now, on stage, Sid is dancing his ass off, but alas, his feet just make a futile thudding sound on the stage… there are no wonderful, rhythmic tap–tap–tap—tapa–de–tap sounds coming from the pit. Harry is snoring comfortably as Charlie Sanford frantically waves his magic baton at sleeping beauty Stitman. After three bars of Sid's dancing feet with no taps, Charlie is still furiously thrashing the air with his baton. Then, in desperation and fury, he bellows out at his brother-in-law,

"Shoes, Harry! Goddamn it! SHOOOES!!"

Since nobody else plays at this point, all the eyes in the orchestra are on Harry as he comes to with a jolt, a jerk and a snort, his eyes still glazed. He grabs for the shoes and unfortunately, grabs at one so that the front of the shoe hits a cymbal, then falls to the floor, while his other shoe is whanging away on the slate.

As a result it sounds like a one-legged man tap dancing his heart out. Sid continues, but works his way close enough to the edge that he can look down into the pit. His face goes through surprise, anger, and consternation… you name it—he looks it. Finally he's had enough! Sid grabs up the poison glass, gulps and collapses. As the audience laughs and applauds, Sid's head comes over the edge of the stage, bounces and jerks a couple of times. He is a consummate pro, and he'll wring every laugh he can out of it.

But for just a beat, he opens one eye, looks down at the frantic Charlie, and Harry, and stage whispers, "What the hell was THAT!"

After the show Harry is summoned to his brother-in-law's dressing room.

Pinky stands around wringing his hands, muttering, "The little mispucha—it wasn't my fault!"

I watch as Pinky waits to see what would happen to his new friend, and whether he'll get blamed for it. Next evening, there is a short inspirational talk by Lou Adrian about the evils of drink on matinee days, while Charlie Sanford glowers at us from over his shoulder in the orchestra room.

CODA

Sid Caesar never did come back to the West Coast to do a show. That was too bad, but I was very glad that Pinky was able to make a new friend. Harry tried to stay in L.A. and work the Civic Light Opera, but when his brother-in-law meal ticket left, Harry found the work scene a little lean and returned to New York, a sadder but wiser little man.

But he was not forgotten… Weeks after *Little Me* closed, we were playing *The King and I*. This production starred Florence Henderson who was as wistful as steel, and it took longer and longer for Ricardo Montalban as the King to die. But we smiled as somebody in the back of pit would whisper,

"Shoes, Harry, Goddammit, SHOOOES!"

TWENTY-SEVENTH CHORUS:
A BIG CHANGE

I've been playing *Little Me* in spite of a bad cold I can't shake. I have twenty private students, and I'm landscaping the back yard. In order to kill the insects I've been spraying the ground with some powerful bug killer. After the show one night, I feel as if my body is divided somehow in two around my waist. It seems that my legs want to go one way and my top half another. I manage to get home and go to bed.

The next morning I'm anxious to get up and get going because I have one of my infrequent record dates. I sit up and feel dizzy. I try to stand up and fall to the floor. Patti hears the thud and comes in to see what's wrong. She helps me up onto the bed, and I know that I've got a serious problem. I ask Patti to call a sub, and then she calls the doctors who were the internists who attended my dad.

The doctors tell Patti to take me to St. Vincent's Hospital. By the time I get there, I am so weak that I can't hold my head up.

The hospital checks me in, and Patti sees me through an awful bout with something called Guillain-Barré Syndrome. I'm paralyzed; all I can move are my eyes. I lie in a bed in St. Vincent's Intensive Care Unit for three weeks. I have a tracheotomy; they feed me through a tube down my gullet. Patti and my mother watch and wait to see if I'll make it.

When I recover and come home, my ideas and feelings about life have changed. I know that I'm unhappy and dissatisfied with everything. I realize just how transitory my grip on life is, and I know that I don't want to go on as I have been.

I know that I want to be single again. Patti is an angel, but there's something I feel that tells me that I don't want to be married any more—to Patti, or anyone else.

One of the hardest things I've ever done is to tell her how I feel.

We divorce, and I don't see her for a long time. I know she's hurt, and I feel guilty, but I still know it's the right thing for me.

All these years later, we have lunch and exchange gifts on holidays. My wife Carolyn and daughter Laura have accepted Patti with affection and caring.

Twenty-Eighth Chorus: Liza's Opening Night at the Coconut Grove

It is the early Sixties, and I have just quit my first job. I have been working in the pit orchestra of the Civic Light Opera at the Philharmonic Auditorium, where we have been playing the musical show *Little Me* starring Sid Caesar. It's a good job: it's a funny show, it pays very well, and I get to work with one of my favorite people, Irving Bush, who is a great trumpet player. There's only one problem—I never get to play first trumpet, and really want to have that chance. I get offered a job with Dick Stabile's band. He is going to open at the Coconut Grove and he wants me to play first trumpet.

I talk to Irving, and he says, "I think it's a good idea to take the job, so you get that night after night experience of playing first trumpet... besides people will get to know you are a first trumpet player, and not just a section player."

Irving always has good advice, so I take the chance, and the job, and we start to rehearse.

In the '60s, rehearsals on steady jobs like the Grove are free, and Dick Stabile rehearses the band for three days just on his dance book. I don't care, because the band is good, and I'm getting to play first trumpet, which is fun and more responsible than just playing in the section. The first trumpet helps to set the style and phrasing, and I'm getting to work with guys that have been on the road with Stan Kenton and Woody Herman, and all I've done is go to UCLA. Oh, I play in rehearsal bands, and the last two summers I played lead trumpet on all the shows at the Cal Neva Lodge at Lake Tahoe—shows like Lena Horne and Tony Bennett and Frank Sinatra.

I know I'm ready for this job. I can't wait for opening night. The show is the first engagement ever for Judy Garland's daughter, Liza Minelli, who is about twenty years old, and just starting her solo career with what everybody hopes will be a bang, here at the Coconut Grove. Dick Stabile tells us that we will rehearse his dance book, then we'll have to rehearse three days on Liza's act music, because it is brand new, and everybody will be learning the music, especially Liza.

So here we are on a warm summer afternoon, in the "World Famous Coconut Grove," where the fake palm trees and the moth-eaten monkeys among the palm fronds don't look so glamorous in the afternoon light. But it really doesn't matter. We all know our band is good, we all get along well, and I really enjoy playing with all these guys.

Liza is a really friendly, nice person, with no pretension; she is a good dancer and she can really belt a song.

We start rehearsing—and rehearsing—and rehearsing. We have now rehearsed every afternoon for almost a week, and we haven't gotten paid a cent. I'm not in trouble, because I still have a little saved up, and besides, it's good experience, but Stu Williamson, the marvelous jazz trumpeter next to me says, "I don't need experience, I need some bread."

♪♪♪

Finally it is opening night. We rehearse one more time, go out and eat dinner, put on our tuxedos, and play a dance set before the first show.

I can't believe the audience that fills the Grove, while we wade through two sets of dance music. Even the veteran guys in the band are impressed to see Judy Garland and her husband, Sid Luft, and her ex-husband (and Liza's father), the great film director, Vincente Minelli, at ringside, separated by a few tables.

I see Sammy Davis, Jr. and his entourage, and Gary Cooper and his wife. Then I see Fred Astaire and Cary Grant and their ladies enter. Everyone is finally seated, and the lights come down on this turnout of Hollywood royalty.

Dick Stabile has fortified himself for this star-studded gala opening with several blasts at the bar with fellow celebrities. It is show time, and Dick walks center stage to the microphone. He tries a joke or two, but nobody is paying much attention, so he figures he'll wow the crowd with our overture, which is "The Man I Love."

He turns to us, and gives us the downbeat. Now, our leader is a helluva saxophonist and he has developed the ability to play in the altissimo register of the alto sax. In this arrangement of his, he plays so high, so long, that dogs from as far away as Beverly Hills are heading to the Grove.

But the audience is like most Celebrity audiences, busy checking each other out. They talk right through this stellar display of a combination of high notes and cascades of notes. Dick hits a high 'Q' on the end of the arrangement, and because of the remarkable inattention his efforts have received from Hollywood's elite, and the fact that Dick is a little numb, he barely acknowledges the sparse applause.

He turns and strides away, sax in hand, to the side of the stage, knocking the microphone over as he departs. Incredibly, he has neglected his most important duty, which is to introduce our featured attraction, Miss Liza Minelli.

Liza is standing one chair's width away from the trumpet section. She is hidden from the audience by red velvet curtains which she is holding nervously, but she's almost the same level and in plain sight of us trumpeters, on our high riser at the back of the stage. She kind of dances around, anxious to get on, as she waits for her introduction. There is none. The drummer has started his roll on the timpani, and Liza is fidgeting around waiting for our peerless leader to make the intro.

She looks over at me questioningly, and asks, "Why doesn't he introduce me?"

I'm almost as anxious to get started as I guess she is, but I feel embarrassed, because we even rehearsed Dick announcing her. All I can do is just nod my head in the direction of Stabile's back, as he reaches the side of the stage and disappears. Liza sees, gasps, and says, "Come back!"

Unfortunately Stabile doesn't hear her.

Liza looks at me, and says, "Somebody introduce me!"

Liza Minelli: "Somebody introduce me!"

I know somebody has to, but I don't know what to do. Somehow I feel it's my responsibility to keep Liza's, and our band's opening night from dying right here, so as the straw boss, it's up to me to do something. I look down at the sax section. Each saxophonist has a microphone in front of his stand, so that the flute and clarinet he also plays (his 'doubles') can be amplified. I get an idea. I look up into the light booth, to Allen the sound guy, and point at the sax mikes.

Allen sees the spot Stabile has left us in, and raises his hands, palms up, asking, "What'll we do?"

Dick Houlgate, the baritone sax player on the end, who we have nicknamed 'Gate' is a great guy, and he always acts really 'cool' about everything; besides he has the loudest voice of anybody in the woodwind section. I make an executive decision—'Gate' is about to become the M.C.

I point to the sax mike in front of 'Gate.' Allen nods, throws a switch and gives me a thumbs up.

Liza is now dancing around, bouncing up and down, and pleading, squealing, *"Somebody introduce me, for God's sake!"*

The tymp roll is thundering away, so I yell down to my chosen man.

"Gate! You've got to introduce her! Use the microphone!"

Gate whirls around, looks at me, and I can see he's not Mr. Cool right now—he's lost it. He looks up at me as if I had told him to jump off the top of the Empire State Building.

He says, "Who me?"

I whisper-yell back, "Damn it, introduce her, or we'll be up here all night! Do it!"

Gate turns back in a panic, grabs the mike, pulls it to him, clears his throat, and bellows into the mike,

"Ladies and gentlemen—*Judy Garland*!"

Liza shrieks, *"SHIT!"*

Liza's pianist gives a downbeat, and we roar into her opening number, "My Name Is Liza with a Z, not Lisa with an S."

As she races down the stairs past 'Gate,' who now is blowing his baritone sax, she bangs him on top of his head with her clenched fist. His sax emits a horrendous 'Squeak,' and Liza Minelli's first opening night is off and limping.

Liza smacks 'Gate.'

♪♪♪

Later that night, Dick Stabile has, I guess, made amends to Miss Minelli; after all, once we got started, the band played the show flawlessly and Liza was a terrific success. The audience loved her, and she got a standing 'O.'

We are playing what we hope will be the last dance set, but there is one couple left. The waiters wait to collect the drink glasses and present the bill, but nobody tries to rush the couple, and strangely enough, we don't really care, either. It's been an unforgettable opening night, the lights are low, and as we play, we steal a glance at Cary Grant and his lady, as they dance close and slow to "Embraceable You."

Liza triumphant

Twenty-Ninth Chorus:
Louis 'Pops' Armstrong & Me

It's opening night for Louis Armstrong—'Pops'—'Satch,' as jazz fans and music buffs all affectionately know this musical legend. It's 1965 and this will be a welcome, relaxing time after Liza Minelli's engagement. She is very nice, tremendously talented and appreciative of our band. Also she forgave Dick Stabile for neglecting to introduce her to her star-studded opening night audience.

I'm glad we only have to play a set of dance music, then turn the stage over to Louie and his All-Stars. They sure *are* all great players. Barney Bigard, formerly of the Duke Ellington Orchestra, on clarinet; Trummy Young, who was a star as a young man in the Jimmie Lunceford band of the '40s; Arvell Shaw on bass; Billy Kyle on piano; and Barrett Deems, billed as "The World's Fastest Drummer."

I have developed a white pimple under the skin in the middle of my upper lip. It started little, but it's getting bigger and making it harder to get loosened up to play. I put Blistex on it, but it persists.

After Louie's first show I decide to ask the great trumpeter for advice. I wait until the crowd filters out, and go back to his dressing room door, behind the bandstand, stage left.

Louis finishes signing an autograph for the last fan. He mops his face with one of his famous big white handkerchiefs. I marvel at this legend. He still plays great, and sings like—well, as only Armstrong can *sing*. And everything he does, whether he plays, sings and entertains, he does it with such infectious good taste and humor that it's just great to watch.

He looks up at me, smiles and says, "Well, hello, Pops!"

Louie seems to call everybody 'Pops' and it's his big warm smile that makes it so endearing. I'll try to respectfully approximate his

Louis Armstrong gives me chop juice.

great New Orleans accent, but nothing can come close to replicating that great gravelly voice of his.

"Louis, I've got a little problem with my chops."

"Well, what's dat?"

"Well, it's this thing on my top lip…"

He comes close, takes a look and says, "Come on into my dressin' room, so's I can see it better."

I follow him in and see the tall stack of folded hankies, a little fan that does its best to cool off the man that practically invented jazz trumpet.

I move close to Louie and the light. He slips on a pair of Ben Franklin specs, and tilts my head back to focus. Then Pops takes his hand and gently squeezes in on either side of my upper lip. He's like a real family doctor with his kind concern as he nods, satisfied and tells me,

"Hmm—oh yes! I had me one' dose a couple'a times."

"What is it?"

"Well, it's jes' a doggone ol' white-head… Now Doctor Pops kin take care'a dis for ya."

He turns and picks up a vial from the dressing room counter, then reaches into a box and pulls out a little cotton swab.

He uncorks the vial and dips the swab as he tells me, "Now dis is gonna sting a little bit, but it'll go away in a second."

I watch in the mirror behind him as he prepares to "paint" my upper lip. He holds the vial close to my face as he starts.

I catch a whiff of the stuff in the vial. It's smells like a mixture of Campho-Phenique, fish oil, and herbs among other exotic aromas.

It does sting, but not bad, as I work my lip around a little. I ask Louis,

"What *is* that stuff?"

He smiles, winks and advises me, "It's somethin' an ol' lady who works healin' spells back home makes up fo' me."

He holds the vial up triumphantly, and proclaims, "Dis heah is New Ah-leans Chop Juice, Jack!"

Louie turn to rummage around in a satchel bag, pulls out a small vial and gives it to me.

"Jes' put dis on yo' chops 3 times a day, an' dat whitehead gonna be gone in a couple'a days."

I grin at the Man as I say, "Thanks Pops!"

"Hey, glad ta he'p another trumpet player… Oh, when ya gets home, you take dis" (he hands me a small tinfoil wrapped square) "b'fore ya hit the sack, and tomorrow mornin' you'll see a big difference."

I look at this small silver wrapped square in my hand. It looks like a square of wrapped chocolate.

"Okay, Pops, thanks again!"

We shake hands and I leave. We play a dance set, Louis and the All-Stars do a second show, and we finish with more dancing.

I get home about 2:30 AM and get a big welcome from Carrie, my wire-haired terrier who's delighted that I'm home. We frolic around a bit, then I get ready to turn in. I daub my lip, then remember the little tinfoil wrapped square. It says "Swiss Criss" on the label and I figure it's candy so I unwrap it and pop it in and chew it up. It's like chocolate with a little extra in it.

The next morning I can't wait to get to the bathroom—Swiss Criss is obviously a very powerful laxative.

When I get to work and see Louie, he gives me a sly smile as he asks, "How ya feelin' Pops?"

"Cleaned out, that's for sure, Louie!"

"Dat's what keeps me goin'—you got ta remember da di-gestive system has two ends—your mouth and—" (he points rearward) "the other end! You got to keep it workin' right, an' den you will feel good!"

"Okay Pops — you are the best!"

Sure enough, two days later the whitehead has disappeared.

I hear that some months later Louis and the All Stars are invited to be dinner guests and then perform at a formal State dinner which the British Royal Family is hosting. Louis places a square of Swiss Criss on each guest's silver setting at the table. He doesn't tell them just what this something special is.

I can only imagine the results that the British Royal family had. I'm sure it was a very moving experience.

♪♪♪

I have remarried after five or so years of being single. Rita is fifteen years younger than I am. I meet her when I'm playing and contracting musicians for Hanna-Barbera Studios.

We are blessed with a son, Eric, and two years later, Laura, a beautiful girl.

THIRTIETH CHORUS:
THE SILVER SCREEN & ME

"Hello, Bill, it's the service. How are you, honey? Hope I didn't call too early."

"No, no, I'm awake. What's up?"

I'm awake... just barely. It's February of 1969, but more important, it's 7 AM. I want to sleep some more. Last night my very pregnant wife, Rita, and I did our Lamaze class, and then we joined the other couples for coffee and talk about expecting and birthing.

After class we drove to our Science of Mind Church for another class in the series Dr. Bendall, the minister, is teaching. It's a class on the power of your mind, and focusing on what it is you want; right now we are learning about treating for prosperity. We've decided that we'll "treat" for $750 a week. It has a nice ring to it, and it's not an impossible dream.

All this after I did a double session... six glorious hours of recording for Dean Martin with producer Jimmie Bowen (of course Dino was there for about twenty minutes—long enough to give the recording band a big smile, a wave, and he was gone). That's why I feel tired I guess.

Rita is seven months pregnant with our first child; that's why she is bleary eyed as she looks up from the other pillow, and asks, "Who is it?"

I want her to know everything is okay, but I know I've got to respond to the service quickly; it may be work, and with a baby on the way, I have to be sure I respond to whatever comes my way. After all, I'm sixteen years older than my wife, and I really feel like I've got to be a great provider and husband and father, when the baby gets here. I'm really excited, and I can't wait to see if it's a boy or a girl.

So I cup my hand over the receiver.

"It's Arlyn's—the service, you know."

"Oh…"

She falls back to sleep. I'm glad—she needs all the sleep she can get. I'm back to Anne, the lady who is on the other end, who puts out the work calls, and I sound as professional and business-like as I can from bed.

"Yes, Anne, what's going on?"

"Malcolm Beelby called from Warner's. He'd like you to come out at 1 PM."

"What is it? Who is Malcolm Beelby?"

"Honey, he's some big shot in the music department, that's all I know. Arlyn says you should go."

Arlyn is this magnificently obese woman with the sexiest voice in the business, who owns and runs the answering service which bears her name, and for which I pay $65 per month. Arlyn knows everything that's going on in the music biz… If she says I should go, I'd better go.

At ten to one, I tool up to Warner's gate in our white Porsche 912. I wonder what this is all about? If this was a regular work call for a film recording session, Kurt Wolff, the contractor would call me direct, with all the warmth and caring and personal contact of an SS storm trooper… I think maybe Kurt is one of those escaped Nazis you read about. He even clicks his heels together when he greets you in his thick German accent.

"Ah Bill, it's goot you could pee vith us today," he always greets me whenever I show up for work. He gives you everything but the "Heil Hitler" salute.

But today, I guess I don't get Uberleutnant Wolff. I pull up to the guard's kiosk.

He says, "Yeah?" (Maybe he's been trained by Herr Wolff.)

Anyway, I smile, "Peterson… Musician."

Now normally this mantra gets you a musician's drive-on parking pass so you can pull on the lot, then drive so far into the depths of Warner's that you could jump out of your car and walk over to Universal, which is the next studio over.

But today? Hey, the guard consults his list.

"Your name is Peterson? Bill Peterson?"

"Yeah."

He gives me the look I can picture is reserved for good-looking starlets and assistant producers.

"Would you pull over there, Mr. Peterson?"

Geez, nobody in a uniform has called me "Mr. Peterson" since I ran my last red light. I pull over and wait.

The guard follows me.

"Mr. Peterson. Mr. Beelby will be out in just a minute."

"What's going on? " I ask myself.

Maybe word has gotten out how good I've been playing lately… maybe Warner's has chosen me to play the Harry James solos in a remake of *Young Man With a Horn*.

My daydream is shattered as a face appears in my Porsche window.

"Hello, Bill, I'm Malcolm Beelby."

I turn to see a large set of teeth, surrounded by a set of smiling lips. The mouth smiles but the eyes don't. This guy looks wary, and his eyes are, well, watchful. He's got his hair parted right down the middle, and greased down.

"I'm so glad you could come. We would like you to interview about a role in a film…"

So that's it! They want me for some stupid sideline bit, where you pretend to play, but you don't; you're just miming to a pre-recorded track made by what I want to be—one of the Hollywood heavies.

"Mr. Beelby, I hate to break it to you, but I quit doing sideline the year after I got out of UCLA and into this business, so I don't want to waste your time."

I key the Porsche's ignition, rev the motor, and prepare to split, but Malcolm's smile almost cracks.

"Oh no, Mr. Peterson… uh, Bill!… We'd like you to audition for a part in a film! Please, won't you talk to the Assistant Producer and the Director, as long as you're here?"

I am curious to see what this is all about, so I look at Malcolm Beelby, sweating on a cold February day, and nod, "Okay."

He wipes his brow with his display hankie, and says, "Will you follow me, please."

He's sweaty but I've got to say he is polite. I put it in first, and crawl after Malcolm. He has a lot of energy, or maybe he really is this nervous. We go down a studio street, hang a left, and Malcolm points to an empty parking spot. I pull in, take out my trumpet case and the mute bag just in case, and follow him into a huge bungalow with deep carpets. Malcolm announces our arrival like he was proclaiming the arrival of the Prince of Wales.

"Mr. Bill Peterson, the trumpeter, is here!" All that's missing is a fanfare. Just then, a nice looking guy, younger than me (I'm 36), pops out, and Malcolm intros me like was going to sell this guy a used car.

"Mr. Ganis, this is Mr. Bill Peterson. He's a very highly respected trumpeter."

If I had been an English major at UCLA I'd call this bird an "Obsequious sycophant," but since I'm just a dumb trumpet player, I mark him down as a "Kiss ass" and let it go at that.

I talk to Mr. Ganis, Sid to be exact, and we hit it off. He has a friendly intensity about him, and his eyes mirror a good sense of humor.

After the hellos and a handshake, Sid tells me, "This is for the role of a cornet player in this movie we're making... do you think you could do that?"

"Look, Sid, I play the trumpet for a living... this is what I do, okay?"

"Great, great, you've got the right look—I'd like you to meet Doc Erickson!"

Now I'm intrigued, and I'm so out of my element that I want to see just how far this nonsense is going to go before they catch on that I'm not an "actorrr!" but just a B♭ trumpet player.

Sid ushers me into the next office. It's even nicer than Sid's, and the carpet is like three times thicker. You could lose a golf ball in this stuff. Sid intros me.

"Doc, this is Bill Peterson, the trumpet player."

Doc smiles, "Hi Bill, thanks for coming."

We shake hands, we chat, we get on well, then he says, "I want you to see Mr. Mankiewicz."

Doc opens the door, and I see Mr. Joseph Mankiewicz, the writer and director and producer of *All About Eve* and other great films that I know. He is at a huge desk in what I guess is his office; all I know is that this room is one size smaller that my whole house.

He peers over rimless gold specs, smiles, and a secretary appears from somewhere to escort me to the great man, in case I get lost in this carpet which is so thick it's like skiing powder at Sun Valley. I follow her, and Mr. M. shakes my hand.

"Glad to meet you, Bill... Oh, is that a trumpet you've got there?"

Good god, I've got to set these guys straight, nobody seems to get it. They must think I'm an actor who happens to have a horn.

"Yes it is... see, I've explained this to your buddies, this is what I do for a living. I don't know how to act in a movie—in fact I barely know how to act in public."

Mr. M. smiles, "Can you play something on that thing?"

Now I'm getting someplace. This is what *I* do! I get cocky.

"What would you like to hear?"

"Can you play 'The Lone Ranger'?"

Aha, now I can jump on him a little.

"You mean 'The William Tell Overture'?"

Now I'm feeling giddy because at last I'm in my field of expertise, and Mankiewicz the great director doesn't even know the correct title.

"Okay, what key would you like?"

Am I nuts? What if he asks for C#?

But he just shrugs.

"Whatever key it's in, I guess."

I whip out the horn, no warm-ups, and play the damn thing, perfectly, by memory and by ear—the double-tongued trumpet call and all.

He's impressed, but he's cool.

"You can play that thing!"

Well, at least somebody's got it.

"This role pays $650 a week when we start shooting your scenes."

Scenes? Geez, maybe I'm going to be a star and don't know it. But I remember our Science of Mind Prosperity class. I take a deeeep breath.

"$750 a week and we've got a deal."

He doesn't blink.

"Okay, Bill, you're going to be in our film, with lines and everything. The first part of the shoot we'll be on location."

"Look, Mr. Mankiewicz, my wife is about seven months pregnant. She has to be with me because we're doing Lamaze child birth, and…"

He jumps in.

"No problem, we'll make arrangements for her. Miss Stafford, will you get Bill a contract?"

Miss Stafford appears magically, wades through the carpet to escort me. Mr. M. shakes my rather limp hand.

"We'll be calling you in a few days."

"Thanks."

I follow her out, numbly… I'm in a movie? We're going on location?

PART I: FROM TRUMPETER TO ACTOR

Two days later, a messenger arrives at our house with an official Warner Bros. package. I tear it open excitedly. It's my copy of the script.

Rita says, "Where's your part?"

I turn pages—I'm not on the first page, or the second, or… I start to flip through; then I see a paper clip on a page. This must be it. Will it be a soliloquy, or what? I read it: first here's a description of a cornet player, that's me. My character's name is… "Gordon Frisbee!" I have lines with a Warden Lopeman.

Rita's into it; she asks, "Who's Warden Lopeman?"

"I don't know, I just got this."

I flip to the front. There, stuck on the first page, is the cast shooting schedule. I see that Lopeman is Henry Fonda. I'm gonna act with Fonda? All of a sudden I realize this as real as it gets; I'm going to says lines to one of the all-time great actors in the movie business? I mean, I can play trumpet with anybody, but that's something I know how to do. But act? With Fonda? Well, it's their choice.

Rita reads, "Henry Fonda?" and looks at me.

I pull myself together.

"So? I'll just do my best, that's all I can do."

♪♪♪

Two weeks later my wife and I pull into a motel in Indio.

Rita says, "This looks nice."

The coming star of the silver screen grunts, "It better be. We'll see!"

I have had to cancel out of studio calls and other gigs, and now this acting thing is not quite as cool and glamorous as I thought. Anyway, we go in. Rita heads for the bathroom, shuts the door. As I start in with the first two suitcases I hear a shriek, a scream, and she comes flying out of the bathroom.

"Bugs! Great big awful bugs."

I go in. There are water bugs as big as small household pets in the shower and on the floor.

I storm out, put my arm around her.

"We're not staying. Don't worry!"

I grab the phone, ask for the company manager, Mr. Harry Issacs, and let him have it. I'm so pissed I can hardly get it out.

"We walk in, my wife's seven months pregnant and the bathroom is full of big black bugs. I'm going home!"

"Now hold on, I'll get you a nice new room. I'm sorry, but these things sometimes happen. We'll take care of it. I'll be right over to help you, okay?"

Harry arrives after a few minutes to deal with me, the new Mr. Temperamental Movie Star. He assures and calms us down, then he escorts us to the motel across the highway, where we see Alan Hale Jr. and Victor French standing by the pool. This room is fine—no bugs, and we settle in. I rehearse my lines. I try it sissified, tough à la Bogart, countrified, everything I can think of. After all, I don't want to screw up.

PART II: I MEET MY FELLOW PLAYERS

Next day is my first scene. A long black limo with a really tall, really blasé driver picks me up at 5:30 AM. I am numb but excited and I pile in with Victor French, who is a nice down to earth guy with a wild sense of humor. Victor finds out I love Laurel and Hardy, and starts talking like Stan Laurel to my great amusement. We roar down the highway to Joshua Tree National Monument. I see a huge rock prison, which looms up right in the middle of a bunch of Joshua trees, cactus and prairie dog holes. We drive down a dirt road, through the gates, and the assistant director takes me over to the costume guys, both good looking, gray hair, both very nice and very gay. They outfit me in a swallowtail coat and striped pants.

Next, Gloria, a chunky little lady with Lucille Ball color hair, makes jokes and says, "Siddown Honey! How ya doin'?" She works on my hair. She wets and combs it, parts it in the middle, then plasters it down with some stuff that makes it as hard as a rock.

By now it's 9 AM. I look at the area where we are going to work just inside the prison gate. All the tech people are getting ready for the shoot. Next I wander over with Sid Ganis, who is now in Levi's and checkered shirt, to meet my on-screen fiancée, Barbara Rhodes. Sid does the honors.

"Barbara, this is Bill... he's playing the part of Gordon Frisbee ... Bill, meet Barbara!"

She is very beautiful, and she is very sick. It seems they just flew her in this morning. She's in costume, and we rehearse. Mr. M. works with us. Now I'm going to get my direction.

But first Mr. Mankiewicz asks, "How is everything? Is your wife here?"

He's really, genuinely interested—asking me about my wife. I feel a real warmth from and for this man. He's a regular guy, even if he has made a whole lot of great films.

So I tell him about the bugs, but I say, "Everything's fine now."

"Good, I want you to be comfortable."

"Now, how do you want me to say this?" I ask.

I give him my sissified bit and start into my country take on it, but he laughs, holds up his hand to stop me, and says, "Look you're supposed to have ridden in a stage coach for five hundred miles to get to this godforsaken place to entertain a bunch of wild prison inmates, because your fiancée, Barbara here, conned you into it. You're pissed off. Just say that first word, 'Horse feathers!' like you're saying 'Horseshit!' Okay?"

I have now been directed by one of the greats.

He pats my shoulder and retreats back by the camera. Barbara and I get into a surrey with a fringe and the driver jolts us at a break-neck pace out into the desert beyond the main gate of the prison. The he turns us around, and away we go. The gate swings opens, the camera just inside. We pull up, inside the 'prison' courtyard.

"Whoa!" the driver yells.

The two horses rear and prance a little, but stop. I look up to see… Henry Fonda!

Mr. Fonda in a gray western suit and broad brim hat limps over to us. (His character has a game leg.) My god! How many films have I seen him in? I mean Fonda won an Academy Award for *The Grapes of Wrath*, and now I'm going to act with him? I don't think so! How can I? My legs are a little shaky and my mouth is dry, but it's too late to flake out: I signed a contract for $750 a week. Now the red light's on, and I've got to do the gig. Besides, it's almost my turn!

Barbara says her lines to Henry Fonda; he takes her hand and helps her down. Now it's my turn. The camera is behind Fonda, but it's aimed at me.

Fonda looks at me, really intent, and I say the lines, "Horse feathers!" and so on.

Barbara has another bit.

Then Mr. M. says, "Cut!"

He goes to her, talks for a moment, then we get back aboard the surrey and we do it again. This happens three times. Each time Henry Fonda makes me feel relaxed because he pays such close attention to my words, like he's really interested in what this cornet player has to say. Finally, after a few more takes, I figure I'm not doing it right. What the hell, I told 'em I was a cornet player, not an actor… I can feel my heart pounding a little. This isn't as easy as it looks. I like Mr. M. and I don't want to screw things up, so I go to him and say, "Look, if I'm hanging you up, just tell me. I'll do it standing on my head if that'll help."

He walks me away a bit, so we're alone, and puts his arm on my shoulder.

"No, you're doing fine. I can't get a performance out of Barbara. She's sick at her stomach or something. Just keep doing what you're doing. You're fine."

My heart stops racing a little, and he walks her around with his arm around her shoulder, He smiles, she looks more relaxed and smiles too.

We get on board, and ride out so we can ride in, and this time, Mr. M. gives us the thumbs up.

He yells, "Print it!"

My god, it's lunchtime, and I've survived my first day as a "legend" on the Silver Screen.

I always greet Mr. M. every morning—one day he tells me he played saxophone in high school so I kid him that if he plays his cards right, I'll get him a Bar Mitzvah gig. He's an easy person to talk with, warm and friendly, and he takes time to show me how he maps out each day's shoot on his legal pad.

Kirk Douglas sees me writing music one day, and asks what I'm working on. I explain that I'm writing a song that I'll show to Mr. M. in hopes it could be a title tune for our film. Kirk, says, "Then you need to understand my motivation for *The Crooked Man*... he sits down and takes 20 or so minutes to explain just what he's thinking, feeling and doing. What a wonderful gift! He is a truly generous man to me, and I always have a warm feeling for him when I see him on the screen.

PART III: I'M "ON"!

Since I took this gig, I've been practicing playing "The Carnival of Venice" on a beautiful old cornet I borrowed from my buddy Irving Bush. I know that's coming up later on, but right now I'm enjoying the rush of being in a movie, in front of the cameras, instead of being in the back row of an orchestra in a studio, playing wonderful music that the audience and most everybody else takes for granted.

I'm kind of enjoying this new challenge. I mean, after all, I spoke my lines right to Henry Fonda, and the camera, and I didn't stutter or fall out of the surrey with the fringe on top. My make believe fiancée, Barbara Rhodes, and I have made it into the full scale replica of a prison that Warner Bros. Studio has built out here in the middle of the Joshua Tree National Monument.

Today is my second day as an actor, and I am limo-ed from the motel in Indio out to our location once again. After Gloria, the hair stylist, parts my hair in the middle and finishes plastering it down, and the wardrobe guys slip my swallowtail coat and gray britches on, I wander over to have morning coffee with Victor French and John Randolph.

They are friendly and Victor asks, "What kind of music do you play?"

"I have to play everything from pop to classical in studio work."

"How about jazz?" I hear Henry Fonda's voice ask.

I turn around and Victor says, "Bill, this is Henry Fonda… Hank, meet Bill Peterson, the trumpet player."

I look into the bluest eyes since Frank Sinatra. He has this relaxed, cool way of speaking, but his smile is warm.

"Mr. Fonda, I'm glad to meet you." I stick out my hand.

He takes it and says, "Hi there! By the way, it's just Hank, okay?"

"Oh sure… Hank," as I almost stumble over it.

He says, "You know, I played a trumpet player in a picture once with Buzz…"

He turns and calls over to Burgess Meredith, who has just wandered up.

"Hey Buzz, you remember when you and I did the trumpet player thing? What was the name of that picture?"

Burgess Meredith who is dressed in a grimy prisoner's outfit, grins, "All I remember is how it made my lip tingle when I tried to blow it."

My new close personal friend Hank, says, "This is Bill, he's the trumpet player… say hello to Buzz Meredith."

I shake his hand, and I think, good god, here I have been in show biz two days, and I'm hanging out with Fonda and Meredith, and calling them 'Hank' and 'Buzz' besides! I can't believe it! I wonder what my high school band director, Mr. Harbaugh would think? Would he still tell me to take business classes if he could see me now?

My reverie is broken as I hear the assistant director bellow through his bull horn to the guys in prison clothing on the other side of the yard, "All you prisoners to the mess hall."

As they slowly shuffle off and start to file inside the mess hall, he comes over and says, "Bill, we need you for the mess hall scene, please."

"Hank… Buzz, whenever you're ready, please."

Boy, does it make a difference how they treat you when you're hanging with the stars. Us stars mosey over, and I get to ask Hank,

"Yesterday when I said my lines to you, you looked and listened to me every time like you'd never heard it before."

"That's what an actor does."

"Some actors... not all," Buzz Meredith adds. "Watch what Kirk does when he works with Hank."

I look at Hank, but he just has this funny little smile; he doesn't say anything.

We go inside, and into a perfect replica of a mess hall. The guys playing the prisoners are a tough looking lot, and they look at me with that kind of "What's with this guy" kind of expression. Suddenly I really am conscious of the fact that I look like a real fancy dude kind of guy.

My on-screen fiancée Barbara Rhodes comes in, looking beautiful. The prisoners reward her with some catcalls and wolf whistles.

The AD settles everyone down with, "All right, everybody, let's rehearse it."

This is my next Big Moment—I have to play the cornet solo, "The Carnival of Venice," no less—all by myself, no band, not even a piano accompaniment. Now is the time for me to come through! After all the fuss I made in making the point to Sid Ganis the associate producer and Doc Erickson the Exec Producer about being a trumpet player and not an actor, I better be good.

The camera glides up to where Mr. Mankiewicz has put me. I stand in front of the table where Hank, Barbara and some other actors who are supposed to be prison officials are seated. I am facing Kirk Douglas, in the title role of *There Was a Crooked Man*. At this point I haven't met him yet, and he eyes me just like the rest of these tough cons.

The prisoners are hungry, but before they can dig into the trays of chicken that the cooks are serving them, they have to sit through me playing the damn cornet, and Barbara Rhodes reciting "Invictus."

Now a bunch of grimy tough guys who haven't supposedly seen a pretty woman for years may put up with a recitation, but they won't take kindly to a guy in a swallowtail coat with his hair plastered down playing a cornet solo. I bring myself back to reality... this is just a movie, and this is what I do—play the trumpet.

The AD yells, "Quiet!"

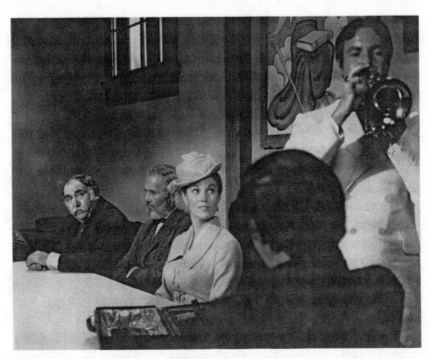

My cornet solo for *The Crooked Man*.

The whole joint gets as still as a recording studio when the red light goes on.

Mr. M. calls out, "Roll 'em!"

Then he smiles at me, and nods, "Go ahead Bill, when you're ready."

Now I have played all kinds of music in every kind of situation, from playing "Taps" for funerals in the Air Force to recording the scores for dozens of movies, but I never faced a tougher looking group than this. My mouth is a little dry. I lick my lips, put the cornet to my mouth and focus on the first note. Thank god it comes out, and so do all the others. I wail through the whole thing; the theme, the double and triple tonguing variations and all, and end up on the high note at the end. I finish, and just like the script indicates, the prisoners just stare and mutter under their breath. The folks at the table applaud lightly and politely, and I sit down.

Mr. Mankiewicz yells, "Cut!"

He comes up to me, and says, "That was fine, but can you not play so good? I mean, after all, you've ridden across the desert in a surrey to this godforsaken place and you hate it, so make a few mistakes, can you?"

"Sure, Mr. M. I'll hit a few clams."

"Good," he says, and goes back beside the camera.

Now they set up and shoot different angles on me and reaction shots on the stars, Kirk Douglas, Hank, Buzz, Barbara and Hume Cronin. I get to play this sucker three times in a row.

Kirk Douglas comes up, and says, "I played trumpet, you know!"

I grin, "Boy, do I remember! I saw *Young Man With a Horn* eight times, and every time you smashed that horn into the back of the chair I winced!"

He smiles, and Hank comes over. He looks concerned.

"How you doing, Bill?" he asks.

"I'm okay!"

"Well, I know how hard that thing is to play, and they've had you playing for almost an hour, so if your lip gets tired, tell 'em you want to take a break."

I guess I look pretty doubtful, because Hank says, "Don't worry, just tell me, and I'll tell 'em *I* want to take a break, okay?"

I can't believe how "us actors" stick together.

Kirk starts a riot in *The Crooked Man*.

Mr. M. re-sets the camera and now they shoot the "Riot Scene." As soon as I sit down, Kirk stands up, says some cynical things to Hank, throws a plate of food at him, and the prisoners start to break out, chasing the beautiful Barbara Rhodes too!

PART IV: LUNCHEON WITH THE STARS

Elaine, my fifteen year old sister in law is at our house and says, "Henry Fonda is just about my favorite movie star. Do you think you could get me a picture?"

"Sure I will."

So, next day I jump into the Porsche for the drive to work at Warner's. For a beat, I fantasize that I am an 'ACTOR,' roaring off to the studio! Then I remember, "Me, trumpet player—Fonda and Kirk Douglas, Actors!" Anyway here I go! Gosh—another appearance before the camera in my budding new career. The daydreaming's over; I pull onto the lot and park and get into makeup and costume and trundle over into the huge old sound stage, where Bogie and Edward G. and Cagney used to chase each around. I see Hank.

"Hank, can I get a picture autographed for my sister-in law, Elaine? She's just turned fifteen, and she's a big fan of yours."

"Of course," says Hank, "but why not bring her right on the set, and I'll give her a picture. Just let me know a day in advance of when she's coming."

"Thanks."

He is really a very considerate man, and this will be very cool for Elaine.

I call Elaine, and all she does is squeal, "Ooooh, oooh, oooh," for a minute.

"When do you want to come?"

"Is tomorrow okay?"

"Well, Mr. Fonda... er, Hank, wanted me to give him a day in advance, so... how about Tuesday..."

I can hear Elaine calling out to her two brothers and sister, "I'm going to meet Henry Fonda! Oh God!"

I figure I've really ingratiated myself with the family, but it's great to see a kid so excited and pleased.

Next day, we are back in costume, me with my hair plastered and glued down, Hank in his hat and boots, and salt and pepper western suit. He's waiting to be called for a scene with Kirk Douglas, and we're sitting in our movie star chairs (mine doesn't have my name on it, like Hank's), right next to the crew setting and lighting the 1870s prison warden's office twenty feet away.

I ask Hank, "Would tomorrow be convenient for Elaine to pay a visit?"

The assistant director comes over, and respectfully says, "We're ready for you, Hank."

"Be right there," says Hank. His blue eyes crinkle into that great slow smile.

"Sure, that'll be just fine."

He uncoils from his chair, and strides over in that Henry Fonda walk, slow, deliberate that I've seen so many times in the movies, and I watch as Warden Fonda and Crooked Man Kirk Douglas, in prison clothes, go to work. It's a great contrast between Kirk's instant intensity, and Hank's more laid back but piercing concentration. I love it! What a treat for a trumpet player turned would-be actor.

♪♪♪

Next day, I see Elaine, in a very pretty dress... this is a kid I've never seen in anything but Levi's or shorts. I get her into the Porsche and we drive to the studio. She stares at the extras walking from costumes to a set, the wind machines, everything, and then I open the big refrigerator-like door onto the *Crooked Man* set. She catches sight of Kirk Douglas and Hank.

We move in closer; they are waiting to work, so it's "Kirk, Hank, this is my sister-in-law, Elaine."

Kirk's chin dimple expands as he smiles warmly, shakes her hand. Hank leans down from his star realm and smiles and takes her hand. I am afraid she may pass out, but she does womanhood proud, She smiles, bobs her head, and stays in control, but boy is she impressed.

Mr. Mankiewicz—Joseph that is, gets a couple of scenes in the can, and it's time for lunch. Hank wanders over to Elaine, who is sitting in Hank's own personal chair, where he has placed her.

I'm about to escort this very excited young lady to the studio commissary, but Hank smiles and says, "Elaine, would you and Bill have lunch with me?"

She manages to stammer, "Y-yes!"

I can see that Hank is way ahead of the game… guys in white commissary garb carry portable tables, chairs and plastic cutlery onto the shooting stage. They get it all together quickly, and serve a lovely chicken luncheon. Hank holds the chair next to him, seats Elaine, and we all set to. Hank has invited some of the crew, John Randolph, Barbara my on-screen fiancée, and Buzz Meredith. The talk is lively; Elaine mostly listens, but smiles a lot. After lunch the tables disappear, we go back to work, and Elaine gets to star gaze all afternoon. At the end of the day's shooting, Hank presents Elaine with an autographed picture. I thank Hank, and Elaine shakes his hand and echoes her thanks. On the way back to the car, I think I may have to hold on to her hand to keep her from floating away.

In the Porsche, she shows me the very plastic knife and fork Hank used, as well as his leftover chicken bones. I'm delighted that she's had a great day, and I'm proud to be associated with such a wonderful artist and gentle man, who would take time to make it special for a young girl.

CODA

Hank was a real pro, without the star ego that some exhibit at times. Years later, while playing a TV show at NBC, I chanced to see Henry Fonda again. He smiled, said 'hello' and remembered our film, *There Was a Crooked Man*. Elaine never forgot her Luncheon with the stars, and neither did I.

PART V: WRAP PARTIES—WITH ALL THE BELLS & WHISTLES

It's September 1969, and two things have recently happened. First of all, my son Eric has been born… August 15, to be exact. Also I've finished my stellar role as the cornet player in *There Was a Crooked Man*.

Now we are treated to the tinsel-town tradition of the wrap party. Mr. Joseph L. Mankiewicz and Warner Brothers combine to throw the party,

My wife Rita reminds, "She's got to be home by one…"

That's for the baby-sitter she's gotten for Eric. Rita, who is not really comfortable with many social scenes, now seems ready to hang out after a month with a newborn. Anyway, I drive our Porsche onto the lot at seven PM, and we enter the *Phantom of the Opera* shooting stage for a really gala shindig which Chasen's has catered.

It's got everything, including all the stars: Hank Fonda, Kirk Douglas, Burgess Meredith, Hume Cronin, my buddy Victor French and of course me. We eat Chasen's ribs and chili, drink nicely chilled champagne by Mssr Clicquot, and revel with my fellow thespians. I even play my piece of resistance from the film, "The Carnival of Venice" with the casual band working the event.

Victor French sidles up and in a Stan Laurel voice, says, "The real party's at my house next Saturday! Please be there, Ollie!"

We tool home, and await our next large social event.

Rita tells me Friday, "I can't find anybody to care of Eric. I guess I can't go."

"No way; we'll take him with us."

"Are you sure it'll be okay?"

"Of course, Victor has kids!"

"But are they babies?"

"Well, they had to be once."

Saturday night we tool down to Studio City find the beautiful old Spanish pad with the red tile roof, and I lift the sleeping Eric, in his car seat, out and put him by the door, with a bottle of cabernet and a note which reads,

"I'm here for the *Crooked Man* party, but *I'm* straight."

I ring the bell, and we step out of the glow of the porch light.

Victor opens the door, picks up Eric, peers around, as he holds out the carrier, and whispers, à la Laurel,

"Ollie, I didn't even know you were repugnant."

Inside, there's a wonderful warm funny group of people, drinking, talking and laughing, and Rita gets to show off our pride and joy.

Everybody oohs and aahs, and Eric responds with smiles and what I swear is a laugh, but is really a gurgle.

Anyway, Victor announces that the BBQ is about to begin, and there is no question, Hank is the chef. I go outside carrying platters of steaks with Victor, Hank Fonda and Buzz Meredith.

After Hank gets the first grill-full going, he and Buzz pull out the fixin's and roll a couple of joints. I mean, Fonda told me about playing a trumpet player, but this is pretty wild. I feel like I'm with a couple of veterans of road bands, kicking back.

Hank rolls expertly. He runs his tongue along the ZigZag paper, and hands it to me...

"See what you think, Bill."

Buzz grins, "Yeah, you should know if it's good."

What they don't know is that I don't smoke grass, but what am I gonna do? I stick it between my lips like I've watched guys do a thousand times, fire it up off Buzz's match, and take a poke. I pass it around, and try to sneak the lung full out unobtrusively. But after the second time, I'm a little less careful, and man, this stuff is potent.

"Sensamea!" says Buzz as he nods. Hank smiles appreciatively.

Then after a few more rounds, Hank asks Buzz, "What're you goin' to do now?"

Buzz takes a really big drag, and as he holds it, he gets out, "I'm going' to the Apple, man!"

"What for?"

"Hank, I'm gonna get to do *Our Town*" (he finally exhales) "...a good new director, and no bullshit... the real thing!"

Hank grins, "That's cool... I got one comin' up too that sounds like it'll be right."

I suddenly realize that it's not that these two great actors smoke grass, it's that they really care about their craft. It's like when you take a gig with a great jazz band or a little combo gig, and the bread is short, but it'll be okay because you're going to play great music with good people. I have new respect for actors in general and these two cats especially.

Later after great steaks and wine, we hug everybody in sight, and go out the door. Eric hasn't cried; he has had a ball, with all the cooing and cuddling and love and attention he's gotten, and Rita seems to have enjoyed it too. Now it really does feel like I'm part of the band... musicians or actors, it doesn't seem to matter. When you're with creative people who care, players of any kind, it's all the same and it's all fun.

Thirty-First Chorus:
Hef, Playboy After Dark,
Playmates Galore & a Grotto Swim

"Hey, my pitch was in there!"

"No way! Plas is closer!"

It's not a ball game... it's even more hotly contested than the Dodgers vs Yankees—we're pitching quarters and if your quarter comes closest to the wall of Stage 5, you win, and it's winner take all!

I raise my hands—I got beat by the best damn 'pitcher' in the orchestra, Plas Johnson.

Oh, sure, Plas is a great tenor saxophonist, but right now this game is what all 10 or so of us players are concerned with, and Plas has taken most of the coin, and cleaned out some of the 'minor league' pitchers already.

There's still a few minutes before our all-day call to play for acts that will appear on the "Playboy After Dark" TV Show, and this game has become a regular weekly happening that all of us pitchers look forward to. Plas picks his latest windfall, when somebody calls out, "Here's Hef!"

We turn away from the field of battle to see Hef's long, sleek Mercedes limo pull up to the stage door. Hef exits the car, waves and says, "Hi, guys!" He goes in, followed by his driver who lugs in a case of Pepsi, Hef's fav drink.

We're ready to go back to our game when a brand new Ferrari Dino coupe pulls up right behind Hef's limo, and we see his current Playmate companion, the beautiful Barbi Benton get out. She smiles at us as Hef's driver holds the heavy stage door open for her.

The driver comes over to us and asks, "Could you guys give me twenty dollars in quarters?"

I point to Plas, "He's the man, but why do you need all those quarters?"

He smiles and says, "Hef wants to play with you guys."

Plas takes the twenty and makes change for the driver. He goes back in, and in a moment, Hef comes out with the quarters. He's a good guy and gets right into it, which means that Plas cleans him out of quarters in short order. Hef's a good sport, shakes hands with our champ, and we follow him into the stage—it's time to go to work.

We enter and climb on the bandstand. It's set up behind a filmy black scrim which shields the band from the replica of the Playboy Mansion's living room. We can see and hear the acts we'll accompany from our place on the side of the set.

We settle in, and the 1st act is Ike & Tina Turner. We've played for them before in other venues... Ike is a controlling son-of-a-bitch who plays guitar and controls Tina, who is the real talent... anyway we play—Ike chomps on his guitar, we play repetitive licks and Tina just lays out the melody and lyric with all the soul and rhythm and feeling anyone could possibly emote.

After Ike & Tina are done, the stage crew has to clear and re-set the set, so we are off for maybe 45 minutes to an hour... we go to the unused sound stage next door to the Playboy shooting stage, where I have set up—ta dah!—a badminton court! Plas and I and the great percussionist Dale Anderson play the game with the rackets and shuttlecocks and net. It's as competitive as pitching quarters—we run and hit and whack the hell out of the little feathered bird and it's great... so freeing from sitting in a chair with your horn and playing the same music over and over till the act or the video crew or the sound guys get what they need.

After a period of 40 or so minutes, one of the other guys from the band comes over and says, "We gotta do some play-ons — come on back..." We towel off, put on our shirts and scamper back to the Playboy After Dark Stage... and so it goes all day.

Now, not all of our colleagues take part in our athletic endeavors... no, some of my buddies in the trumpet section decide to avail themselves of various other stimulants—Three Star Hennessey and bee's honey laced with hashish are the current stimulants of choice.

We return, and now the act wants or thinks they need a really high chord at the end of their performance. When I sit down, the lead or 1st trumpeter, Bobby, tells the 2nd trumpeter, Chuck (who has an amazing ability to play altissimo notes on the horn), "Chuck, they want a very high note on the end of this tune."

Chuck, who is bent over the bottle of cognac, lifts his head with great effort and says, "How high, and how long?"

Bobby informs him, "A double high E♭ above double C, till the leader cuts us off."

Chuck nods his understanding, and we play the tune. When we get to the altissimo ending, the leader points at his trumpet section, and Bobby plays a double high A♭, while Chuck goes for an even higher note, the double high E♭. However, all the stimulants have taken their toll. All that comes out of Chuck's horn is a great gush of air, as if you'd let the air out of a car tire… whoosh! — but no note!

The leader cuts us off, and Chuck, who has no idea of what has just happened, looks up at Bobby and asks, "How was that… ?"

Bobby looks down at Chuck and says, "Perfect, Chuck—just perfect!"

I draw the veil of charity down over this scene, and cut to:

That evening, Hef provides the cast and crew with a lavish buffet: shrimp, crab, lobster, roast beef and all the trimmings, and a bartender serving drinks to all.

My wife has come for the actual show, and she's brought little baby Eric, who's nursing. Of course there are Playboy Bunnies galore, as well as all the guest stars. It's really interesting to watch the bountifully endowed Bunnies when Rita sits down and starts to nurse the little guy. They seem to push up their physical assets while they watch the mother feed the baby. They also seem to be somehow uncomfortable, and they take a look then go off to cluster round our host, the happy Hef. Barbi Benton is one exception; she watches the nursing and stops to ask a few questions of the nursing mother. I join them and it's a nice moment. We play the show (which is live TV), Eric falls asleep, and all goes well.

Now we cut to a few years later: It's 1979, the year of the 25th Anniversary of *Playboy* Magazine.

Once again, I'm a part of the Playboy scene, but this time we are working, if you can call it that, at the actual Playboy Mansion just off Sunset, in the ultra posh Bel Air section of West Los Angeles. Don Randi, who is famous as being the pianist of The Wrecking Crew, is the band leader. (The Crew was a tear it up, burning, rhythm section that included Hal Blaine, the great drummer, and these guys played on literally hundreds of records in the Rock & Roll Era of The Beach Boys, Supremes, Righteous Brothers and countless other great acts and hits.) Don is a great guy who owns The Baked Potato, a club near Hollywood, and today all we have to do is play accompaniment for Hef to sing "Thank Heaven for Little Girls" as a tribute to all the females who grew up to be beautiful additions to our slap happy society which is so ga-ga about glamour.

I arrive in the afternoon, and a valet parks my Porsche. I go in and join the rest of the guys… everyone is looking forward to having a good time, and we are not disappointed.

We rehearse in the Main Hall of the Mansion, Hef sings along, and everything goes smoothly. Then he invites us into the Library where we have a drink. Hef chats about the show and his pad and tells us that we are free to look around.

He says, "My chef is making dinner for you and the bars are open, so have a good time."

The guys wander out but I hang back and mention to Hef, "You have a beautiful pool… would it be okay to take a swim?"

"Why, of course you can!"

He proceeds to lead me down to a locker room, where he says, "Roberto here will take care of you."

Hef leaves and his guy smiles and leads me to a locker. He hands me a key on a cord to same, and gives me a fleecy white bathrobe and towel, and then shows me the entry to the pool.

"Do I need a swim suit?"

He grins at my naiveté as he tells me, "Everyone here swims without anything on."

If that's the way it is, who am I to go against the practice? I strip down, leave my key and stuff on a bench at the Grotto's entry, and enter.

The Grotto is like a marvelous movie set, with 'rocks' and smooth 'lava' projections. There is a constant gentle stream of warm sparkling water which washes over and around the whole 'floor' of the place. The lighting is cool and soothing, with changing shades of gold and brown, and blue and green.

Through this delicious, balmy atmosphere I hear Nat 'King' Cole's smooth voice singing "Unforgettable."

I allow myself to go down the gentle slope of a modified 'water slide,' and I find myself outside, with the green slope of lawn on my left and a 'towering lava flow' on my right.

I swim out and enjoy the view of the Mansion, the peacocks strutting on the lawns, the other exotic animals and of course the Playboy girls adorning the grounds as I move along.

In a moment, I hear a voice calling out, "Hey Bill, what are you doin' in there?"

I look up to see Don Randi grinning at me. He's got a drink in one hand and some hors d'oeuvres in the other.

I grin and tell him, "I'm swimming, man!"

We laugh at the sheer craziness of the scene.

I swim along, enjoying myself, till I realize I'm hungry. I retrace my course back into the Grotto's pool entry, walk up some cleverly designed 'steps' which lead me to the locker area, shower quickly, retrieve my clothes and get dressed.

I get out and join the guys who are now being served dinner on the lawn poolside. I get a drink and we settle in to a lovely roast chicken dinner. After a bit, we get ready to play, as the TV guys set up cameras, lights, sound equipment and all the other impedimenta which goes with doing this show.

Now Hef is surrounded by gorgeous girls for sure, but also he has a good group of Stars to celebrate his magazine's anniversary. The cast includes James Caan, Tony Curtis, Chevy Chase, Buck Henry, Bill Cosby, Dick Shawn and George Plimpton. There are a lot of teasing and laughs, and finally it's time for Hef's song.

As I remember it, I think he's in his trademark PJs. We play the intro and Hef does the song, but it's not sexist really; he gives me the feeling that he really loves femininity and pretty girls of course. It's a nice moment, and the show goes off in fine style.

We all celebrate with Hef and guests and the great Hall is almost awash with champagne and good feelings.

Dick Shawn
Buck Henry, George Plimpton
Tony Curtis

Bill Cosby

Cheri Chase
James Caan
'HEF' sings "Thank Heaven
For Little Girls."

Surrounded by Playmates
& Bunnies

PETERSON

Hef's 25th anniversary celebration

I'll always have a warm place in my memory and heart for Hugh Hefner. Here is a man who carved out a lifestyle which many of us secretly envy, but also projected his own honest philosophy of who he is and what he cares deeply about.

I'm grateful that he made it possible to have one of the most enjoyable times of my musical life, in an unforgettable setting. Thanks, Hef!

THIRTY-SECOND CHORUS: DORIS DAY

I've had an unrequited, unreturned love affair with Doris Day since I first saw her in the 1948 movie *Romance on the High Seas*, and heard her sing "It's Magic" on her hit record. She has that cute fresh faced beauty, and she has a sexy voice, but more than that, Doris has a way of singing whatever song she sings just to me (and millions of other people too).

I have to confess to keeping track of Doris' career, and I even read about her early life. She was born Doris Kappelhoff, to a mother who apparently encouraged her to get onstage and perform.
Doris had some tough times early in her life. She started out as a dancer when she was a young girl but hurt her leg, so she moved on to singing. When she joined Les Brown's band she married young and unhappily, twice. But when Warner's "discovered" her, her career got into high gear quickly; *Romance on the High Seas* was a hit, and she never seemed to look back.
Her marriage to Marty Melcher, who was a manager, was blessed by the birth of her son, Terry, who eventually produced some of his mother's recordings. But after she had made a great string of films and records, more disaster struck her.
Marty and the financial advisor he chose to oversee her finances made some unfortunate choices, and as a result, Doris was faced with the loss of a great deal of the monies she'd earned as a recording and film star.
I have no idea how she dealt with this, and when Marty Melcher suffered fatal heart troubles, Doris Day was faced with almost total financial ruin.
But instead of throwing up her hands and giving up (where does a star go to surrender?), Ms. Day dug in and started doing a steady weekly TV show (which I was happy to play for), as well as getting back into recording and films.

Doris Day

One of Doris' films with Richard Harris is *Charade*. She makes a record of the title tune and I am happy to play on it. Doris does a TV special and I am also in the band. We're working with a large orchestra: an opulent string section, gracing a full brass section, woodwinds (who double on saxes), percussion and a rhythm section of piano, bass, guitar and drums.

For some reason, when we attempt to record one of Doris' most popular hits, there's a note in the violins which conflicts with the very first note she has to sing! Now to help you understand the problem, it's as if you played a 'C' on the piano and tried to sing a 'B' natural while you incessantly struck the 'C'… you probably couldn't sing that 'B,' and Doris can't sing her starting note either.

The arranger/conductor is so overworked, tired and under so much pressure that he doesn't notice the wrong note in the violins which is making it impossible for Ms. Day to sing her biggest hit song.

I finally get up and go to the leader's podium and tell him what's wrong…

He brushes his hair back distractedly and says, "No, no! That note's in the chord!"

"No, it should be 'B♭,' not 'B' natural… You can't have that 'B' natural a half step away from the one she's trying to sing!"

I guess I penetrate his mental fog.

He calls out to the contractor, "Oh! Oh!!… Okay, let's take a break!"

The contractor tells the orchestra, "All right people, take a 'Ten'!"

Everybody gets up to stretch or go to the head, get coffee or whatever.

I head to the coffee machine, together with my trumpet section mates, and lo and behold, Doris Day saunters over, pours herself a Styrofoam cup of what passes for coffee from the big stainless steel vat, and we stand there for a moment.

Now when you've had a secret crush on someone for all the years I've had one on Doris Day, you can't just stand there and not say anything, at least not me!

I smile at her, and she returns the smile. And I'm brave enough to begin, but where? Where else—in the realm of Show Biz! I search my rather addled mind for something—anything! I know the trouble she's had to overcome, and still keep working.

Finally, I say, "I've enjoyed your work for so long... !"

Oh god, that makes me sound like a dumb kid, and makes her seem to be an old lady...

In some kind of desperate embarrassment, I try to continue, "I mean, I've often wondered what it's like working at Warner's, I mean with all the other women on the lot... Janis Paige, Alexis Smith and Janet Blair and so on..."

I stumble to a stop, but she brightens her smile, encouraging me to got on, so, "I mean... is there a lot of... competition?"

Doris takes a sip of coffee, then looks at me with the most straightforward gaze I think I've ever experienced.

She pauses, then asks me, "Do you know anything about Metaphysics?"

Metaphysics? Do I!

I plunge in, "Well, I was brought up attending the Church of Religious Science..."

I fervently hope that this counts for something!

Doris nods with real understanding, and says, "Then you know that the only competition you can ever have is with yourself!"

I stumble on with, "Well, I thought..."

But Doris goes on, serenely, "There *is* no such thing as competition between people... between you or me and anyone else. I did the best I could, and if the writers or the directors and producers liked what I did, they asked to me to do the part and I did the best I could, and it seemed to work!"

I am really affected by her philosophy, and without thinking it through, I blurt out, "That's a good way to look at work and life... I mean, I know you've had some rough patches to overcome..."

She picked up where I trailed off, with, "You know, you can't allow yourself to feel sorry for what's happened. Because every day is a blessing—kind of a miracle, and that's what I believe."

The contractor called for us to come back to our places in the orchestra.

All I could do was tell this wonderful woman of my dreams, "Thank you, Doris...!"

I followed the others back to work, but not before she tells me, in that wonderful soft, husky voice, "You're welcome... !"

Even though it's late at night… probably 11 PM or so, somehow wherever I look, I see things with a new perspective, as if there was sunshine illuminating the dingy old recording studio.

Doris made my Day!

THIRTY-THIRD CHORUS: STREISAND, HELEN REDDY & LAURA— MY DAY WITH THE DIVAS

It's a beautiful day in the Spring of 1976. I'm in my studio, which looks out on the huge back yard and swimming pool of our sprawling red tiled Spanish home.

I take my trumpet from my lips and call out, "Hey Dalton, you wanta warmup?"

I'm calling out to one of my best friends, Dalton Smith, who is sitting on a chaise lounge, poolside, with my four year old, Laura.

He looks up me inside my studio, grins, and shakes his head, with, "Nah, you warm up fo' me! Me and Laura are writin' a song."

It's true, he's got his trumpet case and mute bag beside him, but right now he is strumming a guitar, accompanying Laura, who is singing something, obviously in the throes of creativity, while plunking away on her pink plastic guitar.

I nod and get back to long tones on my trumpet. After a few minutes more, I pack up my horn and step out to join them.

"It's nine o'clock … We gotta be at RCA at ten ayem… We better get going, Dalt…"

Laura stops to glare at me, and declare, in that wonderful combination of Down East accent and baby talk, which she was born with, "Daddy, Dawson and me … We ah witing a song!"

"I know, but Dalton and I have to go to work now, sweetie."

Dalton hugs her, and as all six foot four and two hundred and twenty pounds of him stands up, he tells her in his most charming Mississippian, "Ahm comin' back, li'l dahlin'—ahm barbequing for y'all t'night."

Laura looks at me for confirmation, as I add, "That's right, Dalt's going to do his famous chicken and ribs combo t'night, and you two can work on your song some more…"

Dalton adds, "Ahm makin' my special down home Mississippi B-Flat Barbecue Sauce jes' for you!"

Satisfied, Laura, who at four seems to have mastered the art of womanly wiles when it comes to getting her own way, takes no chances with losing control of her co-writer.

My little Diva orders big ole Dalton, "Weave yo gitar heah den, Dawson."

I ask my budding composer daughter, "What's the name of this song you two are writing, Laura?"

She hugs her pink plastic guitar as she tells me, "'Fwowers on da Moon,' Daddy!"

"Oh, 'Flowers on the Moon,' huh… well, I'll be anxious to hear it."

"Bye for now, li'l darlin'—see y'all latah."

So we pile into Dalton's Porsche 356, and head for Hollywood and the first recording session of the day—a ten-ayem date at RCA studios on Sunset, not far from Vine (now renamed "BMG" in the corporate game of musical chairs).

We park, go through the big double glass doors; the reception/guard sees our horn cases and nods. We move along the corridor to Studio A, the big one, and say hello to the other players already unpacking their instruments. We exchange Hi's and jokes; it's all friendly, mostly—we see a lot of the same people on our daily round of session work in the vineyards of the Hollywood music recording scene. We don't know it, but we are walking into…

ARIA # ONE: STREISAND

Sid Sharp, a stocky, bespectacled guy in his mid forties who is an excellent violinist, is the concertmaster, and also the contractor of the orchestra. He stands up next to the conductor's podium. Now some contractors are a real pain in the ass; they can help or hurt you in this business, but Sid's okay—he's a nice man, and a really fine player himself, and he surrounds himself with other good players.

He calls out, "Hi, everybody, we're working with Barbra Streisand today, and our leader is someone that not all of you have met yet... he's a graduate of Julliard in New York. Please make him welcome... Mr. Lee Holdridge!"

Lee, good looking, in his mid twenties, dark wavy hair, a swarthy complexion and the beginnings of a thin moustache, steps up on the podium as the string players tap their bows on their stands, à la the Phil, while us less 'couth' wind players applaud and yell out "Yeeays!"

Hal Blaine, the most recorded drummer of all time, and the quickest musician in town with a line, looks up from his drum kit, grins at Lee and says, "Hey Lee, the call for Latin Lovers is down the hall!"

Lee blushes, then grins. Sid shakes his head, and we all get to start the gig with a giggle. (It's a good thing we did...)

We get an 'A' from John, the oboist, who lives someplace miles from Hollywood, where he raises goats, but is the most in-demand oboist in town. The strings fiddle away, each in their own private little world, sawing away at some half remembered concerto, till Lee picks up his baton, and says,

"Let's start with 'I Won't Last a Day Without You,' please."

Everybody gives him our respectful attention. He gives a downbeat, and the rhythm section starts. Then the strings and woodwinds come in—it's gorgeous and fresh sounding, and Dalt and I look at each other and smile. The other brass players—French horns and trombones—nod. When you have played as many different kinds and styles of music, it's a pleasure to hear something clean and new, and work with someone good, because believe me, not all of them are.

Suddenly we are roused from our enjoyment of the beauty of Lee's orchestration, as the Control Room door bursts open, and out rushes Barbra Streisand, geshrying at the top of her famous soprano voice,

"STOP! STOP! ... WHAT THE HELL IS THAT?!?"

She races toward the orchestra and Lee, on the podium like a one woman Israeli Army Unit in full Blitzkrieg mode.

Lee stops the orchestra, and we all stare at Streisand—yeah, what the hell is this?

Streisand gets up on the podium, famous nose to new kid/arranger nose, and shrieks, "This is the same old bullshit! I want

The Divas: Laura Peterson (with Dalton), Barbra Streisand,
Helen Reddy

new… I want fresh! THAT'S WHY YOU'RE HERE! Now fix it, goddammit!"

Lou McCreary, one of the trombonists, looks up and says, "Why don't you give the chart a chance, Barbra?"

La Streisand glares at him with a look that would curdle sour cream and snarls, "You just shut up!"

Lou just gestures, palms up and shrugs.

Now we've all worked with all kinds of stars, big names with all kinds of tempers, but none of us have ever heard anything as raw and demeaning as this. This is a new high—or low—as far as I'm concerned, and I know the other players feel the same way! I mean, what Lee wrote is gorgeous, and what the hell does Streisand want? New? Fresh? Has she been digging Phil Spector's "Walls of Sound," or Frank Zappa's BS… or maybe she'd like a little Charles Ives, or Boulez, with a rock beat underneath?

Anyway, Lee is gracious under fire, and says, "Let me try something for you, Barbra…"

Sid, the contractor, stands and calls out, "Let's take a 'Ten,' people…"

Lee grabs a pencil, bends over his score, and starts to change his chart. As luck would have it, the copyists who delivered the orchestra parts are still hanging around, and they rally round our embattled young leader with their copying pens and fresh manuscripts, as he frantically rewrites and re-orchestrates on the spot.

After a little more than twenty minutes, he gives a downbeat, and we play the newly copied page before us… it's good, but no better than what he wrote in the first place. Barbra stands listening, her arms folded across her chest, a sour look which says to me, "It's not as good as I deserve, but I'll allow it…" and we get through the rest of the session, getting three songs recorded with only minor outbursts from the Prima Donna.

On the way out, a lot of the wind players, trumpets, trombones and woodwinds, stop by to murmur 'good job' to Lee. He blushes beneath that olive skin and smiles shyly.

Welcome to Show Biz, Mister Holdridge!

CODA

Barbra is a huge star who wants every one of her performances and recordings to top the last one. She is intensely demanding of herself, and everyone that works with her. Her high standards and great performances are legendary, and her public adores her. The musicians who work for her just go along with her, and play wonderfully well, either because of, or in spite of, the Diva's tirades.

ARIA # TWO: HELEN REDDY

It's now a little past 1:30 PM on the same day, and we have to be out to Warner Brothers Studios for a date with Artie Butler, the little roly-poly mensch who everyone loves, and likes to work with. He's from New York and has a real talent for making arrangements that work. He is also armed with one of the sharpest wits you will ever encounter. We make it onto the lot, and luckily, find a parking spot close enough so that Dalton doesn't have to run in his cowboy boots.

Sid Sharp and most of the string players from the Streisand date are straggling in, still talking about the lady's outburst. Some of the same guys in the trombones and woodwinds arrive, and we settle in to see what we have in store for us on this session.

Artie looks out at us, bemused, and cracks, "I couldn't get my regular guys, but you'll have to do…"

Lou McCreary, the trombonist who plays so well that leaders endure his "take no prisoners" attitude, calls, in a laid back voice, "Oh, that's okay Artie, we thought this was a Nelson Riddle date, but we'll make your stuff sound good anyway."

Okay, tit for tat…

Artie fires back, "Lou, when I want 'stand up,' *I'll* do it, okay? Now fellas, most of you were on Helen's record of 'I Am Woman,' and we wanta make another hit for the lady…"

He looks around and holds out his hand and Helen Reddy steps up beside him.

"Fellas, Helen Reddy!"

She nods to us, and Artie kicks off the first chart, "Ruby Red Dress." It's a cookin' kind of down home chart, and the band gets swingin' immediately.

Helen just stands there, not looking pleased.

We finish playing the arrangement, and she says, "It's not the right key, Artie! It's too high!"

Artie has heard everything that singers or producers can throw at him.

But he just says, calmly, "Ah, Helen, that's the same key we agreed on when we rehearsed—A♭!"

"I don't give a damn what key it is, it's too high! Fix it!"

Artie knows he's right, so he suggests, "Why don't we give it a chance… maybe you'll get warmed up and it'll feel okay… okay?"

Helen snaps, "Well, all right, but I'm telling you…"

That's all Artie needs. He kicks it off, and we roll though it again. She is standing there, covering one ear, and singing along, while she stares at the score. That's funny, because she made a point of telling us proudly that she doesn't read a note of music—she as much as said that it was her God-given talent that put her on top.

We play through the fade ending—the three black sisters and brothers who comprise the back-up group singers are really cookin' —and we finally stop.

Helen tells Artie, "It's still too high! And there's a funny note in there, in the second chorus…"

Helen steps down off the podium to glare at Artie and us members of the orchestra.

Artie holds up his hands in surrender and resignation.

He looks down at our contractor, "Sidney…?"

Sid stands up, shrugs, and with a bemused smile, calls, "Take a 'Ten,' fellas…"

The orchestra gets up, and most head for the coffee. Artie calls his copyists who are also standing around, and they confer.

We look at each other… another tantrum? Maybe it's something in the air… maybe the Russians have really poisoned the water… Anyway, most of band gets up, stretches and moves for coffee.

I sit in my chair, watching, as Ms. Reddy, the self-taught "I don't need no stinkin' music lessons" Diva, steps back up on the podium and starts to scan the score!

I can't believe my eyes! No one else is watching, but I can't resist. I call out to her highness, the musical guru, "Hey Helen, can I check a note?"

The Diva looks up from the study of a score of which she supposedly has no knowledge or understanding, and spins to glare at me.

She knows she's busted, so she jabs her right hand in my direction viciously, with her middle finger stabbing out at me, and yells, "YEAH, BUDDY! CHECK THIS!!"

I smile at the furious Diva, and say, "Thanks, Helen."

After Artie tells us to transpose the chart down a step, we play it again, and now she's satisfied. We go on to record "Ruby Red Dress" as well as "Delta Dawn" and two more songs that were big records for Ms. Reddy.

Dalton and I stop for a taste at his favorite hangout, The Chimney Sweep, and then to Gelson's for dinner fixin's. Dalton has an eye for ladies and enough Southern charm to sweep girls right off their feet, and has the checkout girl laughing and blushing all at the same time.

We arrive home to my house, and Mister "Dawson" pours himself a glass of Absolut on the rocks and I play catch with Eric. Then Dalton and Laura gather up their guitars and move off, hand in hand, back out by the pool. As I fire up the BBQ, I can hear Dalton's soft strumming and Laura's little girl voice, happily singing—singing about "Fwowers on da Moon"… and you know, when I look up there at La Luna, I think I can just make 'em out, too. But it really doesn't matter, because whatever she sings about, she's my favorite Diva of 'em all!

ARIA # THREE: CODA FOR THE DIVAS (LAURA & DALT)

Dalton puts the chicken on the grill with his special Mississippi BBQ sauce. Then while the chicken cooks, he and Laura get back to work on another of their original compositions, on this, another Day With the Divas!

REPRISE WITH BARBRA

The next morning I have another session with Streisand, this time at a much smaller, more intimate studio. As I slip into my chair in the much smaller brass section (minus Dalton), I look in my mute bag to see "presents" from my daughter—two big, juicy looking navel oranges and one of her favorite toy dolls, in case I should want to play, I suppose!

I look up to see Streisand come in. She looks a little grim and maybe unhappy. On a crazy impulse I pick up one of the navels, hold so she can see it, and say,

"... Mornin' Barbra, you look like you could use an orange!"

I make a practice pitch motion, then toss it to her gently. She might throw it back at me, or kick me off the date...

Instead she catches it, smiles and says, "Thanks! You want some?"

"No thanks! I've got another one..."

Then John Bahler, the leader kicks off the first tune, "Let the Good Times Roll"... and they do!

Barbra peels, we play, and a good time is had by all.

THIRTY-FOURTH CHORUS: "HE-E-E-E-RE'S JOHNNY!!

I get a call from the great trumpeter Snooky Young to sub for him on the *Tonight Show*. I'm glad, because I watch the show every night or so; the band roars, Carson is amusing and the guests are usually interesting. Besides, playing with Doc Severinsen's NBC orchestra will be a real treat for me.

I drive over to NBC for the afternoon rehearsal, and park. I enter around back, and walk down the hall to the studio.

The walls are lined with huge blow-ups of photos of Bob Hope, Jack Benny, Danny Kaye... it's a Who's Who of Show Biz Greats. I go into the band room and see Johnny Audino (the lead trumpet player), Conte Candoli (the great jazz player) and Maurie Harris (The Snob).

I listen as the guys exchange good natured insults. I get my trumpet out of its case and grab up the mutes as Al Lapin, the contractor of the band, comes in and says, "Alright, let's go, boys!"

Now Al is a rather short, well-groomed guy in a beautiful suit who is originally from the Lower East Side of New York. He is famous among the musicians who work for him for several things. First of all, he replaced Spike Jones as the staff drummer when Spike started his crazy comedy group, "The City Slickers," many years ago. Al is kidded by the guys about having dinner on him at IHOP, because his son started the International House of Pancakes and Al is a major stockholder. Last but not least is Al's Yogi Berra-esque use of the language. For instance, today Al has just purchased a new car.

Johnny Audino asks Al, "So, Al—what kind of car did you get?"

Al says, a little defensively, "I got a Lincoln Town Car."

Johnny Audino throws him a little dig... "A Lincoln... why a Lincoln...?"

Al draws himself up to his full 5′4″ and tells us, "I'll have you know that Lincoln is the Cadillac of motor cars!"

Now Gil Falco, who is movie star handsome and the lead trombonist of the band, joins in.

He asks Al, "What do you think about this gasoline shortage, Al? What do you think we oughta do?"

Al considers this for a nanosecond, then advises us, "Well, I think you should keep your car fulla gas alla the time!"

With this news flash under our belts we start to rehearse the play-ons and play-offs with Tommy Newsome as the leader... Doc Severinson, the phenomenal trumpeter and leader, is taking Ed McMahon's place next to Johnny.

Johnny Audino spends extra time with me and the trumpets. He wants to make sure I've got the charts down. That's fine with me, but the other guys may not be pleased; Maurie grumbles a bit, but Johnny's the boss of the section, so we plow right through all the play-ons and bumpers that we could possibly be called on to play.

Al consults his Rolex, and calls a dinner break. I wander over with the other guys to the commissary, which is tolerable. The band is made up of veterans of the big bands, and a few guys who came out to Los Angeles when the *Tonight Show* moved from New York to the West Coast.

We come back; everybody's in a suit and tie. We get on the stand, and it's SHOW TIME... There's an audience warmup, but I'm too busy checking that I've got the music in order the way that Tommy Newsome has called it out. Then Doc Severinson in a wild red jacket with sequins gets to the mike, the lights flare up, Ed Shaunessey the drummer rolls on his tom-tom, and Doc yells,

"It's the Tonight Show, starring Johnny Carson, Doc Severinson and the NBC Tonight Show orchestra, and special guests Orson Welles (and some other stars), and now... (Drum roll crescendos...),

"H-E-E-E-RE'S JOHNNY!"

Tommy Newsome kicks off that *Tonight Show* theme that we've all heard so many times—Ed the drummer pounds out an ear-shattering downbeat, and we roar in, led by Audino's sizzling lead trumpet. Believe me, it's a different thing watching and hearing the band play it while you're in your PJs at home, and getting to be a part of that wonderful, sizzling, fat big band sound that greets Johnny and his audience. We play it strong, Johnny comes out between the curtains, grins, and bows, and we play a goofy little ending to the theme that sounds like "Shave and Haircut—Two Bits." Then I relax but Johnny Audino whispers a reminder of what the next music cue will be… the Theme playoff.

I flip over to the next page, then look over at the set… Johnny is doing his monologue, and the audience is eating it up. He's even funnier when a joke dies. His "takes" are priceless, and his audience laughs even harder. Of course his material is sooo timely; he's got a joke for anything and everything… gibes at the politicos in power, whatever is newsworthy, and especially "Show Biz biggies."

Carson is so cool, so affable; he's got this gig so under control. His sense of humor is marvelous, his timing impeccable and his facial expressions so funny and so natural that you might think any of us could get up there and do what he does. And you might think that until you see somebody take Johnny's place as host, and you get to see what an artist Carson is. When he finishes the monologue, Tommy faces us and silently counts off the first bumper, and we swing into it, and we're into the first commercial break.

There's a lot more music actually played on the show, while the TV audience at home is treated to commercials on their screens. But the band keeps the audience in their chairs and entertained during the commercial breaks by playing swinging tunes with great arrangements by some of the guys in the band like John Bambridge and Tommy Newsome, as well as other good arrangers.

I've got a perfect view from the trumpet section (the back row of the band, of course) of the couch where the guests come out and take a seat, and Johnny, at his desk.

Orson Welles is the "Headliner" guest of the show. He's a huge man, confined to a wheelchair. But time and his great girth has not dulled his wit and wisdom. He is clever, funny and quick with his repartee with Johnny. He even manages some "magic" tricks—sleight of hand—and since both he and Johnny are amateur magicians, they have a great time. I can see that Johnny has great respect for this unforgettable auteur. After a commercial break, during which we play a frantically swingin' chart (and Doc? Well, he proves with his soaring, exciting trumpeting that "The Doctor Is In!"), Johnny leads Orson into talking about his days in New York, The Mercury Radio Theater, and then his days as an actor on Broadway.

Orson obviously enjoys recalling the days on stage, and tells us about being in a play with a beautiful, sultry blonde actress and the contest he has with his other co-star, Burgess Meredith, to capture the lady's favors.

He says, owlishly, "…Finally the lady chose my competitor, and I gracefully retired from the field. In fact, I went so far as to offer them the use of my Long Island place for Sunday and the dark day. They thanked me profusely, and we did our Saturday night performance—so, next afternoon, after the Sunday matinee, I dropped the keys into Burgess Meredith's warm palm and bade them 'enjoy' themselves.

"When they returned Tuesday, Burgess cornered me in my dressing room, his eyes on fire, and yelled, 'You son-of-a-bitch!' and other endearments. When I innocently asked what the problem was, he shrieked, 'You know very well! We went to the master bedroom, and after I'd popped the champagne and when we were finally cozy… an alarm clock went off. I jumped up, tracked it down, and shut it off. We settled back in, I invited her to bed, and when she joined me… another alarm clock…'

"I told my rival, 'That's too bad!'

"'The damned clocks were all over the place, in the closet, the bath, and the kitchen downstairs, under the bed…'

"'Oh really…?' I asked.

"'Till Nine AM, you oaf!' he bellowed. 'The last clock was INSIDE the lady's suitcase! How did you manage *that*?'

"'I'm sorry you had so much trouble, really! Were my butler and the maid helpful?'

"At this point he swore a bit more and threw a jar of crème at me which shattered the mirror."

There's some more repartee as Johnny tries to persuade Orson to reveal the lady's name. Orson jokes his way out of that, and refuses to tell. But the producer of the *Tonight Show*, Freddie

Orson Welles and Johnny Carson

De Cordova, comes from the wings to stand with his back to the audience, but in Orson's, Johnny's and the band's line of sight, and writes on a blank cue card with a felt tip. The name is that of an exotic, beautiful blonde star who made several films in Hollywood. The name …?

"Ona Munson?"

Orson's huge face creases in a big smile and Johnny grins.

They share some inside chatter and some card tricks, and the show goes on.

CODA

I'm in awe of what Johnny has… his unassuming charm with the audience and his guests, and the fact that he loves good big band music. Of *all* the late-night show hosts, Mr. Carson is the best that ever graced our TV screen, in my estimation!

Rita gets a job driving a forklift at a brewery. She divorces me in 1980. I pick up Eric and Laura every Tuesday and Thursday, cook dinner and work on homework, or just kick back. Of course I do the usual things, taking Laura to soccer practice, and coaching Eric's baseball teams. I have these two wonderful people every other weekend.

It's a difficult time, but we get through it with love for each other. Eric introduces me to one of his teachers at the Sepulveda Gifted Magnet Middle School, Ms. Mary McMannes.

Eric tells me, "You could go jogging with Ms. McMannes—she runs, too!"

I follow his suggestion and meet a wonderful, lovely woman. We start a long and strong relationship, which became a source of so many good things.

THIRTY-FIFTH CHORUS: BLONDIE

My son Eric pleads,

"Just one more grounder, Dad."

"Okay, okay, but I have to go to work, EP."

"Cartoons?"

"Nope, it's a record date... somebody by the name of Blondie... have you heard of her ... or it?"

My son holds the baseball, and looks at me with new interest.

I seem to have made a dent in his fourteen-year-old "cool," so I ask, "You... know her?"

"It's 'them,' Dad," he corrects me.

Laura has breezed into the front yard, and she picks up our discussion with, "Blondie is Deborah Harry... get a picture will you?"

I head for the house with my two kids, who seem impressed for the first time in many weeks because of my trumpet-playing gig.

"I'll try, but artists don't usually have photos when they're doing recording, you know."

Laura gives me that smile that could make me try to do anything... my 12 year old daughter's got a way with her.

"Oh, you know you can, Daddy."

So I get my trumpet, flugelhorn and mute bag, jump into my Porsche, and head down the 134 Freeway from Van Nuys, onto the 101 into Hollywood. It's just before the afternoon rush, so it's an easy drive. I park close to United Studios on Sunset, and go in.

There's a different vibe about the place today. The studios, A, B, C etc., all seem quiet. Usually some sound leaks out a bit, and there are normally musicians that do sessions rushing in and out. But not today.

I see an engineer wandering down the hall with a cup of coffee, and ask, "Why's it so quiet around here today?"

"Because this group 'Blondie' has block booked the whole place. This is the second month they've been in here... You people'll be in 'A.'"

I mosey down toward 'A' and see Jimmie Haskell, the leader and arranger, come hurrying along past me with an armful of arrangements.

I say, "Hi Jim... what're we doing today?"

He hardly breaks stride as he tells me, "We're sweetening some tracks for Miss Harry and her group 'Blondie.'"

He keeps going but pauses by a young woman leaning against the wall halfway down the hall. She doesn't seem to be doing anything—just leaning.

Jimmie very nicely says, "Debbie, we'll be doing the horn overdubs in just a few minutes."

Jimmie vanishes through the studio door.

I figure this is as a good a time as any to ask for a picture for my kids, so when I get to Debbie, who is still leaning against the wall, staring at the carpet, I stop, smile and say, "Hi Debbie!"

She raises her head and tries to focus on me. It's almost too much of an effort, but I keep pitching.

"My two kids, Eric and Laura, are fans... would it be possible to get an autographed picture for them?"

This doesn't seem to get much of a response. At least she doesn't give a flat-out "No."

I sort of wait, as more musicians come down the hall to the studio, and go past Debbie and me.

Her eyes seem to have a sort of glazed or dazed look. She's still trying to get me in focus, and she kind of straightens up a bit and in a soft, outerspace kind of voice says, "Picture... ?"

"Yeah, I'd sure appreciate it..."

But now it's time to join my colleagues in the studio, so I leave her as I kind of lamely say, "I'll check with you later, okay...?"

Debbie rouses herself a tad and nods as she says very softly, "Yeah... later..."

Blondie's Deborah Harry

I leave her leaning against the wall. I go into the studio, where two trombonists, a tenor sax player and two other trumpeters are getting their instruments out of the cases and joking around with each other.

Everyone except for Bill Green, the bespectacled, scholarly looking African American tenor man—in fact, he *is* a scholar of the woodwind instruments, and a fine teacher as well as being a busy session player. We know he's been studying karate with the same precision and dedication he's spent becoming a fine reedman. He's showing and telling Pete Candoli (the legendary trumpeter who worked with Woody Herman and every artist in Holly-wood) a spinning kick in which Bill's added his own wrinkle. He squats down, quick as a sixteenth note, then spins on one leg, with his other kicking out.

Pete eyes him, smiles and says, "Yeah, that's really cool, Bill."

Pete turns back to chat with someone else; Bill is satisfied, and goes back to slipping a reed on his baritone sax.

It's time to run the charts, while the engineer plays the tracks that Debbie Harry and company have recorded. That's the fun and the challenge of studio session work… you never quite know what you'll be asked to play or what style you'll need to get into. The first chart is a kind of calypso tune called "The Tide Is High," and it's a laid back kind of feel that's fun to play.

Debbie's vocal is already on the track, along with the rest of the group, and we just go with the flow, reading the notes Jimmie's written, and after a few 'takes,' we've got it, to Jim and the producer's taste. Debbie never appears in the control room, although a couple of the members of Blondie do roll in—young skinny guys with long hair, funky looking jeans and T-shirts, smoking cigarettes—and give a listen. We take a break and then come back to play the other tunes.

When we've finished, we pack up and I go back down the entry, but Debbie Harry has vanished.

I never did get a picture for my children, but had the kick of getting the recording for them when it came out and became a hit.

THIRTY-SIXTH CHORUS
A BRUSH WITH BOB DYLAN

Once in a while I get to write music for radio and TV commercials. It's a challenge to come up with a musical hook that will grab the audience, make a statement for the advertiser and please the agency folks and the sponsor, all within 30 or 60 seconds.

An agency calls and I jump at the opportunity.

My gig is to write music that sounds like a Diana Ross hit, but it has to be original. I played for the Supremes when I was working at the Coconut Grove, and recorded with them. And lord knows we all know what the great Diana sounds like. I come up with music that flows with the lyrics that the agency folks have written.

The next step is to choose a singer that can capture the magic of Diana Ross. I already know who to choose. I call the dynamite singer who has graced most recording studios, doing backup vocals for everyone in town, and who sings solo when some star can't make it vocally. Clydie tells me that she's staying in Brentwood with a guy of whom she is apparently very fond. I invite her to bring him along.

She accepts the date, and comes the next day to record her vocal. She has great range, but I check out the key just to be sure, before we cut the track. We're set, and the producer from the agency arrives with her copy in her extra large size briefcase, and sits down at the back of the studio. She sweeps her cold eyes over everything and everyone with a look of faint disapproval. Okay, so she is going to produce and sit in judgement. I figure Clydie's talent will turn the cold to warmth.

Clydie arrives on time, with a slightly disheveled looking guy with wild, unkempt hair. My chosen singer introduces me to 'Bob,' and I realize it's not just any Bob, it's Dylan. He shakes hands, then glances around, and studies the producer. She gets her copy out, slips on horn-rim glasses and pulls knitting needles and wool out of her case. She nods at me and starts to knit. I take it that whatever the deal is, she's ready—she just sits and purls. She reminds me of someone, but I can't quite get it. Oh well, it's time to go to work.

Clydie goes into the studio, slips on her headphones, and we run the track. I don't even need to cue this lady, but she listens, nods and smiles. She's ready to make a take, and I know how good she is—she'll probably nail on one or two takes.

We run the track back, as the producer lady moves up next to me at the console, and her knitting needles click away to her own beat. She doesn't look up at me or Clydie, she just stares down at her flashing needles, and Clydie sings my tune with the agency lyrics with great feeling and perfect style. Dylan is wandering around in the back of the control room, but I can see him listening carefully. Clydie has done some backup for him on some of his recordings, and as he hears her voice, a slow little smile creeps across his mouth. She's that good. The track ends, and I turn to Madame producer.

She looks down at her knitting, and announces in a cold harsh voice, "She doesn't sound right…"

I think she's wrong, but I have to play the role.

"I think she captures the sound, the feeling and style that we talked about. Now is there something that Clydie can do to make it more what you want?"

She doesn't look at Clydie, or me, but the needles keep clicking.

Suddenly my mind clicks like her needles—I've got it. She's like a modern day Madame DeFarge in Dickens' *Tale of Two Cities,* who sits at the foot of the guillotine and knits while the bloody heads roll off into the basket. I shoot a glance back at Dylan. He stands looking at Madame, his head cocked ever so slightly to one side, like he's frozen in disbelief.

Madame finally says, "She doesn't say the product name clear enough."

I shrug, and pass the quibble on to Clydie as a suggestion, on the talkback.

She smiles, nods and says, "Let's do it again!"

That's just what we do, and after that take Madame doesn't like the way Clydie sings the word 'the.' This goes on, take after take; the hour I've allotted for getting the vocal is long gone, while the

Mme DeFarge, Clydie, and Bob Dylan

thing Madame is knitting has grown in length. Finally, after twenty or so takes, Dylan moves slowly up to us at the console. He looks at Clydie, who I know must be getting tired and frustrated, but doesn't show it.

Finally Dylan says, softly, but with great irony, "You folks sure do a simple thing a lotta times, don't you."

The knitting stops, as Madame looks up at the back of one of America's music legends as he turns and ambles slowly to the door.

Then he turns and says to me, "Tell her to come on out whenever she gets done. I'm gonna get some sun."

He's out the door. I look down at Madame.

She seems to have gotten the message, as she says with a cold snap in her voice, "I guess we'll just have to make do with what you've got… now, a couple of things…"

She splits a few more lyric hairs, and Clydie obliges with great good spirit. When Madame finally gives me a curt nod of dismissal, I go in to the studio to Clydie, as our producer sweeps up her copy and her knitting. Clydie looks at me, then out at Madame, who stands, stiff and straight, then strides out of the control room to the phone. Clydie and I start to smile, then giggle, then laugh out loud.

While the engineer prepares for the mix, which is the next stage in the process, I walk Clydie outside. Dylan is lying on his back on the hood of a faded blue Chevy station wagon. He's taken off his Levi jacket, stripped down to a T-shirt and is catching the rays. He sits up as we come up. Madame DeFarge is walking to her Porsche, but turns to look at us, as if passing sentence on the next doomed aristocrat.

She says to me, "I'll see you back at the agency, Bill."

I figure I've had enough of Madame's 'input' for the day, but I'm compelled to tell her we're going to mix now, and ask if she'd like to take part.

She gives me an icy stare and says, "I think you can do that without my help."

All I can think is, "Thank God."

She is about to say something to Clydie or Dylan, but he slides off the hood, and laconically says, "You folks sure make a lot outta a little."

He puts an arm round Clydie's shoulder and they get into the wagon. He keys it and they move off slowly. I leave the parking lot and go back to mix. Incidentally the agency and the client love Clydie's work, and so do I.

I talk to Clydie the next day, and she tells me that Dylan works this way. Writing the song is everything. Then he gets his band together and they play it through till he and his guys are satisfied with the feel and the arrangement they come up with. Then they make one take. He's usually happy with what they've got and it's time to kick back.

Now *that's* the way to work, even without knitting needles for accompaniment.

THIRTY-SEVENTH CHORUS:
A NEW GIG

It has been over forty years since I first worked with Mr. Nat 'King' Cole and I've been asked to become an officer of Professional Musicians, Local 47. There are great players coming to Los Angeles as well as new leaders and things change. I feel that it's time for me to take up this new challenge as vice president with Max Herman, who has been a Union Officer for many years.

After Max serves two years, I'm asked to run for President of the Local. I'm successful, and enjoy several terms in office.

THIRTY-EIGHTH CHORUS: THE SINATRA I KNEW

It's two thirty Friday afternoon, and Carolyn and I are quickly off Flight 19 from New York's JFK. Everything works: the driver meets us at Gate 19, our luggage is first onto the carousel, and we're like a couple of kids in the back seat of the Lincoln town car, laughing, frolicking, just feeling good. I look over at my beautiful, auburn haired fiancée, as she stretches her long legs out. We've been engaged for just a few months, and I'm so happy that we're together. She's a classically trained bassoonist, with a Doctor's degree from Manhattan School of Music, but she has an appreciation of jazz too, as evidenced by the CDs of Monk and Miles in her collection. Our shared passion for music seems to bridge the fact that Carolyn is much younger than I, and we come from different musical interests.

But as Louis Armstrong once said, "It don't matter what kind of music it is, as long as it's good.."

Suddenly a fragment of a tune pops into my head. I lean over, and with apologies to Sinatra, I sing to her, sotto voce, "Once I get you up there, where the air is rarefied, we'll just glide, starry eyed."

She smiles and says, "Ain't it the truth?" and kisses me.

After all, we've just had a wonderful week in the Big Apple, where I put on my AFM Pension Fund trustee's hat to help engineer a 5% raise in pension benefits for all musicians. The Pension Fund meetings were a nine to five responsibility, but after the meeting one night, we got to see a Broadway show. We're both warm with the excitement of this last week, but most of all there's a closeness we feel which grows and glows between us.

The car takes us home. We look round our two story, set on a hillside in Mt. Washington. It's close to downtown Los Angeles, but covered with tree lined canyons and grassy hillsides. It's like

245

discovering our new home all over again. I flip on the CD player, and Sinatra's voice rings out, "I've got the world on a string, sittin' on a rainbow..." It's just how I feel right now. Funny how he always seems to capture what I'm experiencing, happy, sad, good or bad, in just the right tone and texture.

But right now I've got to rush. I have to check in at the office, and I drive down our hill to the Union, where I catch up on mail and return phone calls. I'm anxious to get home. I stride out to the lot, key the Honda, pull out of the lot and head for the freeway. I switch on KLON, the jazz station radio and I'm greeted by Frank Sinatra singing with Billy May's band. "Come fly with me, let's fly, let's fly away..." the tune I sang to Carolyn. I've had the pleasure of playing this arrangement with the man many times. He and the band swing it out, and I'm smiling with the song and the memory of working with Sinatra.

Then Chuck Niles, the voice of jazz in L.A., tells me, "As you probably know, we lost Francis Albert last night, but we'll always have his music... like one of the songs he used to sing puts it, 'For the good times, the sad times and all the in between times'..."

I know he'd been ill. Bill Miller, his accompanist even told me, "I don't think the old man will make another birthday."

But Sinatra is... well, somehow the normal rules never applied to him... the way he sang, the way he lived his life. Somehow too, I never really believed he'd leave this stage he loved so much. I pick up the cellular, dial home. Carolyn's voice answers softly.

"Hello."

"I just heard that Sinatra's... gone."

"I know, honey. I just heard too. I'm so sorry..."

"I'll be home in a few minutes."

When I pull in, Carolyn's at the door. She gives me a hug, and leads me to our dining room. I look out at L.A.'s downtown buildings glistening in the late afternoon sun. But my mind drifts back to the good times I had playing first trumpet at Frank's Cal Neva Lodge. Carolyn gets out the Jack Daniel's and two ice filled lowball glasses. She sits on the dining table, and caresses my face for a moment.

"I remember what you've told me about Sinatra. I thought maybe we should toast him."

"Good idea. We worked all the big stars, but there was never

Frank Sinatra

the feeling I got from anyone like I had with him, right from that first summer in 1959…"

"Tell me about it."

My memory is vivid of that night, as I settle back and tell her the story.

"Well, we'd just played Lena Horne's closing night. Her music was arranged by the great Lennie Hayton, who was music director on *Singin' in the Rain* and countless other great musicals. Her music was challenging, more so because you had to become used to breathing and blowing a horn at an altitude of 6,500 feet in that thin Lake Tahoe air. Anyway, Sinatra, in a tux, was ringside with Juliet Prowse, watching the show.

"Afterwards, Matty Malneck, the bandleader, tells us, in his unique bilateral emission lisp, 'Fellashs, Mishter Shinatra wants to rehearsh at 2:30 thish morning, okay?'

"We're a little tired after two shows, but we nod and say, 'Okay.' After all this is the Chairman of the Board.

"We come back from having a drink at the bar, and get on the stand. Bill Miller, Frank's accompanist, grey-haired and slim, smiles and passes out Frank's books. Irv Cottler, his drummer, settles in at his set. Bassist Ralph Peña checks his tuning as we wait for a couple of minutes.

"Suddenly the front door to the empty showroom flies open and Sinatra comes in, still in his tux, a drink in hand.

"He strides down the aisle and climbs up the stairs to the stage, smiles at Matty, and says to us, 'Hiya fellas.'

"He pulls his bow tie loose, and jerks his head at Eddie, a tough looking Chicago guy who is the maitre d', and who is standing in the wings with a portable bar.

"'Hey Eddie, bring on da booze!'

"Eddie wheels the bar out on-stage, replete with bottles, ice and glasses all on board.

"Then Frank tells us, 'Eddie's our bartender tonight. You just tell him what ya want.'

"I glance at Eddie. Now so far this summer the maitre d' has been as hostile to the band as a rattlesnake to a bunch of mice. I'm loving this.

"I call out to Eddie, 'I'll take a Jack Daniel's, rocks, please.'

"He scowls at us, but Sinatra doesn't see it. The rest of the band takes the cue. After all, when would a person ever turn down an invitation from the Chairman of the Board to have a drink?

"Frank pulls out a pack, lights up, and draws in a lungful, takes the mike off its stand. He asks us as he points at Bill Miller,

"'Did Sunshine Charlie there pass out my arrangements?'

"Bill Miller says, 'We're all set.'

"'Okay. Let's start with, "Come Fly With Me."'

"We get it up out, and Frank counts it off. He stands center stage, not singing, just listening to us run down Billy May's chart.

"Right away it's special. I mean, I'd hired a good drummer who played all the other shows with our band, but Frank's drummer, Irv Cottler, is a veteran who has played with most of the great big bands. He really knows how to boot a band, and what The Chairman of the Board wants, so playing with him is something else. He drives the band, and swings with impeccable time. We hit the last chord.

"Frank nods, looks at the band and says, 'Hey saxes, you can make more of those bent notes—you know, whee-eeh dot wee-dot. Okay, 'Luck Be a Lady…'

"We pull it up, the string section fiddles around for a second, but Frank holds up his hand, and they get as quiet as church mice. Matty gives us a downbeat and Frank sings, off mike, into Matty's ear just enough for him to conduct the rubato section with the strings, and get it together with Sinatra's interpretation.

"Then Irv kicks it into tempo, and we start to swing. Now I've listened to a lot of the man's recordings, but for the first time I really hear and feel the tremendous intensity that he injects into the song when he's singing live, right at you. He creates an 'In-Your-Face' energy I've never experienced with other singers. I mean, Vic Damone has great chops, but he seems to sing to and for himself some of the time. Tony Bennett tells you a story, with great individual style, but nobody has this keen edge of fiery confidence, don't give a damn 'tude, and swingin' style. The whole band responds, biting into the Nelson Riddle arrangement, popping the phrases, swinging like we never have before. We blast into the band chorus; the saxes and trombones have it first. I start counting the four bar rest, when I glance up to see Sinatra move to the band.

"He steps between the lead alto and tenor players and looks

up at me, his blue eyes blazing with energy. He points right at me, then jerks his thumb up toward the ceiling. It's the unmistakable signal, 'Play the next phrase up an octave.' I sneak a peek ahead. Ohmigawd, playing this phrase up an octave means it'll start on high 'D,' then lift up to high 'G's' and 'A's. I mean I practice up to double high 'C' almost every day, but not after two shows and during an all night rehearsal. But this is what I've always wanted to do, play the best arrangements with the biggest star of all. Here I am at the Cal Neva... this isn't Capitol record studios, but this is my chance to do it just like the Hollywood hot shots. I count out the rests, two–two–three–four, three–two–three–four, four–two–three... and I grab the biggest breath I can of this thin mountain air, and I hit the 'D' and wail into the high notes. I make it all, and it feels great, sitting on top of the whole band, an octave higher than the other two trumpets. The guy next to me gives my leg a 'good going' kind of pat. Sinatra flashes a quick grin, and gives me a 'thumbs up.'

"Matty glances at me, with a faint smile. Maybe he's afraid I'll ask for more money. Anyway, we finish rehearsing at about five AM, but it's funny... nobody seems tired now. We polish off our drinks and head for our rustic cabins, but the feeling stays with me, that feeling of swinging with the best."

♪♪♪

I stop and look over at Carolyn. She lifts her glass, and smiles at me, as she says, "Like the man said, '... Once I get you up there, where the air is rarefied, we'll just glide, starry-eyed...'"

We clink our glasses together, as I murmur, "To Frank," and we raise a toast to the Chairman of the Board.

CODETTA

My son Eric loved Frank's style, and he loved to sing along with his records. So when I finish playing a session with Sinatra one night, I'm bold enough to call out to him as the other musicians are packing up just as he is about to leave the studio. I have a snapshot I took from underwater when Eric is a ten year old joyously happy kid, and we're in Maui.

I take it out of my wallet, and call out, "Frank, can I speak to you for a minute?"

He stops, turns, his eyes a blazing blue and hostile, as I hurry to him.

"I worked with you at the Cal Neva with Matty Malneck's band."

Frank smiles and says, "We had some fun up there…"

"We sure did. Ah… my ten-year-old son Eric's a big fan of yours. He sings along with the 'Sinatra and Basie at the Sands' album."

Frank said, "Kid's got good taste. I'll send him a picture."

I said, "That would be wonderful. Eric'll love it… but could you autograph this?"

I give Frank a snapshot I'd taken with an underwater camera, of my son snorkeling in the water off Maui.

Frank grins as he looked at it, and says, "Hey, that's all right!"

He takes my pen and writes on the back of the snap: "To Eric, Good hunting! Best wishes, Frank Sinatra."

He hands me the pen and the pic. I thank him, and he turns and goes out the door. I stand feeling the warmth of this moment of kindness from the man, and remembering the night at the Cal Neva when I first really felt a part of the "Swingin' Ring-a-Ding-Ding" big-time music business.

I worked with Sinatra many times again, in person and on records and TV shows. I know he was as flawed as any of us, but I always felt real warmth for the man. I always loved that special intensity which almost seemed electric every time I heard him sing an uptempo tune, and that deep feeling for the words that lets you know that he meant every blessed one of them.

THE CODA FOR ERIC

Eric died in 1988 at eighteen. He was stricken with a sudden epileptic seizure, and toppled over in the shower at my ex-wife Rita's house. Paramedics, ER, MDs… nothing could save him.

This has been the hardest, most painful thing I have ever had to endure, and my heart goes out to all parents who have lost a child. Mary McMannes came back into my life to help me through the terrible time.

It's not the way you think it should go; your kids are supposed to outlive their parents, but Life has no hard and fast rules. I've heard it said that the way to make God smile is to tell her your plans.

All *I* know I know is that when I hear Frank sing, I can see in my mind's eye my handsome son Eric, smiling and snapping his fingers in time with the sounds of Sinatra.

THIRTY-NINTH CHORUS:
NAT & NATALIE

I have loved Nat 'King' Cole's music, vocal and pianistic, from the first time I heard the man. When I had the opportunity and pleasure of working with him, I was absolutely knocked out. Of course my folks were big fans too, and I have collected his recordings from his trio days on.

In 1988, I am asked to run for office at Local 47, the Los Angeles Professional Musicians' Union. I am elected Vice President, in charge of all "live" performances, from the L.A. Philharmonic to Saturday Night "Casual" bands. I also have the added responsibility of being Chief Business Representative; my responsibility is for all Recording and Studio sessions in our large jurisdiction.

One of the first recording dates I attend is at Capitol Studios, the famous Round Tower on Vine St. in Hollywood, where Sinatra, Nat 'King' Cole, Peggy Lee and countless other stars did so many of their seminal recordings. I enter not as a trumpet player, which I have done for years, but now as a Union Officer. I ID myself with the receptionist and turn left down the hall to Studio 'A.' The red recording light isn't glowing, so I go in.

Bill Holman, the great arranger, is running down his charts for Natalie, who is at work in the vocal booth. The band swings, Natalie swings just as hard, and it's terrific.

When Bill calls a 'Ten,' some of my buddies in the band take the opportunity to lay some friendly, funny insults on me. Then Natalie comes out; she confers with Holman, and when they're done, I introduce myself.

She smiles and is friendly, as she tells me, "I'm going to do a kind of special vocal tonight… it's a duet. If you'd like to come…?"

Of course I would, and I do.

That night, I return, and when I come into the control room, I see that the big studio is empty—chairs and music stands stacked, microphone stands angle up into the air, naked looking without their mikes. I see that the vocal booth is ready, the stand light on. Of course, the musicians' work on the session is done for the day.

I say hello to the engineer, whom I've known since my days as a studio player.

He tells me quietly, "It's been a long day for her. It's the anniversary of her dad's death, and she and the family went to a memorial service."

I move to the guest area in front of the control console. The first thing I see are three cute-as-a-button children sitting on the big over-stuffed leather couch. They are busy drawing and crayon coloring on paper in their individual plastic "artist's kits." The children look up at me, as does the gray-haired black woman who's with them.

It's funny how white hair, and a suit and tie, give you the appearance of someone trustworthy.

I tell the lady, "I'm Bill Peterson. I'm with the Musicians' Union."

She nods—I guess she figures I'm safe. I smile at the kids; they smile shyly back.

Since Natalie hasn't returned from the service, I decide it's an opportunity to make friends with the children and as a parent of a girl and boy myself, I know the best way is to engage them at their interest level.

I ask the tallest child, a bright-eyed little girl of perhaps five, "Would you like me to draw you a 'Donald Duck'?"

The other two turn to watch their spokesperson.

She smiles again and says, "Oh, yes!"

I take my big blue Waterman fountain pen from my coat and the little girl hands me a sheet of her paper. I sit down on the couch and put the paper on the low table. The kids look at their tutor/guide/babysitter.

She nods approval, and they cluster around to watch me draw.

I do a quick line drawing of Donald, shaking his finger in a comical kind of scolding pose. The children giggle and point and laugh.

As I put the cap back on my pen, the kids say stuff like, "Ooh, that's good …ooh neat…"

The little girl who is spokesperson looks at the drawing, then at my pen, and asks, polite but hesitant, "Could I try your pen?"

Now a fountain pen's nib is delicate, and they always say only one person should ever use it, especially when it's getting broken in, but I want her to experience the magic that is a fountain pen!

"Why sure you can!"

I take the cap off, put it on the top of the pen and hand it to her. She takes it very carefully, and draws on another piece of paper. She tried lines, circles, scribbles, and even a flower, and the Waterman faithfully and flawlessly follows her every whim.

Finally, she stops, and replaces the cap, just as she had seen me do. She cradles my pen in her small palms.

As she hands it back to me, she smiles and says, "Thank you…"

As I reach out to accept it, she tells me very seriously, "This is a pen from the olden days!"

I smile and look up to see Natalie enter, with an exquisite little girl of three or so clinging to her finger.

Natalie smiles at me, and says, "Welcome."

I start to recount what just went down. She smiles and says, "I heard…!"

Natalie pats the little spokesperson's head, and the kids immediately switch their focus to the little girl newcomer—smallest of the group.

The producer, Tommy LiPuma, asks Natalie, "Shall we try one?"

"Let's!"

She gently disengages the exquisite one's tiny hand, and tells her, "Auntie has to go to work now, sweetie, so you play with the kids."

Natalie enters the studio, and slips into the vocal booth.

The studio guys turned the lights down low, and Tony asks, "You ready, Nat?"

It hits me like a shock—Natalie is called, understandably enough, 'Nat' too!

Then they roll tape, and the playback sound of the orchestra fills the control room.

I feel another shock and a chill... It is NAT 'KING' COLE'S voice, singing "Unforgettable." Then, like a miracle, there is Natalie singing answers, responses to her dad's voice, then at times, joining in a duet that bridges barriers of time and space... and death. Nat's remarkable voice *is* timeless, for now and forever. I feel the thrill I always got from hearing his soft, warm voice, and his impeccable musicality—and then the tears come, streaming down my cheeks.

All I can remember about it is the wonder of their two voices, father and daughter, combining, interweaving to create the magic of the great recording of "Unforgettable."

Two Nats and a Natalie

FORTIETH CHORUS:
CLINT EASTWOOD RECEIVES AN AWARD

It's 1995, and I've been elected President of Professional Musicians Local 47 of Los Angeles. So I take the opportunity to go out to a place on Ventura Blvd. called Moonlight Tango which features big bands every Thursday night. Now I don't mean that Glenn Miller or Harry James or Benny Goodman have come back. These big bands are local, Los Angeles musicians usually led by arrangers or instrumentalists, and musicians need a place to play, above all.

I enjoy hearing the bands and seeing and talking with the players, so on this evening I arrive to hear Bill Watrous' big band, which features the leader on trombone. Bill W. kicks off the first tune, an uptempo swinger, and as I move over to the bar, I see a tall lean guy with one of the Ernest Hemingway type of long visored caps that you'd wear to go deep-sea fishing. I get closer and recognize Clint Eastwood. He's a pretty good jazz pianist, I hear, and he has endeared himself to jazz aficionados everywhere with his use of jazz in the scores for such films of his as *Gauntlet*, as well as his dark, probing story of the great alto saxophonist, Charlie "Bird" Parker.

I feel a real affinity for the man and his work, so after the tune is over, I introduce myself, then say, "I'm President of Local 47 and you're one of our members…"

He looks at me with those piercing eyes and nods, "Yeah…"

"You've always scored your films here in L.A., and your film, *Bird* helped people understand what being a jazz player can be all about."

"We tried…"

"You did it, and I'd like to present you with a plaque on behalf of the Local for your decision to score your films here. We could do it at a scoring session, if that's all right?"

Clint considers the idea, and has a swallow of his Amstel Light beer. Then his face softens and creases into a grin as he says, "Yeah, I guess that'd be okay…"

I learn when he's going to start, and make arrangements to check in with Tom Rooker at his office on the Warner Bros. lot. We listen to the set and talk about music, and that a friend of mine, Dennis Shryack and his partner, wrote two of Clint's hit films, *Gauntlet* and *Pale Rider*.

He smiles, nods and says, "Yeah, Dennis is a good guy…"

After the set, Clint leaves and I hang for a while with my musician friends.

Next day I have my secretary, Barbara, call and make arrangements for me to attend one of the scoring sessions at Warner's. Clint is working on the scoring of *The Bridges of Madison County*. On the appointed day, I go out with a plaque in hand, but I make a stop to pick up something else.

I arrive at the Warner Brothers' lot, park and go into the big scoring stage. It's always kind of dramatic when a film is scored because when the orchestra plays, the stage is usually lit only by the film shown onscreen and the musicians' and conductor's stand lights. After the "take" is finished, the film stops, and the crew turns on the big overhead lights which illuminate the studio.

I step over to Clint, who is at the podium with conductor/composer Lennie Niehaus (a wonderful jazz saxophonist in his own right). Some of people in the orchestra call out to me. I wave, and shake hands with Clint and Lennie, as I join them on the podium.

I turn to the musicians and say, "It's great to see you all! Now we all know this man is a fine actor, director and producer, but it's a big plus that he loves music and musicians. As you probably know, Clint Eastwood has been scoring films here in Los Angeles for as long as I can remember…"

(I turn back to Clint)

"…So I want to present this award to you, on behalf of Local 47 and all the musicians who have worked with you."

I hand him the plaque. He smiles, accepts it graciously, and shows it to the orchestra and Lennie, as I say, "Now we all know that you have received many awards but I thought this is something you'd enjoy even more!"

I hand a brown paper grocery bag to a puzzled looking Clint. He takes it, reaches in and pulls out an Amstel Light from the six pack. He cracks up and Lennie smiles and laughs with the orchestra.

As we shake hands again, Clint says, "Now that's an award I can get into!"

♪♪♪

A few years later I drop by when Clint and Lennie are working on the score to his riveting film, *Mystic River*. Clint looks up from a desk and smiles at me.

I say, "I don't think you got a picture of the day I gave you the plaque and the Amstel…"

Clint takes the photo, looks at it, then at me and says in that laconic style of his,

"We looked a lot younger then, didn't we!"

We smile and nod our heads at the truth of what he's said.

I present an award to Clint Eastwood as Lennie Niehaus looks on.

FORTY-FIRST CHORUS:
JOHN WILLIAMS HELPS LAURA

I've enjoyed the responsibility of being President of Professional Musicians, Local 47, Los Angeles. The job gives me an opportunity to see and hear many of the composers who produce music for the films scored here in town. There are some remarkable talents at work in this demanding art, but one of my favorites is John Williams. Our relationship goes back to our days in the Air Force, and he has not only honed his craft but expanded his talents to become one of the most performed and in demand composers in the world of music.

My daughter, Laura has been engaged to do a photo shoot at one of John's film sessions. I call John and get his permission for her to take pictures.

I drive out to Sony Studios (the former MGM picture factory), and go into the scoring stage to find John conferring with the recording mixer, while the musicians are warming up. Laura is already at work, taking pictures. Suddenly a man and woman come out from the control room. They rush up to Laura.

The woman, who is the contractor of the musicians on the date, demands of my daughter, "What are you doing? Who told you that you could take pictures?"

The man, John's agent, imperiously continues, "You have no right to take pictures of Mr. Williams. Please leave, NOW!"

Laura looks from one to the other, then turns as John sees what's going on. He breaks off his talk with the recordist, comes over, puts his arm around Laura's slender shoulders, and in the kindest yet most positive tone he tells the two, "Laura Peterson has my personal, express permission to take any pictures she wishes. Is that clear?"

John smiles at Laura, who looks at him with gratitude, then smiles at the other two. He goes back to work; the recording mixer retreats to the control board, followed somewhat meekly by the contractor and the agent.

I come up to John, now on the podium, look up at my old friend and quietly say, "Thanks, John... "

He smiles down at me, and says, "My pleasure... your daughter is charming, and I'm sure she's a good photographer."

I know that the session and the photo shoot will go well. I turn and leave, knowing that John's generosity and good nature are still an integral part of my friend's makeup.

FORTY-SECOND CHORUS: MADONNA

Madonna is a show biz phenomenon... an actress of sorts, a singer and most of all, a self produced, promoted and propelled celebrity.

Madonna has gone through more permutations, transformations and evolutions than a larva that ends up as a butterfly. My experience with her comes not as a trumpet player, but when I am asked to run as an officer of the L.A. Musicians' Union, Local 47. As Vice President, I make an appearance at the recording session for the Academy Awards, the "Pre-Record."

I show up at the sound stage where the librarians are passing out the music parts to the orchestra. The orchestra leader is Bill Conti who is a wonderful conductor and is a veteran of the Academy Shows.

It's a few minutes before the session is to start. This is the time that's usually the most enjoyable part of a session—a time to get a coffee, sit around and shoot the breeze with your fellow players. I catch Lloyd Ullyate, who is one of the premier trombonists in the business, telling his brass section mates about a job in Palm Springs he and his brother Bill's band played. It seems that after the first set, a well-dressed man weaves up to the bandstand. He's obviously the worse for whiskey, but his dark hair is impeccably combed, straight back.

He says to Lloyd, in a laid back midwestern drawl, "Your guys sound real good. I wanna buy you two a drink... C'mon...!"

Lloyd and Bill look at each other, shrug and follow the guy staggering though the crowd to the bar.

As they follow, Bill tells Lloyd, "You know who this guy is?"

"Well, he looks familiar..."

"He's the guy that wrote 'Stardust'... Hoagy Carmichael!"

The co-leaders and the famous composer of hundreds of songs arrive at the bar and put their orders in. The drinks arrive; Hoagy reaches into his pocket and pulls out a huge roll of bills. He peels one off and slaps it down in front of the startled bartender. He turns to the Ullyates with proud yet tipsy grandeur, points at the bill. The guys can see that it's a $1,000 bill he's plopped down as if it were nothing. He's really playing "The Great and Wealthy Songwriter" bit to the hilt.

He says to the brothers, "I'll bet you never saw a bill that big in your goddamn life... huh?"

Lloyd takes a long look at the thousand-dollar bill, then turns to Hoagy and says, "Yeah, I have once before, Hoagy... but it had Johnny Mercer's picture on it!"

Then Lloyd tells us, "We took our drinks and strolled back to the bandstand, leaving Hoagy to think about it, alone at the bar."

The guys laugh at the story as the contractor calls, "Okay guys, let's get to work."

The band members pick up their instruments and start to pre-record the music for the Academy Award show.

Now a pre-record gives the director and producer of the Awards TV Show the opportunity to record the music. This is way before the director and staging people do all those fantastic filming tricks, with the singer floating through clouds, or upside down or whatever brilliant stroke they can come with. All of this is so the folks at home will sit though the three and a half hours of "I wanna thank my agent and my Aunt Minnie..."

The pre-record goes smoothly for the first two hours, till they start on Madonna's songs.

Madonna is one of the featured singers, and maestro Conti has spent hours working with her. He has laid out, talked and played through the arrangements that each featured performer is to sing. Then he and the orchestrators and arrangers write the score of the arrangement. At this point the scores are given to the music prep people, who write out the actual parts for the orchestra to play.

Since all that has happened, the orchestra has rehearsed, re-hashed and re-rehearsed the musical number she's doing. They do a take, then another, then everybody listens to the playback (or, as the orchestra players call it, a "blow-back"), because the drums, synth sounds, guitars and Fender bass almost drown out the acoustic instruments. Each time she finishes listening, Madonna has some comments, and one of her retinue takes notes.

After many more takes and playbacks, and so on, and much time, the orchestra is almost into overtime, or as the film production folks like to call it, "TAA-DAHH!"—GOLDEN TIME!" (This "Golden Time" is really a joke considering what these same accountants, lawyers, and agents who nowadays run the studios pay themselves. If a musician makes six or seven thousand for all the hours they spend, and all the practicing they've done to be able to do this job, it's still a bargain for the studios).

Anyway, there's a final playback for Madonna. Her pencil plucked brow furrows, her lip gloss purses and it is obvious that the Diva of *Dick Tracy* and many other musical triumphs is not happy.

Conti the conductor, producer Gil Cates, the orchestrators and studio staff gather in the control room. Meanwhile, the clock keeps ticking, the time keeps rolling, and voilà! the musicians are into overtime!

Madonna snatches up the notes and proceeds to dictate what she now feels she wants. The arrangement, as it was co-conceived by Madonna and discussed fully with Bill Conti and his people, simply won't do. She outlines massive changes.

"The violins should cut that part where they go 'Ta-da-ta,ta-dum' out!" The very talented and capable Mr. Conti quickly substitutes a new section, the arrangers and the copyists set to work to "fix" the parts with the new notes. This is only the start of Madonna's deconstruction and reconstruction of the arrangement of her song. When she gets finished, it'll be a completely new version.

Even though Bill Conti's staff is among the best at this kind of work, this procedure takes time. The orchestra musicians work on the changes to their parts, then if the changes are massive, the orchestrators and copyists have to create new parts for the players, so they chat, drink coffee or do a crossword. The result is that not a note is played or recorded. The players are almost into the second hour of Golden Time.

Madonna

The producers fume and grumble because "This is costing a fortune for those goddam musicians!" but of course they bend to the Star, Madonna's, wishes.

Bill Conti renders her pronouncements, translating them into instructions that the orchestrators and arrangers and copyists will translate into musical notes. The orchestrator/arranger team write out new score pages and the copyists ink orchestral pages for the players. The whole music crew, except for the players, works with a frantic fury.

All this from a singer/personality etc., who doesn't read notes, and who has worked for probably a week with Mr. Conti, detailing what she wants, and now has trashed it!

Trombonist Lloyd, a veteran in the biz, who is noted for his quick wit, checks the clock, surveys the frantic pace of Madonna's dictation of ideas, turns to his colleagues in the brass section and cracks,

"You know, I've worked for John Williams and Nelson Riddle and Dave Rose, but Madonna is my favorite arranger!"

The guys laugh; the producers scowl. But life goes on... and miracle of miracles, the show airs and gets its usual huge audience, and the network, amazingly, doesn't go broke.

FORTY-THIRD CHORUS:
THE CODA FOR THIS BOOK

So that's my view of "Show Biz from the Back Row." All the people who were or are stars are simply people who act and react to the extraordinary positions and demands to which their talent has propelled them. Being a star has made them make some extremely difficult demands on people who must serve or accompany them on their journey to being a Star.

Sometimes their selfishness or lack of consideration for anything but their own needs and desires seems to be funny, or sad, or rude, or combinations of all of the above. Sometimes these Stars are as loving and giving and enjoyable as anyone could wish.

It is important to remember that they are people like us, with the same fears and the same courage that we possess, the same need to be accepted and loved that we all experience. The folks of whom I write were given a special talent or gift for expressing those emotions that can touch us with a song or a dance, lift our spirits with a touch of comedy or take us into the dramas of Life that lie deep within all of us.

I have been blessed to have done what not everyone has been privileged to do: to play and write and experience music with the most gifted and talented people of Show Business...

I have been able to do what burned a hole in my soul. And I am most deeply grateful for the chance I've had to share those moments with great artists, performers and musicians.

It seems to me that it's important to make a personal history of these Golden Years of Show Biz because these Stars and their times are unforgettable and they will never come again.

ENCORE:
THE AUTHOR AND FAMILY

Bill Peterson today, with his wire-haired terrier Nickie, soon to
be starring in her own book.

Martha Raye (front row) tending bar at the party she threw for the band (see Ninth Chorus). Arrow points to Bill Peterson.

Bill "Bix" Peterson in 1960

Bill Peterson today, working on a score.

Carolyn and Bill

Carolyn and bassoon.

Eric Peterson, 1969–1987
We still miss him.

Eric and Laura.

Laura having fun with the pilot of the plane to Tokyo.

Laura is a free soul who adventures through life.

INDEX

LaVergne, TN USA
12 January 2010
169706LV00003B/105/P